The Women's

Job Search

Handbook

Gerri M. Bloomberg and Margaret Dodge Holden

Williamson Publishing
Charlotte, VT

ISBN 0-913589-49-7

Cover design: Trezzo-Braren Studio
Typography: Superior Type

Manufactured in the United States of America

In memory of our mothers

Alta S. Dodge   *Pearl N. Milhender*

whose work was for their families

To our daughters

Beth Jessica Bloomberg
Jane Perry Amidon
Martha Dodge Amidon

who know they can choose what they want their work to be

Contents

Preface

We met for the first time twenty-one years ago on New Year's Day, and we quickly found that we had mutual interests in politics, social issues, and life in general. We both had very young children, had begun to take on significant roles in our community, and saw ourselves as mothers and community volunteers. At that initial meeting at age thirty, we felt that we had a lot in common and hoped that we could create future opportunities to work together on community and political projects.

A few years later, when we each had returned to full-time work outside our homes, our paths crossed again at the University of Vermont. There, Gerri created the Employee Assistance Program and served as a counselor for faculty and staff, providing psychological, consulting, and career services. Margy worked in the Center for Career Development, counseling and providing other career services for students and alumni. Together, we designed and presented career development workshops and seminars for faculty and staff.

Since then, our families, our interests, and our careers have taken us in separate directions, but we have maintained a shared sense of purpose and a growing interest in women in the workplace. When Gerri was asked by Williamson Publishing Company to write this book, she turned to Margy to coauthor the project. What had begun as a friendship, a commitment to community, and later a professional relationship, progressed to this expression of what we had learned and felt was important to share with other women.

Over the years, we have observed, experienced, counseled, and spoken many times of the roles, challenges, and accomplishments of women in the workplace. We have come to respect the power of women to get work done and to make outstanding and unique contributions. We wanted to write a book combining the practical, psychological, and philosophical that would help women to think or rethink how they perceive their work world, to comprehend their strengths, to understand a deeper self and how that relates to making career choices, and to find solutions to inhibiting barriers. We felt that combining these issues with very practical job search tools and then relating them to finding satisfying work would be an invaluable resource.

We are asking the reader to take a thoughtful journey that more fully defines who she is and how she thinks and acts, and to apply these insights to her job search and subsequent work life. We will be supporters and encouragers in this process. We will also be realistic about attitudes and behaviors that are liabilities and ultimately affect women's chances of getting what they want from their professional lives.

When we interviewed Margaret McKenna, president of Lesley College, she validated our thoughts when she said, "The things that society has seen as women's weaknesses – our ability to relate successfully to people, to see the other side, to think through things before we act, to put ourselves in the other person's place – are really our strengths with which we can make better and more humane decisions. And what we have found out about management is that people are much more productive within these humane systems. Women instinctively bring characteristics to their workplace positions that are incredibly useful."

The path to reaching workplace goals has been a lot clearer for men because the world of work and even the job-search process have always been defined in terms of the male arena. In a sense, men have known since early childhood what was expected of them. Many women have not had the comfort of a clear vision of their future selves. Because women are often charting new territory, we have to be clear about what we feel, think, and want. We need to know how to sell our own special skills.

With the changes and contributions accomplished by women in the workplace come an array of opportunities in professions and jobs that were not accessible to earlier generations. The world of work is less gender-defined. Although real barriers for women do still exist, men and women are increasingly working side by side. The criterion for landing the job is now more likely to be who is the best qualified candidate.

Before we begin, a practical note: We have purposely not created a workbook format for this book, although we have included exercises, activities, and questions designed to help you define and know yourself. We feel that writing down your responses and ideas is not only an effective and important part of the job-search process, but an added dimension to understanding your deeper self. We ask that you use a notebook to accompany your reading. Writing not only will help you to clarify your ideas, but also will give you a valuable record to which you can return to mine further insights and measure your progress.

A journey begins with one small step. We hope that you will take that step, and we wish you well.

Acknowledgments

We are very appreciative of the fine contributions made to this book by Ellie Byers and Joan Smith. Ellie, who wrote chapter 3, "Job Satisfaction: Knowing What You Want and Need," is a career counselor and organizational consultant. Ellie also made a substantial contribution to chapter 2, "Women and Their Work: Myths and Issues." Joan Smith, who is a career counselor, organizational consultant, and author, wrote chapter 9, "Reentry: Women at the Crossroads." We are also indebted to Judith Banker, vice president of R.D. Gatti and Associates, a human resource counseling and placement firm in Boston, for her contributions to chapter 7 on interviewing. These women have made significant contributions in their fields, and we thank them for sharing their insights with us.

We are deeply grateful to the many women and men who took the time to be interviewed and shared with us their thoughts and feelings about the women's job-search process and issues in the workplace. We would like to acknowledge especially Frances Bagwell, Sam Bloomberg, Nancy Blouin, Ninoska Bonnelly, Mari Cosculluela, Laura Fishman, Judith Koplewitz, Tony Leone, Margaret McKenna, Bobbette Scribner, Larry Simmons, Sallie Soule, Jill Mattuck Tarule, and Lori True.

We also want to thank our publisher and editor, Susan Williamson, for her skill, insights, sense of humor, patience, and dedication to the concept of this book. Her unceasing encouragement allowed this project to blossom and take form.

As with all of our lives, there are always people who have meant a lot to our own development both personally and professionally; people who have touched us by their own brand of example, support, encouragement, and love. Some of these people are with us now, others who have passed on are with us in spirit.

########

To my husband, Sam, and my sons, Ethan and Josh, for their love, patience, encouragement, and support while my books and papers increasingly invaded their space.

Joe Milhender, my father, possessed an innate ability to find the positive attributes in people, encourage them, and make them feel good. He applied these principles in his work as a successful businessman. He set an example for me to help others create a more humane and productive workplace in my consulting work. He would be very proud to see this book in print today.

Two women, Sally Spatola and Lois Diggs, whose endless love, devotion, and humor helped to guide me from a child to womanhood.

Nancy Magnus, friend, counselor, and a special woman who had a difficult life. She taught us that adversity can be a wise teacher.

GMB

########

In the writing of this book, the memory of Bob Holden has been with me often: his curiosity and interest in helping people work together, his gentle manner of teaching by questioning, and the enjoyment he would have had watching me work over a hot computer.

The spirit of my father, Wilson S. Dodge, who was greatly respected as an honest businessman, and who always exhorted me to behave like a lady and get the lawn mowed, has been with me as we have written about many of the issues in this book.

My children, who have each made unique and thoughtful decisions about their own careers, are an inspiration to me in all that I do.

Doug Hyde, my dear friend and cheerleader, has, throughout the book-writing process, set an example of how to get things done. He has shown enduring interest, made thought-provoking suggestions, and urged me to "go get 'em!"

MDH

Chapter 1

Women in Search
of Work:
Knowing Yourself

I am part of all that I have met. – Alfred, Lord Tennyson

Before you even think about resumes and interviews, before you let frantic feelings about needing a job – any job – take hold, stop long enough to begin the insightful, careful, truthful process of taking a look inward, into your past, your childhood, your teen years, the times of pleasure, the glimpses of high self-esteem; the times of turbulence, of guilt, of low self-esteem. What you learn about yourself and your past behaviors can tell you a lot about the messages you put forth in your interactions today. Give yourself the time to begin acknowledging the mental and emotional "baggage" you carry around everyday; assess your present mind-set with a view toward keeping those behaviors that have served you well and continue to serve you well, while changing those behaviors that work against you in your life today.

This is a tall order to present to you in the first paragraph of the first chapter of a book whose goal is to help you land a meaningful job. Understand that everything that follows will be much more helpful and bring you closer to your goal if you can at least begin to acknowledge those things you do to help yourself and those things you do – albeit unknowingly – that get in your way. We are not suggesting you put aside your job search and enter analysis. We are suggesting, however, that you open your eyes, ears, mind, and heart, and above all listen to yourself. What you hear may surprise you.

What is a mind-set? A mind-set is a combination of perceptions, attitudes, feelings, and beliefs that result in your *choice of behavior* with your coworkers, friends, and family. It is a point of view, a mental inclination or tendency often stemming from a personal philosophy. Your mind-set is a blending of how you see and experience your world and then how you translate that worldview into your behaviors. A positive personal mind-set allows you to create the most helpful approach to finding what you want in the world of work, both in finding the right job for you (not just any job!) and then functioning positively in it.

Exploring your mind-set is like putting a firm foundation under a new building. It carries you through every step of the job-search process and into the job as well – from planning to resume writing, from networking and interviewing to negotiating for what you need. Everything around you can look different after even a brief inward look. Once you know yourself better, you will find you see the world around you – including interviewers you have never met before – with a new clarity. Acknowledging your mind-set gives you security in the oftentimes unnerving job-search process because you know which feelings are tinged with past responses and which are valid in your present circumstances. For once – perhaps for the first time – you will be able to trust your responses. This is the first step on the way to knowing what actions to take.

When you think about it, this mind-set business is not a lot of meaningless talk. Imagine, if you will, that your vision is very blurry; perhaps, you have just had some drops put in your eyes at the eye doctor's. Someone points you in the direction of the restroom far down the hall, but you have a hard time finding it, making wrong turns, taking false steps, feeling unsure of yourself as you grope along the way. You may even decide that you really didn't need the restroom after all and retreat to the security of the waiting room.

Writing resumes and interviewing without discovering who you really are and what you really want to do is similar to groping around in hallways. However, once you know your mind-set, know what your goals are and why, know what works for you and makes you feel good, then you can embark on your job search with a clear focus. The clarity of knowing where you are going and why brings an air of confidence and energy. This is the aura that those whom you network with and who interview you are looking for. You communicate a strength of purpose that employers gravitate toward, and rightly so, because when a woman gets a job that uses her skills and meets her expectations, she is very likely to perform at a high level.

This is not to say that you don't need interviewing and negotiating skills, because those skills can make a big difference. But the most finely tuned job-search skills may not win you the right job of your choice without the unspoken clarity of purpose you communicate from knowing yourself better.

Think of it! Many people take interview after interview without landing a job because basically they really did not want that job in the first place. Yes, they wanted to be employed, they needed the paycheck and satisfaction, it seemed like a good position, but they didn't truly want that particular job. They simply wanted almost any job. And, though, neither the job candidate nor the potential employer knew exactly what was being communicated, the message came through: "I'm not right for this job." That's how powerful understanding your mind-set can be. It can change the way you see yourself, and thus, how others perceive you.

We have heard many women say that they cannot tolerate books that say, "you can do it," when, indeed, they feel that they cannot "do it." Jane, a client, said, "It is not helpful to read in a book that I have to be confident when I walk into an interview. For heaven's sake! I'm smart enough to know that, but I don't know how to look and feel confident when most of my life I've only felt good about myself within the confines of my own home." Jane has to do more than walk into an interview repeating constantly "I'm confident, I'm confident." She has to come to terms with her past to understand why she unknowingly and habitually chooses to lack confidence. Adopting a more confident attitude is not as difficult as one might think. *The lack of forethought and a well-defined mind-set is the reason why most women struggle with job-search and work behavior issues.*

Examining "where you are coming from" and your personal philosophy is the basis of any successful job-search process. Looking inward is a very practical issue, different from just sitting around and philosophizing about life. *It defines what matters to you.* When you can define who you are and what you want out of your work life by integrating your practical, philosophical, and emotional point of view — your mind-set — then you can attain your goal. On the other hand, if you are kidding yourself from step one, if you do not really know what it is you are looking for, then you will not be happy with where you end up, even if you do get a job. *Getting a job and getting the right job take about the same amount of work,* so why not explore your inner self and get the job that is right for you.

So, grab a notebook and pencil, along with a few quiet contemplative moments, as we begin together the process that most assuredly will place you in a job where you can thrive, not merely exist.

Let us begin by understanding how your way of thinking gives you a frame of reference for how you see the world, because this worldview is ultimately reflected in your approach and success in the job search. Armed with an understanding of this frame of reference, you can then choose to change it or use it as is. Basically, we all have what it takes to be successful in defining our careers, but sometimes we unknowingly adopt behaviors that may actually work against us. Identifying these behaviors allows us to develop strategies to make some changes, as well as to see ourselves and our goals more clearly.

Simply put, your mind is made up of perceptions, thoughts, and feelings — what you see, think, and feel. These impact upon the way you function in all aspects of your life, including looking for a job. The way in which you see or experience life has a direct bearing on how you think, feel, and behave. No matter how you view life, *you always create behaviors to support that view* to help you make sense of things and feel in control. In effect, your behaviors support or substantiate the feelings and thoughts you have about life, not the other way around. For example, if you feel the world is a hostile place where most people are out to get you, then you create behaviors to support that belief. Those behaviors might be defensive, aggressive, closed, nontrusting, and negative. You may actually invite hostility by sending out these messages.

> *Jane approaches an interviewer feeling that she always has to be on her guard, because the interviewer will most likely be there to trick her or ask her questions to expose her worst side. She walks in with a defensive air, revealed by her body posture and facial expressions. (Yes, we really do wear our beliefs on our faces, in our gestures, our attitudes, and in our body posture.) This immediately alerts the interviewer that something is amiss. Picking up on his suspicion, he asks Jane some very hard questions, designed to expose behavior he now suspects might make her difficult to work with. Jane's view of the world created a most unfortunate paradox. What she wants most is to put her best foot forward; instead, she ends up inviting the very thing she fears the most, an unfavorable impression. Jane's beliefs result in behaviors that actually confirm her negative view and thus the vicious circle can begin.*

On the other hand, had Jane felt that life is a gift, the world is basically a friendly place, and that meeting different people provides variety in life, her behavior would very likely have been warm, open, trusting, and accepting. People would gravitate toward her and seek out her company. Just think how comfortable and trusting an interviewer would feel with someone like this.

Imagine how your own worldview, the way in which you experience people, and the behaviors you have adopted to support these beliefs affect your attitude in the job search. Tackling important tasks such as planning, networking, interviewing, and negotiating requires an ability to approach people with clear goals and a confident, trusting attitude. Indeed, even to express yourself positively on paper for a resume, you need to perceive yourself in a positive and confident manner. And once you land the job you want, your worldview will have a lot to do with your degree of satisfaction and success at work.

From your earliest years, you chose how you experienced your world albeit in response to your environment and the people you interacted with. In essence, you created your own individual sense of reality as best you could in order to feel safe and secure. But how did your worldview evolve? What influenced you to make the choices that you did? Again, your mind is made up of perceptions, feelings, and thoughts that are shaped by many influences throughout your life. This evolving mind-set, in turn, affects your behaviors.

Some influences are momentary or situational. These are more likely to change in the short term. Situational influences are such things as how we feel on any given day or what is occurring in our lives in general. These influences – as is true of all influences – can be positive or negative. Did your spouse get promoted or lose his job? Did your kids keep you up all night or did you leap out of bed well-rested? Are things going smoothly with your relationships, your family, your work? Situational influences, then, may impact on your day-to-day behavior, but most likely will not change your deeper worldview.

Past Influences

Past influences are more deeply imbedded within us and are therefore less likely to change without some committed study, introspection, or counseling. Past influences can include the chemistry or temperament we were born with, the environment that we were raised in, or the behaviors that significant people in our lives have modeled for us.

■ **Chemistry or Temperament.** You are born with your own special chemistry, which helps to determine your pace and your reactions. Some of us are more hyper, reactive, and energetic. Others are more laid back, quiet, and slower paced. There seem to be enough of all types to go around to fit the needs of the planet. All are valued.

■ **Environment.** You are influenced by where you were brought up and how you interacted with that environment. Different regions of the country, urban apartment or rural farmhouse, and concomitant community values influence who you are and the choices you made in the past and make today.

■ **Early Modeling.** Early modeling from significant people such as parents, siblings, relatives, teachers, and peers is particularly important. The way you view your world depends largely on early images and sensitivities, based on how significant people in your life treated you, behaved around you, interacted with you and with others, and thereby modeled behavior for you. We all clearly recreate in our adult lives patterns of behavior and communication that were modeled for us as we were growing up. We carry these patterns into both our personal and work relationships. They reveal themselves in our attitudes and approaches toward everything, including the job-search process.

Peg grew up in a family that had endured many financial and emotional hardships. Over the years her parents believed that life was unfair and that no matter what they did, things would most likely not work out. Any attempts on Peg's part to have even small successes were greeted with scorn and derision as the parents modeled their own life experiences for their children. Peg grew up feeling that no matter what she did, it would not be right or good enough. As an adult, Peg has pushed herself hard to achieve and, by most standards, would be considered a good worker, but she rarely feels as if she has accomplished anything. Her colleagues often find her negative and unable to recognize her own achieve-ments. Peg has clearly taken on the perceptions and behaviors of her parents. Through counseling, Peg eventually came to under-stand that the attitudes of her parents toward her abilities really had very little to do with her, but were, in fact, a mirror of their own perceptions of themselves. She took stock of her own talents, honestly examined the negative behaviors she was communicating through her belief system, and set out to develop behaviors that made her a supportive and excellent coworker. She also realized that when she was young, she did not have the freedom or the know-how to develop positive choices, but that as an adult she did.

It is human nature to turn to things that are familiar. Familiarity brings comfort. It is what you know and what you can control. Oftentimes, women choose familiarity, even if the impact is negative. It is very important to ponder how you came to adopt the behaviors you now exhibit as an adult. You need to discern if you are responding to your adult environment with old familiar patterns of communicat-ing and perceiving, or if you are choosing to perceive and behave in new and perhaps more appropriate ways.

We create our own experiences through our perceptions, thoughts, and behaviors. *We often cannot choose the events that occur in our lives, but we do choose how we will perceive and deposit them in our bank of experiences.* What an awesome thought it is that you can actually control your responses to events, as well as the resulting actions you decide to take.

Laura and Mary have both been terminated from their jobs at the First Federal Bank due to a reorganization and ensuing staff reduction. Laura is devastated and goes home, unable to function for nearly a week. She believes that she has really been fired and that she will never be able to get another job. Mary is angry when she receives her notice and feels that way for most of the day. However, the next morning she sits down at her desk to pull together her resume. She feels the need to make contacts, as well as to seek out the availability of other positions. She checks the morning paper for jobs and begins a series of phone calls to reactivate her network of friends and work acquaintances. Both these women are understandably angry about what has happened, but each has chosen to take a different path. Laura's actions involve an historically familiar choice of feeling hopeless about things; on the other hand, Mary's choices involve action and moving on.

These two women are good examples of how we give meaning to the people, things, and events that surround us. We decide how we will experience our interactions with people and events. We do, in fact, decide if the proverbial glass is half-full or half-empty. That awesome, far-reaching power rests solely with each of us.

As you create your own behaviors, you must realize that others do so also. It is important to avoid internalizing negative behavior that other people sometimes direct at you, for it is theirs to own. In other words, it is their problem, not something you did. A person who is short-tempered and grumpy with you is revealing more about what is happening in her own life than anything about you. A person who feels good about herself usually does not yell and scream when she does not get her way. Rather she deals with the issues in an understanding and reasonable manner. A former counseling colleague always reminded us that *when we speak, we almost always speak about ourselves.* After all, what can we be speaking about other than our own thoughts, opinions, and experiences? So, at any given time, your words reflect how you are feeling on that particular day. Women often have a tendency to internalize or take ownership of other people's behavior, as if it were their own. This may translate into, "that interviewer seems irritable and short-tempered with me; what am I doing wrong? I don't have a chance," rather than, "Uh-oh, that woman seems to have gotten up on the wrong side of bed today. What can I do to get her attention directed in a positive way, so I get what I want out of this interview?" Women who are feeling insecure or victimized by the workplace are easy targets for choosing to blame themselves for the behaviors of others.

It is never too late to challenge your perceptions, make positive changes, and build a more satisfying future. At this point it is important for you to look at what your mind-set has been. How have you been thinking about and perceiving your world? What was modeled for you by the significant people in your life, and what did you learn from them? (Be objective rather than judgmental. This exercise is about learning and growing, not about blaming.) You can begin to answer these questions by working through the following exercise. The first part of the exercise deals with earlier parts of your life, and the second part asks you questions about the present. The purpose of the exercise is to help you define the mind-set that you acquired in early years; the second part helps you see which characteristics you have chosen to carry into the present and which you have chosen to let go. Take out your notebook and write down the answers. If you are tempted to skip this section, please don't. All of us can benefit from it at any point in our lives.

Revisiting the Past: An Exercise

1. This question will show you which characteristics were modeled for you by those who brought you up. Use words or short phrases to describe the following (these questions pertain to whoever raised you):

Mother's or female role model's characteristics:

Level of her self-esteem	Way she felt about you
General nature or temperament	Attitude toward work
General attitude toward life	Ability to listen
How did she get along with her peers?	Patience
How did she get along with other family members?	Encouragement of others
	Sense of humor

Father's or male role model's characteristics:

Level of self-esteem	Way he felt about you
General nature or temperament	Attitude toward work
General attitude toward life	Ability to listen
How did he get along with his peers?	Patience
How did he get along with other family members?	Encouragement of others
	Sense of humor

Your characteristics as a child:

Level of self-esteem	Earliest career thoughts
General nature or temperament	Ability to listen
General attitude toward life	Patience
How did you get along with your friends?	Sense of humor
How did you get along with your parents and siblings who were living with you?	Feelings about your appearance
	Feelings about school

Which characteristics seem to be like one or both of your parents?

Which characteristics are unique to you?

2. More specifically, comment on your experience with the following:

   ★ Which parent did you identify with more closely?

   ★ Were your opinions respected by your parents and your siblings?

   ★ How did your family handle conflict or disagreements?

   ★ How did you feel about your role in the family?

   ★ What kind of values did your family model regarding work, making changes, taking risks, success, and potential? What did you learn from those values?

3. Based on the characteristics and facts you have now identified from questions 1 and 2, write down how you perceived yourself as a child, based on your system of beliefs about the world around you.

4. Now identify those behaviors or actions you exhibited as a child that support those beliefs.

Examining the Present: An Exercise

1. Use words or short phrases to describe the following:

Your characteristics as an adult:

Level of self-esteem   Present career thoughts
General nature or temperament   Ability to listen
General attitude toward life   Patience
How do you get along with your friends?   Sense of humor
How do you get along with your parents,   Feelings about your appearance
   siblings, or other family members?   Feelings about work

2. More specifically, comment on your experience with the following:

   ★ How do you get along with roommates, spouse, significant other, or children?

   ★ How do/did you get along with your boss and coworkers?

   ★ How do/did you handle your workplace conflict or disagreements?

   ★ How do/did you feel about your role at work?

★ Are/were your opinions respected by your boss and coworkers?

★ What has been your experience with job hunting, networking, interviewing, negotiating, and meeting new people?

★ What are your values today regarding work, success, and potential?

3. Based on your answers to questions 1 and 2, write down what you now believe about yourself and the world around you.

4. Write down those behaviors or actions you presently have, as a result of your beliefs.

5. In the three columns below, identify those beliefs you have already changed from childhood, those you would like to keep, and those you wish to change for the future.

Changed in the Past   *Would Like to Keep*   *Change for the Future*

At this point you have some insight into your present mind-set and can see how it might be impacting on your job-search process or your attitude and behavior at work. You may also have identified perceptions and behaviors that do not work for you and that you want to change. Many clients, after doing good work on understanding their mind-sets or how they came to see and experience the world, say, "I know I have views and behaviors that are not working for me, but I have no idea how to change. Now what?"

A woman stands in a familiar field. She is a frequent visitor to these surroundings. She takes in the smell of the tall grass after the rain, the tall poplar trees swaying in the wind, and an occasional wildflower here and there. The wind gusts and briefly brings a sweet, fresh, unfamiliar fragrance. She turns and looks off in the distance toward the direction of the gust. At the end of the field is a small stream with a footbridge leading to yet another clearing. The grass there is covered with a display of wildflowers so magnificent that it momentarily takes her breath away. She feasts her eyes on the variety of hues; some rich in color, others subtle and pastel. Beyond the flowers are a few pine trees that gradually increase in numbers and melt into a dark forest. The sight of the forest breaks the spell of her fascination with the extraordinary vision of color. She stands, leaning forward, as if trying to decide whether to explore this new land. She lingers a moment, turns, surveys her familiar field, and with the vision to her back returns to her car for the brief ride home.

Oftentimes women resist change simply because it is unfamiliar, and they are unable even to imagine anything different. They choose to remain in their known and safe surroundings. Sometimes women remain in known surroundings, even though they can see that a more promising field beckons or they know that beyond, in the dark forest, lies a marvelous and challenging adventure. They are paralyzed by the realization that change can bring the promise of richly colored hues, but also the unknown territory of the dark forest. Yet, any woman, no matter what her personal or job history has been, can move beyond her present mental state, visualizing and then attaining a job that is both meaningful and sustaining. The major obstacles standing in the way are the walls we erect in our minds. Those walls, however, can be taken down or have wonderful picture windows cut in them. Doorways can be formed and pathways leading from them can bring a brighter, more satisfying future.

In order to make architectural changes in the mind and thereby create a more positive worldview, women can choose to enhance perceptions and behaviors that do work and change those that do not. Some women do this with personal self-help methods, while personal or career counseling may be an option for others. If the choice is counseling, a woman should choose an experienced counselor to help her acquire the tools to solve both present and future problems. Whatever avenue a woman pursues, it will require that she be vigorous, consistent, and patient in her journey to change. Perhaps you remember practicing the piano or an athletic drill when you were younger, wondering when you would ever improve. Then one day, after weeks of persistence, you found that suddenly everything had fallen into place and you were playing much better. It takes time and hard work. We have seen clients give up too soon, feeling that change should come in a matter of days. Each person's timetable for change is different. We cannot tell you when, but we can tell you that if you calmly and patiently persevere, change will come. Remember that you cannot make the river go any faster than it already flows.

Two methods of changing and gaining clarity for personal, workplace, and job-search purposes have worked for many women. The first is the process of visualization; the second is assistance with clear rational thinking that helps reduce anxiety and tension. Visualization is particularly helpful in defining and clarifying what you really want in your work life. The rational thinking approach is helpful in removing the barriers and fears that often impede the job-search process. We like to encourage women to use both approaches.

Visualization

We talked previously about creating pathways that can lead to a brighter future. First, visualize that future. Form in your mind the picture of what kind of person you want to be in your work life. What do you want that job to look like? Where will you be working? In what kind of environment or at what kind of desk? What will you be wearing? What kinds of people are around you? Create the most satisfying picture of yourself and then concentrate and hold that vision in focus. On a daily basis, reaffirm that vision and hold onto that projection of your future self. Once your ideal job is visualized, then set out to draw in the tasks necessary to reach that goal. What would a woman in that position have done to get there? What would her job-search plan look like? How would she best project herself in a resume? How do you think she would create her ideal network? What would her ideal interviewing or negotiating stance for that job be like? After you create the vision, hold onto it firmly, without compromise, and build a plan to get yourself where you really do want and deserve to be. And don't settle for anything less!

Here is some help with visualization. Visualization is a lovely and focused way of breathing life into a goal. It gives clarity, color, form, dimension, and vibrancy to your goal so that it comes alive. The basis of this technique is the wise old adage, "you are what you think you are." Visualization meshes and enriches the philosophy of your worldview; if you have a positive and richly defined worldview as you enter the job-search process, then the behaviors and actions you create to support this personal viewpoint will ultimately help you attain your goal. In addition, the visualization process helps you to experience a deeper, inner self that often stays hidden in the pace of our daily lives. It is in that deeper, inner self that you can discover many of the additional talents and capabilities you may have hidden within the walls of your mind.

Let's try some visualization together, so that you can get the hang of it. A completely relaxed mind is best. An easy start is to envision a place where you have experienced total calm and peace. Try to recall the scene, fix it in your mind, and then add the dimensions of temperature, sound, smell, touch, and emotion in detail.

> *With her eyes closed and feeling relaxed, Marie described the following scene. "I am lying on the sand under a palm tree by the side of the ocean. The palm tree has cast its shadow, so that I am in the shade. The air is deliciously warm with a gentle breeze. I lift my hand, extend it from the shade into the sun, and let the breeze run through my fingers. The ocean is a turquoise color with the sunlight glistening off the ripples. The waves break onto shore with a regular, comforting sound. I can see an island that must be twenty miles away. It has a mountain range that reaches into the clouds. The beach extends for miles, and I look both ways to take it all in. To the left are palm trees, their branches hanging over the sand. It looks almost desolate. The sea breaks into shore differently*

there, as it climbs over underwater reef formations and finds its way to the shore in a series of white-foamed layers. Two native fisherman stand to their waists in the water, pulling in small fishing nets. Occasionally I can hear the distant excited sounds of their voices when they discover a net full of fish. Off to the right the beach turns gradually like the shape of a cornucopia, and two miles down I can see a point with large rocks, waves crashing off their structure in the midst of the ocean. Above this scene, as the beach reaches up to form a green hillside, I see many small dwellings carved into the side of the hills. I reach my hand down by the side of my chair, pick up a handful of sand, and let it run slowly out. It feels warm with fine grains and a few pieces of broken shell. I lay back, take a deep breath that I let out slowly and feel totally and completely relaxed. I seem to sink lower into the sand, as I experience a total union of myself with my surroundings."

After Marie experienced this scene, her counselor asked her to hold the vision for five minutes. At the end of the five minutes, finding the scene so satisfying, Marie asked if she could continue the image. When she gradually put the vision aside, she was ready to begin work on creating a new image for herself of what she wanted to be like as a prospective job candidate and also what she wanted for the future. She sees herself as a confident, calm, and thoughtful person, who plans with forethought, researches each company, and asks the right questions during an interview.

Marie had been a successful administrative assistant, taking care of the many details of the offices in which she had worked. Although she had experienced much job satisfaction, attempts to break into other fields had been haphazard. As she relaxed her mind, closed her eyes, and visualized her next job, she found herself in a museum, working with artists, museum officials, and art commentators from magazines, newspapers, television, and radio. When asked for more details, she saw herself arranging exhibits, coordinating all the functions necessary to bring the artists' work and the public's interests together. When asked how she was feeling about that work, she described intense excitement about the creativity involved. With great insight, she then shared that this vision completed a hidden artistic part of her that would like to combine both her creative instincts and her love for planning and organizing. On a daily basis, she practiced holding onto that vision. In addition, she affirmed her new creative, thoughtful, calm self every morning with quiet meditation. And that newly discovered Marie was the person who pursued the job search. She laid out a plan, spent a month researching possibilities and creating a network, and in three more months, she had landed a job very much like the one she had envisioned.

Much has been written about visualization. One well-known book, *Creative Visualization* by Shakti Gawain, is helpful for people who are comfortable using their imaginations and who wish to develop their inner selves and their spirituality. It is a very rewarding, relaxing, and lovely way to stretch the mind. For the purposes of the job search, visualization is also a very helpful step, as you begin the planning process in chapter 4.

A Rational Approach

Let's look at the rational, tangible approach to dealing with emotional barriers or stressors in your work life. Again, this approach is an appropriate adjunct to exploring your mind-set, because here you look clearly and analytically at your irrational behaviors and thoughts, formed earlier in your life, but kept alive just because they are familiar. This approach helps you to understand that your feelings and thoughts trigger emotions which result in behaviors to then support those emotions. This approach also leads you to examine your thoughts as you interpret your life events and to question their validity and appropriateness to what is really happening. Grab your notebooks, for here is an eye-opening exercise.

Let's Get the Facts Straight: An Exercise

Basically, we will be dealing with defining an issue or assumption, examining the resulting thoughts and feelings, and then looking at the behaviors that have been developed to support those beliefs. Before you try this exercise for yourself, let's look at an example.

> *Angela, feeling depressed and hopeless about her future, went to see a counselor. She had spent a month combing the papers with no job in sight. After determining that her depression was related to her present job situation and not from severe long-term issues, her counselor talked about the realities of the job search and what she had to do to make it work for her. She was asked to fill out the following exercise. (Notice, in the outline, how Angela's present thoughts, feelings, and behaviors have occurred in other situations before.)*

> 1. *What is happening (event, stressor, or belief)?*

I look in the paper and there is no job available that I want.

2. *What are you telling yourself (your ruminations, "self-talk")?*
I'm no good at this – not smart enough. I won't find anything; I'm so scared I won't be able to do anything.

3. *What has been your response in the past when things looked like they might not work out?*

   a. *Example:*

Incident	Thoughts	Feelings	Behavior
Afraid I wouldn't get in college	I'm not smart; they won't want me	anxious, worried, scared, depressed	inactivity, sit around, complain to friends and family

   b. *What were the results (what actually happened)?*
   I got into the second college of my choice.

   c. *How did you feel after the situation resolved itself?*
   That I worried too much, lost time from my studies and other activities I like to do by sitting around and worrying too much.

4. *What are your feelings today about the present situation?*
anxious, worried, depressed

5. *What behavior is resulting from your feelings and thoughts about the present situation?*
inactivity, complaining to friends and family, feeling sorry for myself

6. *What evidence supports your negative feelings?*
I have heard that the job market is poor. There are no jobs listed in the paper.

7. *Do you see any relationship between the behavior resulting from your feelings and thoughts today and that of issues, stressors, or beliefs that have been present in the past?*
Yes, in the past I have felt low self-esteem, paralyzed, become inactive, and sat around worried, anxious, and depressed.

8. *What is the worst thing that could happen?*
not get a job, go broke, have to move

9. *What are some possible positive things that could occur for each of the worst things listed in the previous question?*
look into another field, move to a new place, make new friends

10. *What could you try that you aren't trying?*

Get out and volunteer so I can meet people and improve my skills.
Set up a job-search network.
Visit or call directly companies that are not listed in the paper.
Research more companies.
Look into other fields that could use my skills.
Read books.
See a job or career counselor.

One of the helpful insights that came out of this exercise for Angela was the realization that these irrational thoughts came from her past and really had little to do with her current excellent talents.

So now, let's begin this exercise and see what you can learn about thoughts and habits that work for you and those that you might want to change.

1. What is happening (event, stressor, or belief)?

2. What are you telling yourself (your ruminations, "self-talk")?

3. What has been your response in the past when things looked like they might not work out?

    a. Example:

Incident	Thoughts	Feelings	Behavior

    b. What were the results (what actually happened)?

    c. How did you feel after the situation resolved itself?

4. What are your feelings today about the present situation?

5. What behavior is resulting from your feelings and thoughts about the present situation?

6. What evidence supports your negative feelings?

7. Do you see any relationship between the behavior resulting from your feelings and thoughts today and that of issues, stressors or beliefs that have been present in the past?

8. What is the worst thing that could happen?

9. What are some possible positive things that could occur for each of the worst things listed in the previous question?

10. What could you try that you aren't trying now?

Being Confident and Centered

We have been examining your worldview and the potential for change as a way to gain and maintain a positive attitude in the job search. Please note that the fact you are in a job search means that some change is already occurring. Change such as that experienced in this journey can bring new and wonderful challenges, but it can also bring risks and the unknown. With both the challenges and the risks, we are asking you to bring a positive attitude, be confident, and feel centered. Being centered means having your thoughts, feelings, and behavior in harmony. Feeling centered enables you to be strong, purposeful, and able to move ahead with positive determination to achieve your goals.

Feeling centered is difficult during times of transition, and especially so with the added pressures of a job search. Anytime your familiar, second-nature way of living is disrupted, you are apt to feel off-center. These disruptive events can be moderate, such as having a change in coworkers, or they can be severe, such as being fired and having to seek a new job. For changes that are mild to moderate, you may experience some unsettling feelings for a few weeks, until you make new adjustments. Severe events that threaten to change your life more dramatically can cause extreme anxiety or a state of panic. Mood swings may evoke uncontrollable behavior causing embarrassing tears or inappropriate laughter. Increased impatience or intolerance and an inability to think clearly or rationally may occur. Concentration may become extremely difficult, and tasks that used to be performed routinely may become burdensome. The usual ability to plan or prioritize your daily activities may seem to be gone. The familiar trappings of your life may become unknown territory; you may feel disconnected, like a kite whipping uncontrollably through the breeze, separated from the familiar hand that provided the steadying guide. When you don't feel centered, you don't feel good.

And, yes, these feelings are not unusual at the beginning of a job search. The initial enthusiasm in looking for a job may wane as time passes. This is especially true if you have left a job that was very dissatisfying yet do not have one to replace it. The initial feelings of relief from leaving a bad situation and finally doing something to make a positive change often give way to anxiety and depression. Since many of us define ourselves by what we do, we fall prey to feeling lost or unworthy when the usual routines of life disappear.

When you encounter these periods of feeling anxious or uncentered, go to a place where you are usually content. For some, that is a physical place like home; for others, it is a place in the mind, focusing on memories, sights, sounds, or spiritual connections. Some women feel more connected by reaching out to friends or supportive family members. Other women prefer to be alone. Some connect with nature. Long walks, absorbing the details of the scenery – trees, branches, leaves, fields, clumps or blades of grass, small creatures – often seem to be comforting. If you live in the city, try to find a large park or river where it is safe to walk and contemplate. Music or art often provides comforting connections. A concert, a saunter through a museum, or a good book can be helpful. And don't forget exercise – brisk walking, running, aerobics, swimming, racquetball – can quickly release anxious feelings.

If you can't sleep, don't lie in bed at 4:00 A.M. worrying about not sleeping. Try some progressive muscle relaxation or relaxation tapes (available at many stores), such as the kind with soothing music in the background. If you still can't sleep, get out of bed, read an inspiring or comforting book, watch an old movie on the VCR or TV, or listen to some soft music or an audio book tape. Use the techniques of visualization and rational thinking to keep your thoughts clear and positive during lonely hours. Avoid dwelling on irrational thoughts, especially the negative type you may be working to change. Try some slow stretching to relieve tension in your muscles. After an hour or so, you probably will start to feel drowsy. If you can catch about two more hours of sleep before morning, you probably won't feel exhausted during the day.

Periods of feeling uncentered can go on for a few weeks. If, after a few weeks, you cannot snap out of these feelings or they are getting worse, you may want to consider going to a counselor for more in-depth support. The following are some signs to watch for: If you find yourself feeling increasingly more depressed or more tired, having less energy, unable to eat properly, increasingly sleepless, debilitated by lack of concentration, and increasingly less interested in your spouse or lover both emotionally and physically, it is appropriate for you to seek help. You should see a clinical mental health counselor or social worker, psychologist, psychiatrist, or psychiatric nurse, either in private practice or in a public mental health center. Often your friends or physician can help you find the right person. You can also call a local university counseling center for an appropriate referral.

Finding a job certainly can tear at self-esteem; the journey can be very negative and frightening. But it doesn't have to be that way. The job search is a wonderful opportunity to learn the art of self-appreciation, self-reliance, and self-encouragement. (And you thought you were just getting a job!) Practice controlling your own worldview, by seeing your world in ways that support you and build strength. Avoid trying to change things over which you have no control. Instead, begin using your inner strength to develop a peacefulness that can make you more creative, feel better about yourself, and less frantic. A woman who understands her mind-set has a true sense of herself, feeling anchored and competent no matter what happens in her environment. This centered woman is motivated internally, has a clear sense of her role in events, can maintain a view of relative calm, and then decide how she will react to events. This is the ideal centering for which to strive.

All of us can take positive steps to move toward this goal. Understanding your own mind-set is a significant step, as you create harmony and success for yourself in both the job search and the workplace.

Chapter 2

Women and Their Work:

Myths and Issues

Behold the turtle. He makes progress only when he sticks his neck out.
— James Bryant Conant

Certain themes, characteristics, feelings, and attitudes have woven their way into the fabric of women's lives, impacting upon the job search and work journey. Some of these issues follow us because of growing up in an atmosphere that might have been nonsupportive, neglectful, or even abusive. Other issues, thought patterns, and popular misconceptions involve societal messages about women that falsely tell us that we have certain limits and must behave in certain ways. As women, we have come to believe these repeated messages and ultimately they have inhibited our ability to hear our own voices. We feel it is important to identify some of these themes, particularly for women who have experienced uncertainty and difficulty in the job search and in the workplace. We encourage you to record those issues that seem pertinent to you in your notebook, and to begin to plan how to minimize their impact. Draw on your increased self-awareness developed in chapter 1 to help you isolate why some of these myths and issues have hampered you in the past.

The Big Issues

In the past decade, as women have carved some inroads into the male-oriented world of work, certain issues have gained near monumental prominence, while others remain powerful though never directly spoken of. These issues deal not only with our psyches, but with how the working world views our psyches. When women feel discriminated against, these are the issues that they tend to focus on, because so often what is acceptable in our male counterparts in the working world is either not acceptable in women or is assumed to be missing from the repertoire of women's experiences. We address these important issues here, not with a sense of blame, but because all of us, men and women alike, must confront these misperceptions in order to eliminate them from our work lives.

Body language, what you say, and how you say it communicate your sense of your own power. Unfortunately, many women are extremely uncomfortable with the whole issue of power. Either overtly or subliminally, the message is that the display of power in women is unfeminine and offensive to men. As one woman we interviewed said, "Women shy away from power, because it sounds nasty, dirty, unbecoming, male, and macho," so women dance around the power issue as if barefoot on hot coals. There is a tendency to think of power as a club that is wielded to get people to bend to your wishes, and it is this kind of interpretation that is distasteful to many women. Actually, there may not be many positive models of power in your life, but if you define power as the ability to influence people to accomplish positive goals, then power is quite appealing.

Another woman we interviewed, who is now a college president, had been the second ranking lawyer in the White House. She said she never felt comfortable using power to obtain personal privileges, such as having the White House operator make dinner reservations. When it came to social policy, however, such as placing women and people of color on the federal bench, then she would use every bit of power she could wield.

The state of Vermont elected its first woman governor, Madeline M. Kunin. She went on to serve for three terms. When she decided not to run for a fourth term, the *Burlington Free Press,* Vermont's largest paper, ran the following comment in an editorial discussing her decision not to run. "Being governor – issuing orders, duking it out with opponents, leaping from crisis to crisis – has not come naturally to Kunin. It isn't that she's done a poor job (history won't deliver its verdict for some time yet), but that she often seems as uncomfortable with authority as a man in a badly fitting suit." Kunin acknowledged the stress of power in a revealing speech to a group of women politicians. "Women can acquire the technical skills of politics with relative ease," she said. "What is more difficult to define and to acquire is a comfort level with power itself . . . We are still learning the culture of public life – dealing with conflict, going into battle and emerging from battle with the strength to continue the fight . . . Each day we go through not only outer skirmishes, but inner ones as well." Kunin has stated the struggle that women have with power very well. Her own style of being dignified, low-key, and well-acquainted with the issues was so different from her male predecessors that she was sometimes criticized as lacking leadership. To many, it would seem, power has as much to do with delivery as with achieving goals, and those who are used to male delivery may be uneasy with female methods. Obviously, this does not necessarily make female methods less effective, unless we choose to continue to view them as such.

Go back into your personal history and see how you perceive power. You may have learned when you were young that it was not appropriate to speak up for yourself. You may even have been punished when you tried. But, as they say, that was then, and this is now. Today, power is positive; it is only a question of how you choose to perceive it and to use it. Power is useful in all phases of the job search, but particularly in networking and negotiating. Projecting power, confidence, and success is helpful in the negotiating process, whether it be for salary or for other job benefits or conditions. A woman who is well-prepared, speaks with command and measure to her voice, and keeps her eyes straight ahead on the person she is addressing is powerful. Her language is assertive and to the point. She avoids seeming meek, being apologetic or hedging, and does not allow unnecessary interruptions. And, in the job search, the other side of power – how you react to others with power – is also extremely important. Obviously, the power rests with the person in the position to hire; if you retreat around authority, you are unlikely to win the job and the conditions you need.

A woman related this story to us.

> While in a grocery store recently, I approached four impeccably dressed men in dark business suits, speaking with serious, digni-fied voices, looking as if they were discussing high level, powerful issues. The first thoughts that ran through my mind were that they were there to make decisions on the future of the store. As I got closer, I saw that they each had small grocery items in their hands, but had not yet gotten into line because they were examining and discussing the mechanics of an electronic beer ad that was directly in front of them. I had been sure they were deciding the future of the store, and yet they were actually shopping, just like I was. The power these men were projecting from their dress, concentration, voices, and stance determined my perception of the situation. I had not heard a single spoken word before drawing my conclusion!

How do you react to power? How do you react to authority figures in general? Do you feel comfortable when you are in a position of power, or do you quickly find a way to diminish your position? Were there any female models of power in your childhood? Did your mother or female care-giver make the many, many daily decisions and then wait for Dad or the male care-giver to come home to decide on anything important? Jot some notes or even a brief story about a lasting impression you have where power was the issue.

Some issues exist more in people's minds than in the realities of human interactions. Team play may well be one of those issues, but because it often has sexist overtones – overtones that reflect negatively on women – it becomes a very real issue for women in any organization and in any job. A workplace team shares a basic understanding and appreciation of each other's talents, strengths, and shortcomings. Team members are supportive of each other's work efforts. The result is a mutually productive and satisfying work site in which the tasks of the group are accomplished in an effective manner. Positive team efforts can result in a superior job done in an efficient and timely manner. Being a successful team player involves setting aside individual goals and joining together with others to produce the greater result. As in anything, some people function well in a team; others do their best work independently.

Many books describe the differences between men and women in the workplace: their management styles, ability to be team members, thinking styles, interpersonal styles, and so on. Men and women still bring different behaviors to the workplace and the job search; some of those distinctions are diminishing as years progress, and others will never change. Vive la difference! But differences tend to breed stereotypes, and it is these stereotypes that are damaging to women in the job-search effort. Here's how it goes: Because women have not generally participated in team sports, they do not know how to be team players. Actually, there are many excellent female team players in the workplace (and on the athletic field) who bring a true spirit of encouragement, support, energy, and cooperation to a team project. And, too, there are male team players who are so competitive that their groups make little progress because of lack of cooperation. And, yes, there are men in the former situation and women in the latter situation.

Women are team players, but they need to demonstrate their ability to function well as part of the work team in their resumes, when they are networking, interviewing, and negotiating. (Avoid getting in your own way by tripping over the argument that women should not have to prove their team worthiness if men don't. Better to get the job, get on the team, and dispel prejudices by example.) Women can use their natural empathic, encouraging, cooperative, and intuitive skills to be excellent team players without ever having picked up a bat, slam-dunked, or been part of a successful fifty-yard touchdown pass. A lot of us have played sports; many of us have observed them as spectators. Women aren't fools. We know how to size up a situation. Don't let anyone tell you you're deficient, because you weren't a "real" sports player.

Be savvy about this "team player" stuff. Western male culture tends to glorify the benefits of sports teams, but what people learn from playing sports isn't necessarily about working together to make a touchdown, basket, goal, or home run. The lessons of the sporting arena don't necessarily transfer positively into the workplace with everyone pulling together toward a common goal. Consider such terms as the squeeze play, end run, quarterback sneak, the fake, full court press, or psyching out your opponent that describe moves where the players use deception, very aggressive tactics, ganging up, and clever tricks to accomplish their goals. And, too, personal glory is often part of the prize they are out to win. Many team players have brought these experiences from the playing field into the workplace. Be aware of this kind of negative team behavior. When it comes to interview time, team playing is idealized, and you need to demonstrate your abilities to support a team effort, but don't be naive about the realities of team spirit.

When the team play becomes unfair in your eyes, but is just part of the game to the person who values these tactics, how will you react? Many men enjoy competitive jousting in the workplace. They do not think anything of it, and they would be amazed if they were accused of "doing in" the next guy. It is just a game to them – nothing personal. Women, however, when exposed to this kind of behavior can become frightened, very defensive, and plan a counterattack that goes right for the jugular. Here is where the men and women who enjoy competitive sports may have an advantage. They are used to having the battle be a game that they can put away at the end of one day and start fresh the next. Lawyers are often in this kind of competition as they battle it out in the court room and then play a friendly game of tennis together in the evening. For the most part, when a man loses a battle, he regroups and moves on to the next challenge. Many women, however, take their defeats very personally, not viewing them as a game at all, but rather as a personal affront. Defeat may affect a woman in such a way that she becomes obsessed about the outcome and feels like a failure.

The skills required in team play are the ability to work with others: to listen, be flexible, communicate clearly and effectively, give and take constructive criticism, and provide support and encouragement to other team members for their efforts. In addition, employers are looking for candidates who can be creative, but when necessary, for the good of the team and its goals, also be able to conform.

How do your tendencies, past behaviors, and insight into your mind-set mesh with these ideas about team work? Using creative visualization, create your own sense of a team in detail and write it down in your notebook. Later, when you are interviewing or talking to a prospective boss, you will be able to draw on this image. It will help you to feel comfortable and prepared, and, thus, be impressive.

Humor on the Job

There is a place for humor in almost every area of our lives, and the job search is no different. (By humor, we mean the ability to laugh and express pleasure and joy – not to provide entertainment by clowning and belittling.) If you are basically a hard-working, task-oriented person, it may be difficult to recognize joy, laughter, or humor in work situations. Today, in the workplace as well as in the job-search process, the lack of humor can be a very real detriment in achieving your objective. What's more, the whole issue of humor and its appropriateness can be complicated by gender differences in both appreciation and expression of humor.

Humor helps us feel connected with others in a warm and friendly manner. In the workplace, those with a sense of humor are valued and sought out by others. Humor plays an important role in creating an atmosphere where morale is high and people are self-motivated and productive. Humor helps people be better listeners; it breaks the ice when there is tension; it provides a gentler language for the expression of constructive criticism. Humor helps create a common ground where class and educational differences are minimized. It helps us to be more receptive to learning and more insightful and creative in job-search tasks and decision-making. Generally, people with humor have a much easier time connecting with others in a meaningful way that says, "I would like to work with you and get to know you better."

> Jeanne was an administrative assistant in a medical support ser-
> vices group. The space she had to work in was a mere cubicle, one
> of those rug-coated dividers that graces many offices today. She
> could stand in the middle of her space and touch the divider walls
> in all directions. Most people could not have tolerated it. However,
> the job was a good one with lots of visibility, interaction with
> others, and the possibility of advancement. Jeanne decided to
> make the best of it and decorate her space with all kinds of
> humorous items. She had a small vertical fish tank in which the
> fish swam up and down instead of across. The dividers were
> adorned with a collection of cartoons, humorous photos, and
> cards. Her coworkers were always peeking their heads in to see
> the latest additions. Jeanne was a no-nonsense worker, but her
> relationships with her colleagues were extremely gratifying to her
> and to them. Elizabeth had recently been hired for an administra-
> tive position and her temporary space was near Jeanne's. After
> Elizabeth had been on the job for just three days, she was called
> out of town on business. Jeanne was aware that Elizabeth was
> new and trying to get to know others in the division. While Eliza-
> beth was gone, Jeanne spread artificial spider webbing all over her

space. When Elizabeth returned to the office, everyone was waiting to see her reaction. It truly broke her up as all her new colleagues joined in the prank. Not only did it have the effect of sharing laughter together, but it also helped bond Elizabeth to her coworkers much more quickly.

Jeanne was the catalyst in the office for team spirit and positive relationships. She is the kind of person who is sought after by prospective employers, because of her ability to bring others together, as well as being very productive in her own work.

There has been an incredible interest in humor in the last decade, much of it as a result of Norman Cousins' book, *Anatomy of an Illness,* and numerous studies showing that humor stimulates greater creativity and problem-solving ability in individuals and in work groups. People with a sense of humor have always been valued in the workplace. But now with the increasing awareness of the positive effects of humor, being able to look on the light side is one of the things that interviewers look for in prospective candidates. The use of positive humor during tense moments in a meeting or job interview is often very helpful in dispelling tension. But it is important not to belittle an issue that is important to a person with whom you may be negotiating or interviewing.

Women and men often perceive humor differently, which can lead to misunder-standings. Avner Ziv, a noted researcher on humor, noted in his book, *Personality and Sense of Humor,* that women laugh more and have a greater appreciation of humor, while men make more jokes and tend toward more creative humor. Men seem to indulge in some hard-hitting kidding in the name of humor, while women are less comfortable with "direct hits" and the "quick comeback" if the comments seem hurtful.

It is important to remember that an interviewer may actually test you to see if you have a sense of humor, and you need to be aware that it may not be the kind of humor that you are used to experiencing. If the humor seems harsh, corny, or simply not funny, try to let it go or at least not be judgmental. Listen to it, observe, and try to learn something from it. Remember that the way a person uses humor also tells something about that person. Humor can indicate a desire to share, warm up to someone, break the ice, create distance, or indicate discomfort. You certainly don't need to be a professional humorist to have a sense of humor or an appreciation of humor. Some of us are better at delivering the humor; others are better at receiving it. Both are valued at any stage of the job search or in the workplace.

But what if you truly feel that you do not have a sense of humor? This belief may be a perception you have carried out of your past and needs to be reexamined. Offer yourself some new choices and try humor out in different situations. You can start by observing what makes other people have a sense of humor. What do they see or say that is funny? Build a sense of humor about yourself at work and home that fosters positive feelings, for good feelings often lay the foundation for spontaneous humor. Begin by covering walls and desks with humorous things such as Jeanne did. Or make a point of sharing the lighter moments (which tend to be comical) that have happened to you recently.

An issue of the *Office Professional,* states, "Anyone can learn to be funnier than he is now by immersing himself in humor, going to funny movies, reading funny books, hanging around with funny people. Paying attention to the kind of things that make people laugh helps develop the ability to see the funny things in life." Humor joins, it heals, and it inspires. A sense of humor enriches and broadens our lives. It provides a tool for developing attitudes that make us more personally creative, which makes us more valued in the workplace.

Personal Battles

Some issues affect every aspect of our lives, and when they spill over into our job search efforts, their negative impact can be destructive and debilitating. We each can take steps to regain control of these aspects of our behaviors and redirect the energy to more positive use.

Guilt

A therapist once observed that of all human emotions, guilt is the least useful. The only positive use of guilt is as an indicator of conflicting thoughts, emotions, and goals. The task is to look at the conflicts, resolve them, and dissolve the guilt.

Child care is one issue that causes many women to experience ongoing guilt. Sometimes women feel guilty because they have an uneasy feeling that their children deserve or need better child care. If these feelings seem to haunt you, ask yourself if you have taken all logical steps to assure the best child care you can afford. If you have, then you have behaved very responsibly. If you continue to feel guilty, review what you have done, ask if there is anything else you could reasonably do, and unless there is new information, remind yourself that your guilt is unwarranted, and may be stealing your energy both from your job and from your time with your children.

Ongoing guilt may indicate you are responding to old, possibly outmoded ideas of what is appropriate behavior for a parent. Oftentimes, the guilt working women experience is not really about the quality of child care at all, but rather, indicates a belief that no child care, except that which a mother can personally give, will ever be adequate. This kind of guilt is often experienced by women who feel they really "don't have to work." If our mothers stayed home with us, many of us feel that we are somehow failing our children, no matter why we are in the workplace.

Many of us were brought up in households where our mothers were waiting for us when we got home from school. As children, we may have turned right around and gone off to play with friends, but the message from our mothers' example was "moms stay home."

> Kathy's mother said to her that she thought one of the most important things she did for her three children was to be home every day when they arrived home from school. Even though Kathy stayed home for ten years when her own children were small and then held jobs where she had the summer off for six more, her mother's message always made her feel guilty. Unevaluated, untempered by any of the other things Kathy did with her children, that remark sat there, making her feel bad. Her experience of her children's childhoods was tinged with guilt. Once the children were safely off to college, Kathy told her mother how much she had tried to make up for the fact that she wasn't home when her children arrived from school. Her mother's response was an astonished, "Why? Times are different and I would never expect the standards of my time to apply to yours!" What a lesson in the damage that old, unexamined statements and models can do!

Be alert to this kind of guilt from old messages. It can apply a mean set of brakes to your forward progress! Guilt is a barrier slowing us down, making us feel less accomplished, stealing energy. Guilt feelings are warning signs. If you notice them, stop and ask yourself what is going on? Try to sort out the old belief systems behind the feeling. Then question the belief. Is it still valid today? Does it reflect your values or someone else's? Just because you received these messages does not mean that you need to keep them. You can decide that an old message accurately represents the way you want to live and reaffirm it. You can also decide that it does not correlate with your beliefs or circumstances and change it. The power is yours. You can choose to be the victim or the manager of old models.

Social Apprehensions

Feeling socially uncomfortable or not knowing how to act or what to say is a frequent complaint of women, and these feelings of social inadequacy are exacerbated by the verbal exchanges required in the job search. Feeling this way impedes a woman's ability to interview, negotiate, research, and network. Some women only feel apprehensive when they are in new social situations, such as in an interview with a stranger. Other women always feel shy or uncomfortable in the presence of other people. They often prefer to work alone and have minimal contact with others. These women can be just as highly competent as more outgoing individuals, but they do not advance through the hiring process, because they have problems communicating their competence, their ideas, and their enthusiasm.

Women who feel socially ill at ease come from varied backgrounds, but the common theme running through their memories is that verbal exchanges were either infrequent or unpleasant. Oftentimes, these women come from backgrounds where parents were also extremely shy and very little social exchange took place between family members. Others feel culturally out of place, because they, perhaps, come from a rural area and now find themselves in an urban environment. Still others are adult children of alcoholics who experienced wild swings in communication from abusive language one moment to warm approval the next. It is no wonder that these women feel apprehensive about verbal communication.

An overwhelming sense of social discomfort, causing excessive shyness or aggressiveness, can result from not knowing how to act with people. We initially learn how to behave and interact with others from watching the significant people in early life. But if you were raised in any type of dysfunctional family, you may have had to learn behaviors that protected you at that time, thus leaving you feeling deficient today in the social skills you never learned. As if learning new social skills is not enough, you also have to unlearn behaviors that are not applicable to situations you find yourself in now. It is very important to examine how much of your reaction to people and conversation is based on the present and how much is based on past experiences.

If you feel extreme discomfort or even terror in an interview, negotiation, or other interpersonal situation, examine the meaning you have given to the situation. Challenging questions from an interviewer can trigger unconscious feelings from the past that have no relevance to your present situation. If you have taken the time to understand what kinds of behaviors in people trigger old responses from the past for you, it will be easier to keep focused on your present environment, diminishing your fears and feelings of entrapment. With a few positive experiences, you will begin to realize that you have the power and the freedom to give positive meaning to what is happening in the present. As a child, you may very well have been powerless or without appropriate models in your family, but now, as an adult, you are free to choose new, more appropriate meaning and behaviors to the social and professional situations you find yourself in.

Some of the women we interviewed for this book were adult children of alcoholics. They were successful adult women who had done some important self-examination in early adulthood (often with the help of a therapist or counselor) to develop a more positive mind-set and have been able to move far beyond their early childhood struggles. Although these women realized how difficult some of their childhood years had been, they refused to let the past dictate their ability to have successful and meaningful lives. Sheldon Kopp, in the preface of his book, *Who Am I . . . Really?* says, "Some childhood experiences are unavoidably unhappy, but they need not extend into sorrowfully enduring adult images of ourselves. Empathetic reexamination heals the wounded child within. If we are willing to explore the early anguish, then later on, our stories can end more happily than they began. *An unhappy childhood may be a good reason for grown-up misery, but it makes a poor excuse.*" (Italics are ours.)

Need for Approval

A job search is a time when some people do say no to us. The more we need constant approval or affirmation, the harder the rejection is, even when we intellectually understand it. One of the greatest gifts we can give ourselves is the ability to provide solace, support, and wisdom for ourselves, no matter what is occurring around us. If the happenings of the day have generally gone in the wrong direction, yet we are still able to affirm what went right and what we learned from the day (even if the lesson was hard), then we truly have a skill that will hold us in good stead.

Unfortunately, many of us seek approval and affirmation from outside sources and end up disappointed when we don't get the affirmation we want. To make matters worse, the need for constant approval gives the impression to others that we are needy and often impulsive in demands and behavior. Displaying this kind of behavior during an interview session ("How am I doing? Are my answers okay?") may make the interviewer wonder about your level of confidence and your ability to be a self-starter. Displaying needy behavior during a negotiation can place you in a position of weakness, especially if the behavior results in nervous talking. In the hiring process, prospective employers are looking for people who can get involved in the job with minimal disruption to the existing staff. Employers don't want an employee who continually interrupts the manager, supervisor, or coworkers looking for approval for every phase of a project. The director of a university career development center said that when he interviewed a candidate for a job, he was "always looking for someone to hire who could hit the ground running."

> *Carla was the fifth born in a family of seven children. Her parents were both hard-working people who often worked long hours to support their family. Carla constantly scrambled for her parents' attention when they came home, trying everything she could muster. Her parents were often tired and became exasperated by Carla's attention-getting behavior.*
>
> *As an adult, Carla had great difficulty getting what she wanted and needed for herself from employers, coworkers, and especially from people in authority. People treated her well initially, but then shunned her after awhile. In her previous jobs, she always had the sense that her managers would run in the other direction when they saw her coming. Even though she was bright, educated, and well-trained, she could not seem to advance in any company she worked for, and usually stayed with a company for only a year or two. Carla felt she never seemed to say or do the right thing in job interviews, and, in fact, she had not been offered a job after eight months of searching.*
>
> *Carla eventually recognized that it was her frantic, needy behavior, learned as a child seeking attention, that was interfering with her interpersonal skills, both on the job and in her job search. She admitted feeling unimportant and without value in her family. She later came to realize, that contrary to what she felt, her family had indeed loved her. Their behavior toward her was more related to their own feelings of overwork and pressure. Carla eventually came to understand that as an adult she was still behaving as she had as a child, constantly seeking attention from authority figures in interviews, in negotiations, and at work. As a child she had been powerless to change situations, but as an adult, when these same anxious, needy feelings arose during an interview or job negotiation session, she could quickly identify where they came from, settle down, evaluate the circumstances, and proceed to get down to the business at hand.*

People who need continual affirmation and approval often fight to make themselves the center of attention without really understanding why. If you see yourself exhibiting these kinds of behaviors, ask yourself where they are coming from.

Women who have these tendencies need to practice calm behavior. Practice sitting with people, and instead of talking, force yourself to do some very active listening and observing. Listen as if you were going to be graded on the content of people's conversations. Be attentive and speak only if you are asked an opinion or question. Notice that when you are not constantly fighting to get a word in edgewise, you actually experience calmness. Practice being more of an observer and less of a participator; you will be amazed at what you can learn.

Anger

Anger is one of the most difficult emotions to deal with. When it spills over into the job search, it can wreak havoc with even the most effective job-search plan. In truth, anger is a topic worthy of a whole book in its own right, but we wanted, at the very least, to call your attention to how misdirected anger can permeate all of your interpersonal interactions.

Harriet Braiker, in her book, *The Type E Woman* (where *E* stands for Everything to Everybody), refers to anger as the most problematic emotion for women to express, the one women feel most guilty about expressing. Repressed anger often triggers depression, which is why depression is often referred to as anger turned inward. When anger goes underground, it can break through in the form of irrational responses and behaviors or as physical complaints such as stomachaches, headaches, intestinal upsets, dizziness, and fatigue. We have worked with women who are extremely afraid of expressing a contradictory or angry thought. When this happens in the workplace, a relatively simple situation can escalate to a cold war, paralyzing not only the individual involved, but also the whole work group. How much better it is for everyone when anger is expressed, rather than hidden, denied, or rationalized.

We carry all levels of anger around with us. Angry people project feelings of hopelessness and powerlessness, none of which endear them to future employers. On a job interview, repressed anger might come across to the interviewer as a "chip on the shoulder," that intangible quality that makes the interviewer feel less than comfortable. A good interviewer will pick up on this, knowing that an angry person in the workplace exhibits negative behavior that lowers the morale and thus the productivity of those around her. Talk to those around you about your angry feelings, and begin to learn to recognize those feelings, deal with them, direct them at an appropriate source, or work through them with a counselor, and then get on with the task at hand. Don't let anger be the insidious force that keeps you out of the job you deserve.

When Your Spouse Moves

You have found a job you really look forward to every day, the kids are in great schools, and all of the recreational things you like can be done where you live. Then your husband or partner comes home and announces he has been transferred or that he has decided on a career change. Now, the decisions and the planning begin all over again. A generation ago, some of the decisions were automatic. You packed up, went with your spouse, and began again. Today, there are more options. Commuting marriages are more common. Many women make a higher percentage of the total family income, making it possible for their careers to determine geographic location. Some women are on a career track that they want to continue and therefore choose to delay a move to join their spouse until a more opportune time.

It is important, as the person who is not precipitating the decision, that you know what is crucial to you. What do you have to do to maintain your sense of yourself in a transition? Be clear with your spouse in defining how you feel about the move and let him know that you expect him to acknowledge your feelings. Ask your husband to enlist the help of his company in finding a job for you, if this seems appropriate. New hires or transfers often request assistance in relocating a spouse these days. Acknowledge your feelings of anger, grief, and loss, if you experience them, and discuss these feelings with a friend or your husband. When your husband's career is dictating your move, planning is another way of fighting those feelings of helplessness, anger, or depression that result from having no control over what happens. When you write a plan, you are back in the driver's seat. Given certain parameters, you define what you want to do.

If you have never gone through a personal planning process, now is the time to begin. As you define goals and objectives, some of the options you and your husband have will emerge as better alternatives to accomplish what you want. If you are facing a move to a new community, writing a job-search plan (see chapter 4) is one way to keep on track. In a new place, without the familiar anchors of your old community, a plan becomes a kind of anchor providing a thoughtful method of approaching the job search and maintaining the kind of balance you want between life's activities.

Women, Age, and Jobs

A woman making a career choice at age thirty faces a different set of issues from a woman making the same choice at age fifty-five. A lot of the differences have to do with the adult women in our own lives and what behaviors they modeled for us. And even though we have come a long way, children in grade school today will still face conflicting feelings between what they are told they can do and what they observed the significant women from their childhoods doing with their adult lives. Only recently have young girls in elementary and junior high school been challenged to think about what they want to do when they grow up. While still in school, they feel that the world is their oyster. They can do virtually anything – from business, construction, teaching, engineering, and medicine to human services. The options are manyfold. Paradoxically, these girls have mothers who have role modeled putting others' needs and wants first. So while these girls can conceptualize "I can do what I want," they have a hard time believing it completely for lack of appropriate models.

As a result of career decision making being introduced at a young age, women coming out of high school and college today are very concerned about their futures. Many identify themselves by the career they intend to pursue and have a very strong need to believe in their future independence and self-sufficiency. Many of these young women have observed their mothers dedicate their lives to family responsibilities. Some of these children have seen the marriages of these full-time parents and wives unexpectedly end in divorce. Their mothers, now in their fifties, struggle to identify who they are and what they want to do with their lives. They never expected that they would have to prepare for and choose a career to support themselves, because their goal had been to marry and work in the home. Young women, seeing their mothers and other important adult figures struggle in their fifties, recognize that they must learn to take care of themselves to avoid having this happen to them.

During their twenties, women struggle to establish their own sense of identity separate from that of their family. They also work to establish financial independence and freedom. This can be a very trying period in a woman's life. The "Who am I?" and "What do I want?" questions loom large. Twenty-year-olds may still be making choices about college and career to please parents. How her mother dealt with work and family may have a strong influence on how a young woman deals with this time in her life. For the most part, however, women in their twenties today are focused on establishing a career and getting themselves launched in the right direction before considering marriage and family.

The issue becomes more complex for a woman in her thirties. Many women in their thirties are wrestling with the question of how to balance family with career. This is a very challenging task in our society, as women are usually expected to be the primary care-givers to their children. Most organizations and industries are not set up to support women in their child-care role. Job sharing is still viewed as a new and cumbersome option. Part-time opportunities are limited and tend to slow down and interfere with a woman's career path and growth, as well as pay scale and benefits. Many women are faced with the conflict of rising through the ranks to the top of their career ladders or being the kind of mother they want to be. Other women in their thirties may have pursued a career so rigorously that they feel burned out. They may need to take a long vacation or sabbatical, or they may want to start a family and put their careers on hold for awhile. On the other hand, it's not uncommon for a woman in her thirties to feel that she has spent most of her twenties floundering, trying a variety of things out, never having hit the one thing that she really wanted to do. Her goal now is to find a job that will have long-term potential and that she can really commit herself to. The thirties can be an enormously confusing time. It's very important that women think about and focus on what it is they really want to do next.

For many women, their forties, as their children are growing up, is a time when they are ready to go back to work full-time. These mothers struggle to give up their identity as a parent and to decide just what it is they are going to do next. Other women in this age group started a family later in life, still have small children, and are contending with the issues of balancing family and work. Still other women in their forties are hitting their professional stride, feeling proud of their many years of effort and accomplishment.

As mentioned, more women in their fifties and sixties are entering the work force, either for their first time or for a second time, after a long absence while being a full-time mother and wife. They are often afraid and tend to have low self-esteem. What can I do at my age to support myself? What marketable skills do I have? Not all older women work for financial reasons. Some pursue new work for personal fulfillment; others to have something to do that gets them out of the house and in contact with other people. Regardless of the reason, older women often have the most challenging time identifying who they are and what they want, having spent most of their adult lives caring for others.

The issues outlined here are not necessarily specific to a particular age. A woman in her thirties may feel the same sense of lost identity as a woman in her fifties. Regardless of age, the issues affecting a woman's career choice all have the same impact: They tend to make it more challenging for us as women to be connected with who we are and what we want. Yet, to be satisfied in our careers, we must make choices that do, in fact, support who we are and what we want.

In your personal journey in search of the right job for you (chapter 3), you will be asked to identify what you want in a job to ensure your satisfaction. If asking for what you want is difficult for you, start doing one thing a day that you really want to do. It may not be career related, but it should be something that will allow you to begin to strengthen your ability to take action on your innermost desires and wishes. Perhaps you want to get yourself a massage or spend time with someone that you really enjoy. Perhaps there is a movie you want to see; consider going to it alone. Maybe there is a book you want to read, a course you want to take, a concert you want to attend. Every day see if you can take time – from five minutes to a few hours – to do something you really want to do for yourself. The more you get used to making choices from your heart, and acting on them, the greater your chances of achieving a satisfying career life. The older you are, the more challenging this may be, because you may have spent a lifetime nurturing others. Stick with it and get support if you need it. (You may want to explore local women's groups and organizations.)

For all women, regardless of age, it is still a challenge for us to recognize what we want, who we are, and what our strengths really are. As women, we tend to make enormous concessions with ourselves and with the choices we make. As we enter the twenty-first century, let us hope that we will feel better supported in expressing who we are and what we want, and that we take the action necessary to fulfill our life goals and dreams.

What are the issues you are having to contend with, given your age and current life circumstances? List these in your notebook. How might you resolve them? Do you trust your ability to know what you want in life or in a job? List some activities you might get involved with that would help you become more accustomed to knowing what it is you want for you.

Doing for Others

In learning to listen to our own hearts and minds, we need to watch our tendency as women to put others' needs and desires before our own. Women have learned to be peacemakers and nurturers. Here's how these roles get played out in the job search process.

★ One woman doesn't work because her husband doesn't want her to.

★ Another woman moves, disrupting her own career, because of her spouse's relocation.

★ Another woman pursues occupations (secretarial, nursing, or teaching) that involve nurturing and caring for others when these may not be her true interests.

★ Another controls her success (including not making more money) to avoid upsetting her significant other.

★ Another won't ask for a raise or confront a coworker because of the displeasure this might arouse.

Our actions are dictated by our concern to please others and receive approval. Often we do what we think everyone else wants us to do.

Along with pleasing others, women have also learned through the socialization process that the way to progress in life and to know that we're doing well is by doing a better job. Many women have not learned the important skills of negotiating and networking (how to talk with people and to use resources) to get where we want to go. Instead, we tend to believe that if we just work hard and do a great job, we will be rewarded with a promotion. Such is not always the case. Successful career people make their goals known and strive for promotions within their current place of employment. They know that by building strong relationships with their coworkers and employer, they improve their chances of career growth and advancement.

Sometimes, we feel guilty when looking for a new job because we believe it means we are not being loyal to our employer, leaving him or her in the lurch with a set of unresolvable problems. Do not be a rescuer. You are replaceable. You can be committed to what it is you are doing now and still take care of yourself by looking for other opportunities. The axe can fall at any time. No job is a guaranteed, secure situation. A wise person knows that nothing is forever. The people who seem most satisfied in their work are those who are happy with where they are, but also have some ideas about where they want to go next.

A final comment about doing for others: Many women continue to wrestle with an inner voice that states a good woman does work that involves nurturing and caring for others. This is particularly true for older women who struggle to recognize that there are careers outside of care-giving. While being nurturing is a positive quality women bring to the working world, a woman must *choose* whether or not she wants to be part of a care-giving profession. It is okay to do work that does not involve helping those in need. Women need to open their eyes, ears, hearts, and minds to the myriad of jobs available. For women, especially, this is an important part of the job-search process.

How do you put others before yourself? Have you made choices (either career or other) to please somebody else? Write notes in your notebook about how this issue has been relevant in your life.

Fear of Failure

Many women fear change because they are afraid of making the wrong decision and failing. Consequently, they don't identify their career goals because they are afraid of taking risks that they perceive might lead to failure.

There is no such thing as a wrong career decision, only decisions from which you can learn and grow, if you use your positive mind-set and choose to look at them that way. People who are self-employed frequently acknowledge that the experiences from which they have learned and grown the most have been those in which they have fallen flat on their faces, done a lousy job, lost a client or customer, or failed. They've used these experiences to remedy their weaknesses and build on their strengths.

The hardest job change for most people is the first change. Our fear of change usually greatly exceeds the actual experience itself. Fear comes from an imagined consequence: "If I leave my job, I'll end up in a worse situation," or "I'll never get another job," or "I'll end up in bankruptcy." Usually our worst fantasies don't happen.

> I remember a client who had been on the third shift in a manufacturing plant. She had two small children and a husband whom she virtually never saw because of her work schedule. She had been on this shift for twelve years, and she felt very comfortable and locked into the wonderful organizational conditions and paycheck that she had grown used to over the years. But she was bored with her job. She was afraid of the prospect of starting a new job and leaving a job she'd known most of her adult life. Through our work together she discovered that what she really wanted to do was to help people, perhaps in a counseling capacity. She arranged some informational interviews and called me after a month's time to say that she had accepted a job selling life insurance. I was concerned that selling life insurance probably wasn't compatible with who she was, and that she would have a hard time recreating the sense of security that she had in a larger corporation. She thanked me for my feedback, but stayed with her choice.
>
> Three months later, I heard back from her. Selling life insurance had been a disaster, but she had not felt it was the wrong decision. Taking the insurance job had allowed her to leave an occupation that she had felt stuck in for years. She learned that she could survive happily without it. She left the sales job and went on to a position as an office manager with a trucking firm, where she experienced a lot of autonomy and acknowledgment that came with being associated with a small business where she felt she could make a difference. Her first decision had not been a mistake; it had helped her to move forward.

Learning to face failure and to deal with it successfully is more valuable than learning how to avoid it. Many courses that help women learn how to take risks are available. Consider looking into courses at your local college or university, particularly through continuing adult education programs. Outdoor adventure courses, such as ropes courses and Outward Bound, are also beneficial. Many resorts now offer such courses on a week-long and weekend basis.

Have you had any failures in your life of either a personal or professional nature? How did you deal with them? What did you learn from them? If you felt defeated by them, how might you deal with them more productively in the future?

The Popular Myths

A myth is defined by Webster as "any fictitious story . . . any imaginary person or thing spoken of as though existing." As women, our heads are filled with myths regarding our career development and job potential. As we become more aware of these myths as well as our own historic tendencies to respond in certain ways, we can quickly see how certain thoughts block us from identifying, seeking, and achieving satisfying jobs. We will look at some of the more popular myths that have clouded job search and career growth, that have followed us from entry level positions and now threaten to keep us out of boardrooms. What is truly alarming is that many of these myths are widely accepted as fact. What is truly encouraging is that women such as you are now confronting them head-on. Awareness is the first step toward overcoming these blocks.

Who I Am Is What I Do

Think for a moment what happens when you are at a social gathering and someone meets you for the first time. They ask that infamous question, "And what do you do?" And we respond with "I am a stockbroker" or "I am a teacher" or "I am a housewife and mother." We fill in the blanks with our occupational title and reinforce the belief that *who we are is what we do*. We become accustomed to being identified by our job title. Although who we are really is separate from what we do, giving up a career may feel like giving up our identity. As a lawyer considering a career change put it, "For fourteen years I have been identified as a lawyer. Now, when I talk with people at a party, if I'm not a lawyer, who am I? No longer will people give me those strokes that have kept me hooked into an occupation that really doesn't satisfy me." The less we can learn to identify ourselves by our jobs, the freer we will feel to consider other options. Who you are is not what you do. Hopefully, what you do supports who you are and is a vehicle for your self-expression. There are not only other careers, but also other areas in your life where you can express the essence of your being.

In your notebook, jot down thoughts you have about who you are. Do you think that who you are is what you do for work? What else do you do (or would you like to do) that might act as a vehicle for expressing who you are? The next time you're at a party, how would you like to answer the "What do you do?" question?

Change Is a Threat to My Financial Survival

Money is too often the ruthless ruler in our lives. Because of our financial obligations, most of us will not consider making a job change, unless we are either extremely unhappy and uncomfortable with the work that we're doing or get laid off. And, too, many of us won't take the time to do a thorough job search, because the pressure is on to get a job and a paycheck. Job decisions are frightening because, in large part, what we do for work is closely allied with our financial survival. If we start a new job or change to a new field, we risk taking a pay cut and starting lower on the totem pole. This kind of thinking leads people to feel trapped in their jobs. We assume that what we've got is as good as it's going to get. Unless forced out, we might as well stay where we are.

This is how most people cope in unhappy work situations. Of course, money is an important reason for working. To assume, however, that we have to stick with a job or career path solely for financial reasons is to deny ourselves the opportunity to find more meaningful work. Often women believe they can't do what they want and also make money. Unless you're willing to explore and research the possibility of finding work that is both fulfilling and pays the bills, you'll never learn if this is a fallacy.

To help with these survival fears, many women have found it useful to have a so-called security skill: a skill that is readily marketable and employable, something they can do to make money, no matter what, even if the work isn't the passion of their life. When we know we can take care of our financial needs, we feel freer in our thinking to find out what it is we really want to do. We feel we have more options. Think about what you could do to generate money if you had to do something new tomorrow (unexpectedly or by choice). Perhaps you could apply your cooking skills in catering or at a restaurant. If you know how to type, you can easily learn word processing, a skill that is readily marketable for both temporary and permanent positions. Substitute teachers may be in demand in your geographical area.

You may want to develop a specific marketable skill to take care of your financial needs while you explore what it is you really want to do. Many women today are receiving training at vocational centers associated with their local high school in trades such as carpentry, plumbing, and electrical work—jobs traditionally held by men that are better paying and provide greater financial security. Developing computer skills also will contribute to your being more employable. You may want to check with your state's Department of Employment and Training to find out what job areas are in need of qualified people and where you could develop those skills. Pursuing further training is not necessarily costly. Many institutions can provide tuition assistance. And if the thought of taking a course scares you, know that many women discover that being in a classroom is a far more satisfying experience as an adult than it was as a child or adolescent. If you have any enterprising leanings, you may want to consider selling your skills on a self-employed or consulting basis. A self-employed typist or tutor can often make better money than those employed by someone else.

Most of us quite simply can not afford taking much time off to conduct the ideal job search. We may have financial obligations to children and perhaps even parents who are dependent upon us for their care. If this is the case for you, it is important to recognize that finding fulfilling work may take longer than it otherwise would with savings in the bank. Making a career change while working full-time is like having two full-time jobs. You'll need to follow the job search plan you develop in chapter 4 even more carefully to be sure that your goals don't get squeezed out in the press of time and responsibilities. Experimenting with new fields on a volunteer, part-time, or moonlighting basis may open up doors to you. Pursuing jobs through a temporary agency may also lead to new work opportunities. As one woman returning to the working world after being at home for twenty years put it, "I was anxious about getting dressed up and going back to work. Could I do it? How would I be accepted? What if I failed? Going to work on a temporary basis eased me back into the world of work and allowed me to build up my self-confidence. I found the diversity of temporary jobs helpful to me in clarifying my career goals, as well as in paying my bills. Now I'm not afraid to try new jobs and have discovered through my own experience that there are a lot of opportunities out there if you're willing to give them a try!"

Being financially responsible does not have to preclude exploring new careers. If you are looking for work and need to accept the first job offered to you for financial reasons, consider in your own mind taking it as a temporary measure—something you're going to do for the time being, while you continue to look for what it is you really want to do. Think about and talk over with other people what you can do to take care of your financial commitments while pursuing a new career. And remember that the possibility exists for you to love what you do for work and make money doing it!

How much money do you need to generate to meet your financial responsibilities? Work out a budget in your notebook. What are some jobs you could go after tomorrow if you had to for financial reasons? Look through the want ads of your local paper, visit a temporary agency, talk with people to help you identify your survival skills.

My Job Should Make Me a Happy Person

A dangerous standard that emerged in the 1980s was the need for a job to fulfill everything and anything a woman needs to feel good about herself. Feelings of self-worth come from within and are not dictated by external factors. To expect that a job will fulfill you in every way possible may be setting yourself up for frustration and disappointment.

In any job, there will be problems: interpersonal conflicts and misunderstandings, tasks that may be boring but necessary, and beautiful sunny days when you'd rather be out playing than inside working! It is important that you have a realistic clarity about what you need and don't need in your job to feel satisfied. Likewise, do not settle for conditions and responsibilities if they feel abusive to you. While a job cannot ultimately fulfill you, it can nourish and build your self-esteem. The right amount of support plus challenge can help you to feel better about yourself, but no job can make you an intrinsically happy human being. There is an important difference between being happy in your job and having your job make you happy.

Review your notes from chapter 1 concerning persistent behaviors that are no longer in your best interest. Are you currently dissatisfied with other aspects of your life? List these in your notebook. What actions might you take to remedy these sources of unhappiness? How might they relate to expectations you may have for a job?

I Have to Remain in My Job
for the Rest of My Work Life

No, you don't! In fact, because of our constantly changing world and our need for some sense of fulfillment in our jobs, people are changing jobs on the average of once every two to three years and changing careers three to five times during the course of their working lives. No longer are we making a career choice in our early twenties that we then have to stick with until retirement. How can you know now who you'll be and what you'll want ten years from today? You can only focus on who you are and what you want now, and based on that, begin to move toward what you want to do next.

Fortunately, we're starting to break some old societal rules regarding when in our lives we should be in school, be in a job, and take time off. No longer are we adhering to the education from age four to about eighteen to twenty-one, work from age twenty-one to fifty-five, and retirement from age fifty-five until death plan. Avoid any rigid thinking and planning that causes you to limit your options. Women are going back to school at forty, starting a family at thirty-five, re-entering the work force at fifty, taking time off to travel at thirty. As a seventy-year-old woman, starting a new career in writing, put it, "I've still got a lot in me to offer. I'm not ready to be put out to pasture yet!"

Perhaps what is next for you is a new career. Or maybe you'd like to take some time off to travel or pursue further education and training or spend time with family and friends. More and more people are taking breaks in their careers to pursue other life goals. Many are never retiring, but instead are changing to more satisfying jobs for the first time in their lives. In today's world, women and men are less willing to postpone those things that they really want to be doing now.

Are there things you'd like to do next that may or may not include a job or career change? Is there a job or career you'd pursue no matter how little money you had available? What would you like to do for yourself and for the world around you? Write these in your notebook.

"If Only . . . Then I Could!"

"If only
   . . . I had gone to college."
   . . . I were younger."
   . . . I lived somewhere else."
   . . . I were a man."
   . . . I didn't have kids."
   . . . I had known as a kid what I wanted to do."
   . . . My guidance counselor had done a better job."
   . . . I had lots of money."

. . . etc., etc., etc.!" Our thought patterns frequently justify staying where we are, rather than initiating a job search. "If only I were different in some way, then I could have a job that was satisfying." This is not to say that your age, background, geographical location, and other factors may not pose some realistic challenges and barriers. You need to distinguish for yourself those barriers and blocks you are imagining from those that are genuine considerations. And a real barrier does not have to stop you from going after what you want. Any barrier, once acknowledged, is a lot less threatening.

A similar myth is "there's someone more qualified than I am." That may be, but comparing yourself against a fictitious someone else leads to self-defeating behavior. Which is more satisfying: Having your reasons or having results? Get support in pushing past your "if only" assumptions. You will encounter road-blocks and rejection while seeking a happier career life, but don't personalize these events. Keep moving steadfastly toward your goal, and you'll achieve results despite any real or imagined barriers.

What are your "if . . . then's"? Brainstorm in your notebook all of those assumptions you've made about yourself that, if changed, would permit you to pursue a rewarding career. Don't be embarrassed by what you come up with — we all have our hidden thoughts about ourselves. Look over your list. Cross off those that are not based on fact. How might you overcome those that remain on your list? How important are these in attaining your goals. (A college education might help get that job, but is it necessary? In reality, is past experience just as valid?)

Sometimes looking at our fears and doubts can be uncomfortable. Congratulations for having the courage to look at how your perceptions may block your job-search options.

Chapter 3

Job Satisfaction: Knowing What You Want and Need

Ellie Byers

Be patient to all that is unsolved in your heart, and try to love the questions themselves. – Rilke

"What do you want to be when you grow up?" Most of us have given considerable thought to this question. No longer is it enough for us to work solely for money and to establish financial security. We want more from our jobs. We want the satisfaction that comes from autonomy and decision making on the job; doing work that makes a difference in other people's lives; having variety in our job tasks; having contact with people; receiving recognition for our work; and feeling that we are growing and learning new things throughout our careers. We want our work to be a vehicle for self-expression, to be a place that we look forward to going to on Monday morning.

As adults, we are growing and evolving. We aren't ever going to "grow up" in the sense of reaching a magical age where who we are and what we want are carved in concrete. What we seek in our work lives changes over time. What we want in our twenties is different from what we want in our forties. Life's circumstances change.

Not only are we changing, but so also is the world of work. Two-thirds of today's kindergarten students are going to be in jobs in the future that don't even exist today. The business world is constantly in flux. No longer can we expect the company or organization that employs us to take care of us for the rest of our working lives. Women are learning not to expect that marriage is a guarantee for future security. True security exists when we can unconditionally trust our own ability to generate and maintain financial independence and personal happiness.

How have you ended up where you are now? Here's what some women have said:

> "I fell into it (my career)."
> "It's what I thought I could do."
> "My father, mother, teacher, sibling, spouse, boyfriend, friend said I'd be good at it."
> "I got offered the job, so I took it."
> "My husband wanted me to take it so that I could support him in what he's doing."

In this chapter, we'll begin the work of making career choices. We'll begin setting goals and making changes where necessary. *You'll be identifying what you want to do next in your work life, not what you're going to do for the rest of your life.* The information and tools provided are intended to teach you what you need to know to take charge of your work life so that you'll be better equipped to make all of the work-related changes you can expect to encounter throughout your adult life.

I have quoted some of the comments clients have made while working through these exercises, because I want to emphasize the importance of actually doing the exercises, not just reading through them. Many of these exercises ask you to highlight your responses in the book, jot notes in the margin, and write in your notebook. It is important to do these exercises because they are part of the self-discovery process.

The Career Identification Process

The Bigger Picture

The process of identifying what you want to do and can do for work involves making a series of smaller choices based on who you are and what you want. Many questions need to be answered to help you figure out and identify work that will meet your needs and desires:

★ Who am I now and how do I trust myself to know that what I think I want is what I really want?

- ★ What motivates me in my work?

- ★ What does my heart tell me about what makes me happy?

- ★ What blocks me from having what I want in work (see chapters 1 and 2)?

- ★ How do I balance work with my role as a parent, wife, partner, volunteer, friend, student? What about my personal free time?

- ★ Is what I want to do job-related or more of a hobby?

- ★ What kind of work is best suited to my needs?

- ★ How do I translate what I want into reality? Can I do what I want now or will it have to wait until another time in my life?

- ★ How will work fit in with my other life goals and priorities?

You are the one with the answers to these questions, though you may not know it yet. Nobody else can know or tell you what would be the best career for you. To be truly satisfied with the choices you'll make, the process requires that you explore your inner feelings, motivations, and present mind-set to discover what it is you want to do. Focus on listening to yourself and discovering what is in your heart and mind. As you become more certain of what you want, you may choose people to give you feedback. The satisfied woman of the 1990s will be the woman who makes choices consistent with who she is and what she wants to do.

The Career You Want: The Three Cs

While there are broad questions to be considered, figuring out what you want to do also involves identifying specific preferences necessary to ensure your job satisfaction. Areas that need to be clarified in order to better understand what you're looking for in a career include the three Cs: Content, Conditions, and Compensation.

Content: The content of a job addresses the question of what you want to do on a day-to-day basis and what area(s) of expertise you want to use. The content of your job consists of tasks and responsibilities you enjoy in a field that you find stimulating.

Conditions: What are the job conditions that will help you do your best work? These include size and nature of the organization you work for (or perhaps self-employment), schedule, environment, location of the work site, geographic location, types of people you work with, dress code, and travel. When the conditions feel right, you will be able to focus your energy on the job itself.

Compensation: How much do you need to earn – not only for paying bills, but also for your own self-esteem? What benefits, perks, vacations, health packages, child-care provisions do you need to make your job feasible and rewarding?

Each of us has certain criteria in each of these three areas that, if met, will help ensure job satisfaction. It is important that you are stimulated by the content of the job, that you like your working conditions, and that the compensation is both adequate and rewarding.

The exercises that follow will help you make the many decisions involved in identifying what the three Cs are for you. While doing them, watch for those influences that may alter your thinking and take you away from what's true for you. Are you choosing something because you think you should? Are you choosing something because you know you can do it, even though you may be capable of doing a lot more? Are you selecting something because you feel driven to prove something about yourself when, in fact, it's not what you really want or like to do? Be true to yourself. Listen to yourself. Trust yourself.

Some of the exercises may be difficult to complete, because you haven't had much past experience to draw from. For example, you may not know whether you'd want to work for a small or a large organization, if you have never worked for either. Take the best guess you can, and don't waste too much time deliberating over these items. If you think something may prove to be important to you, learn the pros and cons by talking it over with someone who has had experience with it.

Be patient with yourself. Much of this work may be new to you. Warm up to a comfortable pace gradually. Do the exercises in a number of sittings. Go back over them. Change your answers as often as necessary. Go ahead and choose two items that may seem contradictory to you like needing "security" and "self-employment." It is usually advisable to do the exercises when you are feeling okay about yourself, and when you are not feeling emotionally upset. If you're having a bad day, save these exercises for another time when you're feeling a bit better. Examples have been given to help you understand how to approach some of the exercises, but they are just examples, not prototypes of the ideal responses. The comments are provided to give you varying perspectives. No two people have exactly the same results and experiences. We all have our personal combination of preferences!

As you work through the exercises, you will be compiling your personal comprehensive ideal job description in your notebook. Your job description, when finished, will be a picture of the kind of job you'd like, based on the content, conditions, and compensation you envision. When you reach this point, it will be valuable to begin contacting people in your network (see chapter 6) to share your job description and begin gathering ideas of job areas that would meet your needs. We'll coach you on how to identify and research job options to determine what type of work would be most compatible with who you are and what you want. A well-made job choice is based not only on what you want, but also on getting the facts about what the job really entails. This part of the process requires thinking about how to match your needs and wants with the real world of work. Once you've identified a viable job objective, you're then ready to plan your job search, network for job prospects, put together a resume, interview, negotiate, and prepare for the job itself.

What I Need and Want in My Work

Exercise 1: My Ideal Job Description

"When I first saw the Ideal Job Description, I thought 'No way! I'll never be able to answer all of these questions.' Wow! Was I amazed (and proud of myself) when I did! The exercises were a lot of work, but they were definitely worth it."

Here is where you will enter all the conclusions you reach as you go through the exercises in this chapter. You'll be referring back to these written responses throughout the book. Transfer the following statements into your notebook, leaving plenty of space between each statement to allow adequate room for the answers you develop as we work through this chapter. When you complete these exercises, you will actually know what you want and need in a job.

My Ideal Job Description

■ **Conditions**

A. What I need in my work to keep me motivated (Exercise 5):

B. The specific conditions I want to work under (Exercise 6):

C. My ideal team of coworkers (Exercise 7, Part A):

D. My ideal boss (Exercise 7, Part B):

E. Other types of people I'd like to have contact with (Exercise 7, Part C):

F. The types of organizations I'd be interested in working for (or starting myself), because I like the kind of product/service they provide (Exercise 8):

G. Other conditions that are important to me:

■ **Content**

H. Aspects of my personality that are important for me to express (Exercise 9):

I. What I want to be doing on a day-to-day basis (Exercise 10):

J. The areas of knowledge I most want to be involved with in my work (Exercise 11):

■ **Compensation**

K. What I need/want for compensation (Exercise 13):

■ **Other Items**

L. Other items I need and/or comments I'd like to make about what the ideal job would look like for me (Exercises 2, 3 and 4, and whatever is left that you have yet to acknowledge regarding Conditions, Content, and Compensation):

My Past and Future: Factors Affecting Career Choice

An assessment of your past can give you clues about what you may want in a future job. What has enabled you to feel fulfilled in past experiences? In addition to assessing your past, knowing what you want your life to look like in the future can help you make smarter choices now. Exercises 2, 3, and 4 are designed to help you identify job-related preferences, given your experiences and your hopes.

Exercise 2: Job Likes and Dislikes

"I found this exercise somewhat cathartic—like I was letting go of my past. I was struck by how I've yet to have a job I really liked. I've since learned from sharing with others that I'm not alone—a lot of people I know don't like their work. Well, I'm going to find something I do like!"

Identifying specifically what you've liked and disliked about previous jobs and work environments can be valuable in revealing what you might want or need in a future job. Starting with an assessment of your past allows you to know what you want now, based upon a known experience.

■ ·Step 1. In your notebook, list no more than six jobs you've had. A job can be something you did and got paid for, a volunteer experience, a role you've played (such as parenting), or any life experience that was significant for you. For each job, indicate what you liked and disliked about its Content (what you were doing), the Conditions (where you were doing it), and the Compensation (salary and/or benefits, if applicable). Feel free to combine several similar jobs into one category (for example, "waitressing" or "child care"). Finally, be as specific as you can. If you did not like your boss, elaborate why. Here is a sample chart to help get you started; complete your information in your notebook.

Job #1: Waitressing	Likes	Dislikes
Content	· Meeting people · Being physically active	· Waiting on rude customers · Cleaning up at the end of a shift
Conditions	· My coworkers were fun · Working part-time	· Working late at night · My boss never gave me any positive feedback
Compensation	Big tips!	Small tips!

■ Step 2. Now that you've acknowledged your likes and dislikes from as many as six previous work experiences, let's clarify how that information can assist you in future career choices. Review your likes and dislikes lists. For each item in the likes column, ask yourself "Given that I liked this item in a past job, is it something I would continue to want or need in a future job?" For each item in the dislikes column, ask yourself "Given that I disliked this situation in the past, what does it tell me about what I would want or need in a future job?" Those likes and dislikes you feel indifferent about, simply discard.

Example: The following items could be identified from the likes and dislikes of waitressing: In a future job, I know I want to meet new people, have work that includes physical activity, have a boss who acknowledges me, and have a salary plus commission or tips.

List the items identified from all of your jobs' likes and dislikes below Statement L ("Other Items") on your "Ideal Job Description."

Exercise 3: Lifetime Accomplishments

*"This exercise was hard for me. I couldn't think of any accomplish-
ments for four days! I realized I was setting my standards too high
and needed to relax them a bit. Then they started coming ... like
the time I took a trip alone, and finishing high school during a
tough time. I felt good about myself when I came up with five
accomplishments that really meant a lot to me."*

An analysis of your accomplishments assists in identifying specific work-related
successes that contribute to your overall job satisfaction and to your feeling
successful at work. Be sure to take credit and enhance your self-confidence while
reviewing your accomplishments.

■ **Step 1.** List in your notebook up to ten accomplishments over the course of
your lifetime. These are general or specific experiences that you – and perhaps
others – have acknowledged as achievements, including awards; big risks; special roles; leadership; talent; degrees; promotions; significant decisions; creations;
parenting; work-related, volunteer, and family accomplishments; and personal
growth. Go for those accomplishments that have been the most heartfelt; the
ones that have been most satisfying and left you feeling proud, energized,
connected with who you are. Draw a chart in your notebook and list your
accomplishments. A sample follows.

Accomplishment	Why Important to Me	Potential Job Relevance
Buying my house	Independence Commitment Took a long time	Big challenge Independence Work on goals
My relationship with my daughter		
Implementing a new computer system at work		
Traveling abroad		
Being the top sales representative for three consecutive months		
Surviving my divorce		
Being elected chair-person of the fund-raising committee		

■ **Step 2.** In the second column, explain or describe why each accomplishment feels like an achievement to you. What is it about that accomplishment that makes you feel good about yourself? What was so successful about that experience for you?

■ **Step 3.** In the third column, identify what aspects of each accomplishment you would want to carry over into a future work situation. Is it a feeling? A type of result? A particular interest or skill?

Feel free to come back to your responses and add to them if ideas should come to you later regarding your accomplishments.

List the items from the potential job relevance column on your "Ideal Job Description" under Statement L ("Other Items").

Exercise 4: Life Goals

> *"My goals in life? I've just been bumping along in my life, letting things happen to and around me, rather than making things happen. This exercise opened me up to a whole new way of viewing my life. I also discovered that setting goals wasn't as hard as I'd thought it would be."*

Before tackling the three Cs, you need to address the bigger picture – your life. Your work should be compatible with your other life goals and priorities. What do you want to accomplish in the arena of relationships, health, well-being, home life, further education, geographical location, travel, other leisure pursuits, finance? How does work fit into the picture?

Goal setting is tough for most of us. A goal is something you'd like to see happen in your life; it encourages a positive attitude and anticipation of the future. Life goals are personal desires. The best goals are those that would make you – not somebody else – happy. They can be simple like, "I want to live in a new house," or more involved like "I want to communicate better with my son so that he doesn't rebel against everything I ask of him and instead takes more responsibility for his actions."

In this exercise, don't worry about quantity. If you come up with only one goal, that's fine. If you can't think of any, it may be helpful to look at other people in your life who are doing things that you'd like to do someday. *Don't worry about how you're going to accomplish your goals. For now, just think about where you want to go with your life.* Project yourself into the future.

Use the creative visualization discussed in chapter 1 if you find it is helpful to you.

■ **Step 1.** In your notebook, jot down how old you will be five years from now, and the life goals you would personally like to accomplish by that age. Let yourself go with this exercise. Where do you really want to be in five years? What do you want to have in your life? Jot down between five and ten goals without worrying about practical issues like how you are going to reach these goals.

> Examples: I'd like to have a stronger network of friends.
> I want to travel abroad at least once.
> I want to have all of my debts paid off.

■ **Step 2.** Now, on a separate sheet, jot down five to ten goals that you would like to accomplish within one year's time. Be specific, if you can, with these goals, but if not, general or vague ideas are fine, too. Clarify as best you can what you want in the next year of your life.

> Examples: I want to spend more time with my kids.
> I want to work toward a new career.
> I want to take a computer course.

■ **Step 3.** Now look over your five and one year goals. For each goal, what are some content, conditions, and compensation items you would need in a job to help you reach your goals? Jot these down. For example, if you want to spend more time with your children, perhaps you want a job with a work schedule that allows you that time. Or if you want to pay off debts, what does that mean in terms of the kind of income you need to be generating? List these factors under Statement L ("Other Items") on your "Ideal Job Description" in your notebook.

Good work! Now you're ready to move on to the next set of exercises. If you haven't taken a break, you may want to at this point. Keep in mind that "By the inch, it's easy; by the yard, it's hard!" – Robert Pante

Conditions

Exercises 5 through 8 will help you clarify what types of job-related conditions would be ideal for you.

Exercise 5: Job Motivators

"I liked all of the motivators, but found it helpful to narrow them down to the most important. I had to shed the 'shoulds' and really figure out what was important to me in selecting the final ten."

People have different reasons for wanting to work. The most obvious is the need to earn a living. You may have other needs, however, which, if met, would help keep you motivated in your work.

■ **Step 1.** Read through the list of motivators below and highlight those that seem important to you. Choose as many as you'd like!

★ Ability utilization: I want to do work that will utilize my best skills and talents.

★ Aesthetics: I want to do work that makes things appear physically more beautiful.

★ Belonging/affiliation: I want to work somewhere where I feel like I belong to a group of people working together.

★ Creativity: I want to be able to express myself creatively through my work.

★ Expertise: I want to be an expert in something – to be recognized for my knowledge and talent in a particular field.

★ Fun: I want to have fun in whatever it is I do for work.

★ Identity: I want to do something that identifies who I am and that other people recognize as mine.

★ Independence/freedom: I want to know that I can always take care of myself regardless of the conditions of my life (marital status, economy, etc.).

★ Leadership: I want to be in a leadership role regardless of what field I'm in.

★ Making a difference: I want to make a difference in the world and to know that my work is directly improving the quality of people's lives.

★ People contact: I want a job that allows me a lot of contact with people.

★ Personal growth: I want my work to further my emotional and spiritual growth.

★ Physical challenge: I want to be physically challenged in my work.

★ Prosperity: I want to earn a lot of money and achieve a prosperous lifestyle.

★ Respect and recognition: I want respect and recognition from other people for the work I do.

★ Risk taking: I want ample opportunity to take risks and confront challenges in my job.

★ Self-expression: I want to do work that is a direct expression of who I am.

■ **Step 2.** What other reasons do you have for wanting to work? Why do you want to work? If you have other needs not covered above, list those motivators in your notebook.

■ **Step 3.** Drawing from both lists, select up to ten motivators most critical to your future work satisfaction and list them on your "Ideal Job Description" below Statement A ("What I need in my work to keep me motivated"). Do not be concerned about priority.

Exercise 6: Working Conditions

"I wasn't sure on a lot of these, so I had to guess. Some of them, like company size, didn't matter that much to me. I realized I didn't have to sweat the small stuff."

Listed below are a multitude of working conditions – those circumstances that would satisfy you and help you do your best work. They are categorized into four groups to facilitate your decision making.

1. *Organizational conditions:* These conditions describe the ideal type of organization for you.

2. *Specific job conditions:* These are the conditions that most directly affect how you do your work.

3. *Physical environment:* This group addresses the physical conditions of your working environment.

4. *Work location:* Work location describes the logistics of where you live and where you work.

■ **Step 1.** Read through all of the conditions in each group and highlight those that seem important for you in your ideal job. Feel free to highlight as many as you'd like. You may feel indifferent or uncertain about some conditions because you've never had any experience with them. Either disregard these or mark them with an asterisk, as a reminder to talk them over with someone who has experienced them.

1. *Organizational conditions*

I would like to work:

★ for someone else

★ for myself (be self-employed)

★ for a large business or organization (100+ employees)

★ for a medium-sized business or organization (30-100 employees)

★ for a small business or organization (2-30 employees)

★ for a domestic business or organization

★ for an international business or organization

★ for a nonprofit, public organization

★ for a private, for profit business

★ within a well-structured, less flexible business or organization

★ within a flexible, minimally structured business or organization

★ within a competitive structure

★ within a cooperative structure

★ within a traditional, hierarchical structure

★ within a progressive, egalitarian, consensus structure

★ for an intimate, feeling-oriented business or organization

★ for a formal, professional-only business or organization

★ for a business or organization with a casual dress code

★ where frequent staff meetings occur

★ where few or no staff meetings are necessary

★ where my work life and personal life are very separate (I don't take my work home with me and I am not interrupted at home by work matters)

★ where my work life and personal life intermingle or overlap

★ for an organization that provides on-site child care

★ other: _____

2. *Specific job conditions*

I would like to:

★ work alone most of the time

★ work as part of a team most of the time

★ work alone _____% of the time and work with a team _____% of the time each week

★ use self-direction, determining on my own the most important tasks to be completed

★ have moderate supervision with occasional guidance and feedback

★ have extensive supervision where my work is closely and constantly monitored

★ work on a part-time basis (_____ hours per week)

★ travel in my work (how frequently: _____)

★ work with strict deadlines

★ work with a flexible, open-ended time schedule

★ work a fairly regular 9:00A.M.–5:00P.M., Monday through Friday schedule

★ work varying hours and have a changing work schedule

★ have a lot of change in the content and/or pace of my work

★ have a routine set of tasks

★ have work that is fast-paced

★ have work that is done slowly and steadily

★ work under a lot of pressure

★ work under low to moderate pressure

★ produce longer-term, slower results in my work

★ produce short-term, more immediate results in my work

★ have a great deal of responsibility in my work for people/projects/the overall success of the organization

★ have little to moderate amount of responsibility in my work

★ have decision-making authority over others

★ other: _____

3. *Physical environment*

I would prefer to work:

- ★ in my own work space/have my own office
- ★ in a common work space shared with others
- ★ in a noisy, active area
- ★ in a quiet, peaceful area
- ★ indoors most of the time
- ★ outdoors most of the time
- ★ indoors _____% of the time and outdoors _____% of the time each week
- ★ at a desk or work area (seated) most of the day
- ★ away from my desk or work area most of the day/out of the office frequently
- ★ in a nonsmoking environment
- ★ in a smoking-permitted environment
- ★ with natural lighting/windows
- ★ in an environment that is decorated in a particular way (please specify: _____)
- ★ with adequate disabled-access areas (ramps, restrooms, parking, lounges, etc.)
- ★ other: _____

4. *Work location*

I would like to:

- ★ live and work in an urban setting
- ★ live and work in a rural setting
- ★ live rurally and work in an urban setting
- ★ live in an urban area and work rurally

★ commute (up to how far one way: _____)

★ be able to walk to work from my home

★ work at home (how much of the time: _____)

★ other: _____

■ **Step 2.** From all of the conditions you have highlighted, select up to ten conditions you most want and need in your next work situation to ensure your satisfaction. List these on your "Ideal Job Description," below Statement B ("The specific conditions I want to work under").

Exercise 7: Working with People

"I felt guilty about my preference to work more with adults than with kids. I felt like I should want to work with all kinds of people. I had to be honest with myself, though."

Regardless of what you end up doing for work, contact with people is very likely, though some jobs certainly involve more interactions than others. But what kinds of qualities do people need to have in your ideal work situation? Be honest about any preferences you may have. Most of us are most productive when working with particular types of people. Remember: Go for what's important to you!

Part A: My Ideal Coworkers

■ **Step 1.** If you anticipate working with coworkers, you can expect to work with a core group of people, regardless of the total size of your organization. In an ideal job, how large or small would you like your core group to be? (Giving a range is fine; i.e., 5-10, 10-20, 20-40.) Record this in your notebook. (If you don't anticipate working with coworkers, skip this section.)

■ **Step 2.** In describing your core group more specifically, highlight your preferences from the list below:

I would prefer to work with:

★ men only

★ women only

★ about equal numbers of men and women

★ more women than men

★ more men than women

★ individuals of any age

★ individuals within a specific age range (specifically: _____)

■ **Step 3.** Next, in the list below, highlight the five to ten characteristics you'd most like your coworkers to possess:

· ambitious	· cooperative	· humorous	· organized
· attractive	· creative	· independent	· professional
· challenging	· decisive		· progressive
· committed	· dependable	· industrious	· resourceful
· communicative	· efficient	· innovative	· responsible
· competent	· enthusiastic	· intellectual	· self-directed
· competitive	· friendly	· loyal	· supportive
· considerate	· honest/	· motivated	· trustworthy
	integrity	· open-minded	

■ **Step 4.** Using the preferences you have chosen in Part A, summarize your ideal core group of coworkers under Statement C of the "Ideal Job Description" ("The ideal team of coworkers").

Part B: The Ideal Boss

Drawing from the characteristics listed above, describe the type of boss you would like to have under Statement D of the "Ideal Job Description" ("The ideal boss"). (If you would prefer not to have any boss at all, skip this section.)

Part C: Other People I Want to Have Contact with in My Job

■ **Step 1.** You might have contact with a variety of types of people other than coworkers, such as associated vendors or people in other organizations. Highlight those listed below that you would like to interact with through your job. (If you would prefer working only with coworkers, skip this section.)

★ *Customers:* people who have purchased and/or are using a product(s) produced by your employer

★ *Clients:* people who are using a service that you and/or your employer are directly providing to them

★ *Students:* people who are in a learning, educational situation

★ *Patients:* people who are needing health-related care of a physical, mental, or emotional nature

★ *General public:* citizens from the community at large

★ *Vendors/sales representatives:* people who provide products and/or services to your organization

★ *Colleagues:* fellow professionals who do primarily the same type of work you do, but work for someone else

★ *Off-site coworkers:* people who work for the same company/organization as you, but work at a different site (perhaps out of state)

★ *Members of other organizations:* any other professionals you would interact with who work for other organizations

■ **Step 2.** More specifically, how would you describe the types of people you'd want to work with that are highlighted above? Use the list below to highlight your preferences:

I would like to work with customers/clients/students/others who are:

★ individuals (one-on-one)

★ in small groups (up to ten people)

★ in large groups/audiences (ten or more people)

★ infants

★ children

★ adolescents

★ young adults

★ adults

★ senior citizens

★ males

★ females

★ well-educated (college)

★ minimally educated

★ high-income people

★ low-income people

★ professionals

★ nonprofessionals

★ dealing with a particular type of problem

★ other types of people: _____

■ **Step 3.** Describe under Statement E in the "Ideal Job Description" ("Other types of people I'd like to have contact with"), the types of people you would like to work with drawing from all of Part C.

Exercise 8: The Ideal Organization

"I used the yellow pages of the phone book to help expand the results of this exercise. Although I ended up with a short list, I got to see very clearly where I definitely do not want to work!"

Many people have found that they enjoy their work more, if they like or support the product or service their company provides. The following exercise lists types of businesses or organizations for which you might like to work.

■ **Step 1.** Highlight those organizations you'd be interested in, even if it's not that important to you what type of company employs you. (For those of you considering self-employment, mark those types of businesses you might want to own and run.)

- Accounting firm
- Airlines/air services
- Airport
- Amusement center
- Animal care provider
- Art gallery
- Automobile dealership/
  service station
- Bakery/deli
- Bank
- Beverage warehouse
- Book store
- Carpet dealer
- Caterer
- Chamber of Commerce
- Church
- City, state, or

federal government
- Cleaning company
- Clothing store
- Collection agency
- Computer dealer
- Conference center
- Construction company/
  contractor
- Consulting firm
- Cosmetic distributor
- Counseling/mental
  health agency
- Day care center
- Delivery service
- Department store
- Dry cleaner/
  laundromat

- Electrician
- Employment agency
- Engineering firm
- Environmental agency/
  firm
- Farm
- Florist/gardening center
- Food distributor
- Furniture store
- Government agency
- Grocery store
- Hair salon
- Hardware store/
  distributor
- Health club
- Hospital/medical office
- Hotel/motel/inn/B&B

· Household appliance store	· Newspaper/magazine	· Real estate agency
· Human service agency	· Nightclub/bar	· Research laboratory
· Investment firm	· Office supply store	· Resort
· Law firm	· Parking garage	· Restaurant
· Limousine service	· Parks/recreation	· School/college
· Machine shop	areas/campground	· Sporting goods
· Mail-order company	· Pharmaceutical	company
· Manufacturer (of _____)	company/drug store	· Tailor
· Mass transportation	· Photography store	· Television station
· Military	· Plumber	· Theater/cinema
· Museum	· Political organization	· Travel agency
· Music store/recording	· Publisher	· Utility company
studio	· Radio station	(phone, electric, etc.)

Please note: This is not an all-inclusive list. If you discover that only a few – and perhaps none – of these interest you, don't despair. There are lots of other types of organizations that are more unusual in nature and are not covered here. This list is only meant to spur ideas. Use *The Occupational Outlook Handbook* to discover additional types of jobs.

■ **Step 2.** Transfer the organizations you've selected under Statement F of the "Ideal Job Description" ("The types of organizations I'd be interested in working for, because I like the kind of product/service they provide").

Exercises 5 through 8 have dealt primarily with the conditions you want to work in. Are there any other conditions that would be important that you have yet to acknowledge? List any that you can think of under Statement G of the "Ideal Job Description" ("Other conditions that are important to me").

Content

Visualizing the content of your ideal work is a particularly challenging part of the job-search process. For most of us, it is far easier to identify the kinds of conditions ideally we want to work in, and more challenging to identify just what it is we want to be doing in those conditions. To help you with this, we're first going to discuss skills.

A skill is any quality, ability, or knowledge that enables you to accomplish a task and produce a result. What makes you unique is that you have an unduplicated formula of qualities, abilities, and knowledge. Nobody else has exactly the same set of skills that you have. To assist you in the following skills identification exercises, an understanding of each of the categories of skills and how they relate to the job choice is useful.

■ **Quality.** A quality is a skill that describes the kind of person you are. Qualities are personality traits, those characteristics that you bring to anything you do. Qualities are adjectives that describe who you are. Being aware of your qualities not only will help you select work that is compatible with who you are, but also will assist you in projecting a positive self-image when networking and interviewing. Examples of qualities are creative, honest, extroverted, analytical, patient. Ideally, what you do for work will allow you to express those qualities that you value most in yourself.

■ **Ability.** Abilities – also known as transferable or functional skills – are those skills you have that identify the things you do well that are transferable to a variety of different fields. In any job, you are paid to do certain tasks and to produce results. You use your abilities to accomplish your work. These are skills that tend to come automatically for you and are frequently difficult to pass on to someone else. Abilities are verbs that identify what you can do with data/people/things/ideas. Examples of abilities are organizing, managing, teaching, counseling, working with your hands, calculating. Ideally, what you do for work will allow you to utilize those abilities that you most enjoy using.

■ **Knowledge.** Knowledge is a body of information that you have learned regarding a particular topic or subject area. You demonstrate having knowledge in an area by being able to converse about it with someone. In any job, there are specific areas of knowledge you need in order to do the work. Knowledge deals with the technical aspects of a job. Knowledge is a noun. Examples of knowledge are: accounting, finish carpentry, market research and analysis, animal care, parenting, and children. Ideally, when choosing a career, you'll want to be excited by the knowledge areas your field entails.

In summary, the content of a job will be satisfying for you if the qualities necessary for job success are a match with who you are; the abilities needed reflect things you like to do; and the knowledge brought into or acquired on the job is interesting to you. In Exercises 9 through 11, you will assess your qualities, abilities, and knowledge, identifying those skills you'd most like to utilize in your future work situation.

Exercise 9: My Personal Qualities

"I'm not always sure that who I think I am is who I really am. I made copies of this list and had friends and colleagues fill it out

according to who they think I am. I was delighted to learn that I know myself better than sometimes I think I do."

■ **Step 1.** Read through the following list of qualities and highlight every trait you feel describes you to any degree.

· active	· dedicated/	· influential	· playful
· adventurous	committed	· intellectual	· powerful
· affectionate	· dependable	· intuitive	· practical
· ambitious	· detail-oriented	· investigative	· precise
· analytical	· disciplined	· kind	· realistic
· articulate	· down-to-earth	· logical	· resourceful
· artistic	· efficient	· methodical	· self-aware
· athletic	· energetic	· modest	· smart
· capable	· entrepreneurial	· motivated	· spontaneous
· careful	· expressive	· natural	· strong-willed
· caring	· flamboyant	· neat	· supportive
· compassionate	· friendly	· nurturing	· systematic
· competent	· helpful	· open-minded	· thoughtful
· confident	· honest	· orderly	· unique
· courageous	· humorous	· organized	· witty
· creative	· idealistic	· outdoor-oriented	· other:
· critical	· imaginative	· patient	
· curious	· independent	· perfectionist	
	· industrious	· physical	

■ **Step 2.** Read through the list again, and circle the fourteen qualities you feel describe you most accurately. Put an asterisk next to those qualities you would like to develop.

■ **Step 3.** Identify the qualities you would most like to integrate into your work life. Feel free to include qualities that you did not highlight or circle. List these qualities (about ten) under Statement H of the "Ideal Job Description" ("Aspects of my personality that are important for me to express").

Exercise 10: Abilities Exercise

"What a great list! Now I have the words to describe what I'm good at and what I like to do. I noticed how much I take my abilities for granted and don't give myself enough credit for what I can do."

In work, you inevitably deal with people, data (information, numbers, facts, computer data), things (objects, tools, plants, merchandise, animals, products, equipment, machinery), and ideas (concepts, plans, creative endeavors). The degree to which you work with each of these four categories depends upon the nature of the content of your job.

■ **Step 1.** The abilities in the following exercise are organized under people, data, things, and ideas. Read through the lists and highlight those abilities you think you have. Use the space on the right to make any comments regarding where and/or how you've used that ability in the past.

Abilities I Have with People

I am good at

- ★ collaborating with others

- ★ acting in front of audiences

- ★ entertaining people through a creative endeavor

- ★ demonstrating a sense of humor; making people laugh

- ★ modeling clothing

- ★ singing alone or with a group

- ★ telling stories

- ★ advising people on particular problems or areas of expertise

- ★ mediating between conflicting parties; negotiating agreements

- ★ being sensitive to others' feelings; being intuitive and responsive to others' needs; empathizing

- ★ coaching to improve another's performance

- ★ communicating through writing; writing to or about people

- ★ communicating verbally; articulating and expressing myself clearly

- ★ communicating in a foreign language

- ★ confronting others with difficult questions, feedback, issues

- ★ counseling people in dealing with personal problems; facilitating personal growth

- ★ educating others in a special area(s) of knowledge

★ explaining new concepts or ideas clearly

★ facilitating meetings and other group functions

★ team building; fostering a cooperative atmosphere

★ giving constructive feedback

★ guiding people through a process

★ helping others in need; being supportive

★ hiring new staff or employees; recruiting talent

★ inspiring and motivating people to take action

★ instructing people; getting information across to others in understand-able terms

★ interviewing; asking good questions

★ nurturing people who are in crisis or need special care

★ listening to people

★ being a mentor and role model

★ observing behavior and personalities

★ organizing people in a joint effort; coordinating projects or programs

★ promoting an individual or organization

★ representing others; being a spokesperson; relating to the public

★ lobbying; advocating on someone else's behalf

★ recognizing nonverbal cues and responding accordingly

★ reconciling differences and resolving conflicts

★ rehabilitating the handicapped or disabled

★ serving others; providing hospitable services to guests or the public

★ speaking conversationally

★ supervising others in their work

★ translating a foreign language into English

★ tutoring individuals with learning difficulties

★ managing projects, departments, or other groups of people with an equal focus on task completion and the human element

★ empowering others to make changes

★ selling ideas and/or products; generating new business

★ evaluating people and their actions

★ researching using people as resources

★ leading people through action; taking the leadership role when necessary

★ connecting individuals to people who can be helpful and resourceful; networking

★ influencing the ideas or attitudes of others

★ persuading people to take a particular course of action; arguing effectively

★ meeting and establishing rapport with strangers

★ consulting individuals or organizations; making recommendations; giving expert advice

★ running for an office or position; politicking; winning campaigns

★ delegating responsibilities to others; enabling others to be successful at what they do

★ heading up volunteer groups or organizations; directing

★ encouraging others to take risks

★ enrolling others to participate; recruiting volunteers

★ public speaking; making presentations

★ talking with people over the phone; telemarketing

★ nursing; taking care of people's physical needs; treating; curing

Abilities I Have with Data

I am good at

★ concentrating on detailed tasks

★ coordinating activities or projects

★ copying materials

★ designing and utilizing organizational systems

★ documenting and accounting figures

★ filing paperwork

* financing projects
* following through on projects and tasks
* getting things done; producing results
* improvising for speed and clarity
* interpreting complicated information
* logging data
* managing data
* manipulating numbers and figures; calculating; computing
* meeting deadlines
* memorizing information, numbers, or statistics
* organizing data and information
* planning activities and events
* producing results
* proofreading and editing written material
* recording information and numbers; keeping accurate records
* scheduling workers
* setting-up conferences; handling events' logistics
* making travel arrangements
* sorting written material
* systematizing procedures; arranging things systematically
* taking notes during lectures and meetings
* thinking methodically; thinking intellectually
* typing manuscripts or letters
* administering projects
* assembling items of information into a coherent whole
* budgeting money, managing finances
* gathering and compiling information or data
* estimating job costs; finding ways to reduce expenses
* inventorying merchandise or supplies; keeping track of inventory

★ ordering merchandise or inventory; purchasing

★ analyzing data; extracting the important information; defining cause-and-effect relationships

★ conducting inquiries or medical exams

★ evaluating data and information

★ monitoring data and results

★ obtaining the facts about a situation

★ processing data or information

★ word processing; entering data into a computer

★ retrieving data from a computer

★ reporting information

★ reading books or periodicals; studying new information

★ consolidating and summarizing data

★ testing the reliability of data

★ using data to gain insight

★ working with technology

★ examining and comparing to find similarities and dissimilarities; determining the important from the unimportant

★ estimating the time necessary to do the job

Abilities I Have with Things

I am good at

★ assembling parts, technical apparatus, or equipment

★ being athletic or physically fit; playing sports

★ building things; constructing

★ doing physical labor

★ driving vehicles

★ eliminating unnecessary objects

★ enduring physical danger or hardship

- ★ enforcing regulations, policing
- ★ fixing broken objects or gadgets; repairing
- ★ handling plumbing, electrical, or mechanical breakdowns
- ★ handling products or packages
- ★ inspecting products
- ★ increasing production
- ★ lifting and moving objects
- ★ making things
- ★ managing things (tools, products): keeping track of where things are
- ★ navigating charts
- ★ operating machinery
- ★ overseeing production
- ★ piloting boats or planes
- ★ preventing destruction; maintaining the quality of an object
- ★ producing tangible results
- ★ projecting objects into space
- ★ protecting things or people
- ★ taking apart; disassembling
- ★ receiving merchandise, shipments, inventory
- ★ reducing the volume of things
- ★ rescuing people or animals from danger
- ★ restoring and renovating things
- ★ sewing with fabric, knitting, weaving, handcrafting
- ★ shaping wood, metal, plastics, etc.
- ★ operating heavy equipment or machinery
- ★ showing how things work
- ★ supplying materials
- ★ surveying land
- ★ thinking mechanically

- ★ working with animals; caring for them; training
- ★ using things
- ★ tinkering with engines and machines
- ★ working outdoors
- ★ working with the land and its resources
- ★ wallpapering, painting, staining
- ★ working with plants
- ★ working with office machines and equipment
- ★ working on an assembly line; running manufacturing machinery/equipment
- ★ setting up displays, merchandising
- ★ setting up machinery
- ★ making models
- ★ working with high-tech testing equipment and other
- ★ scientific apparatus

Abilities I Have with Ideas

I am good at

- ★ creating new ideas; using my imagination
- ★ defining words, concepts, information
- ★ detecting and examining problems
- ★ developing solutions; devising remedies
- ★ diagnosing symptoms or problems
- ★ discovering new facts and ideas
- ★ experimenting
- ★ explaining new findings
- ★ hypothesizing; theorizing
- ★ innovating new technology
- ★ inventing new things
- ★ investigating; researching

- ★ predicting future occurrences
- ★ programming computers
- ★ questioning; challenging the status quo
- ★ troubleshooting problem areas
- ★ utilizing resources
- ★ creating new masterpieces
- ★ striving to be on the "cutting edge"
- ★ creatively using words and language
- ★ writing jingles
- ★ designing fashions
- ★ devising advertising schemes
- ★ displaying objects creatively
- ★ drawing; illustrating; sketching
- ★ painting pictures
- ★ photographing objects or people
- ★ playing a musical instrument
- ★ preparing works of art
- ★ printing letters by hand; doing calligraphy
- ★ printing on various mediums
- ★ thinking intuitively and creatively
- ★ writing stories
- ★ composing music
- ★ deciding what should occur and when
- ★ planning and developing projects or programs
- ★ devising new business ventures
- ★ designing educational events
- ★ establishing policies and procedures
- ★ expanding possibilities
- ★ formulating new strategies

- ★ identifying new areas to pursue
- ★ implementing new ideas
- ★ improving upon existing circumstances; making things better
- ★ initiating action
- ★ judging results; monitoring outcomes
- ★ preparing reports
- ★ projecting ideas into the future
- ★ setting goals and creating a vision
- ★ raising issues
- ★ recommending solutions
- ★ promoting programs or business
- ★ responding to problems, issues, crises
- ★ risking
- ★ selecting the best (and rejecting the worst) ideas
- ★ undertaking challenging opportunities
- ★ turning problems into opportunities
- ★ working with color
- ★ having a good sense of rhythm
- ★ modifying and applying what others have developed to a new situation
- ★ conceiving new interpretations
- ★ visualizing

■ **Step 2.** In going through the abilities you have, you may have run into some abilities you don't think you have, but wish that you did have. Go back over the list and put an asterisk to the left of those abilities you wish you had.

■ **Step 3.** Remember that ideally you will enjoy using the abilities that your job requires. Circle those skills from all four categories that you would most like to use in an ideal job regardless of whether you feel you can do those things now. Pick as many as you want! List these under Statement I of the "Ideal Job Description" ("What I want to be doing on a day-to-day basis").

Exercise 11: Knowledge Exercise

"My final list was such a mishmash of knowledge areas. I had to decide which areas I wanted in my work life and which in my personal life. Narrowing down the choices also helped me to feel more focused with my interests."

■ **Step 1.** Using the categories listed below, brainstorm in your notebook areas in which you currently have some knowledge. You need not be an expert, have a degree in the area, or have written the definitive book about it. Anything that you know something about and can converse about with someone for two minutes or more is fine. Keep in mind that knowledge usually reflects interests you have.

    1. Knowledge I gained in school and from seminars

    2. Knowledge I learned from jobs I've had

    3. Knowledge I picked up from reading and conversation

    4. Knowledge I developed from my hobbies

    5. Other knowledge I've gathered along the way in life

■ **Step 2.** What knowledge would you be interested in learning? If you were to take a course tomorrow, what would you like to learn about? Brainstorm new areas of potential interest in your notebook and mark each one with an asterisk. Also asterisk any areas of knowledge you already have that you would like to learn more about.

■ **Step 3.** Look over your lists for Steps 1 and 2, highlighting those bodies of knowledge you have any interest in being involved with to any degree as part of your job. Highlight as many areas as you like – even if they all seem to be totally unrelated to each other. Also, you don't need to be currently knowledgeable in any of the areas you select. Just pick what you'd like from your heart!

■ **Step 4.** While your highlighter is still hot, go through the following list and repeat what you just did for the areas of knowledge under Steps 1 and 2. Choose any areas you'd be interested in integrating into your ideal job. Don't worry if your list is eclectic!

accounting	adult development	anatomy/physiology
accounts receivable/	aeronautics	animals
billing	agriculture/farming	anthropology
acting	air and heating systems	antiques
advertising	alcoholism/drug abuse	architecture

armed forces/military
art
art history
astronomy
automobiles
banking
biology
bookkeeping
books/literature
botany
budgeting
chemistry
child/adolescent
  development
clerical/secretarial/
  office work
colleges/universities/
  higher education
color
computers
construction/carpentry
consumerism
cosmetology
cost estimating
counseling
crafts
crime/corrections
customer service
dance
death/dying/hospice
dentistry
ecology
economics
education
electrical wiring
electronics
energy
engineering
engines
entertainment/
  performing arts
environmental science
family systems/parenting

fashion
fine arts
firefighting
food/beverages/
  culinary arts
foreign cultures/
  international affairs
forestry
fund-raising/development
gemology
genetics
geography
geology
gerontology/aging
government
graphic arts/commercial
  art
heavy equipment
  operation
history
home economics
hotel/resort work
human relations
human sexuality
importing/exporting
industrial psychology/
  organizational
  effectiveness
insurance
inventory control
investments
journalism
labor relations
landscape design
law
law enforcement
library science
machinery/mechanics
management
manufacturing
marketing
mathematics
mediation/arbitration

medicine/medical
  technology
metal work
metallurgy
movies/film/video
museum work
music
nonprofit administration
nutrition
oceanography
office management
organizational systems
outdoor recreation
outdoor survival skills
personnel/human
  resource development
petroleum/fuels
pharmacology
philosophy
photography
physical conditioning
  fitness
physics
piloting
plants/gardening
plumbing
poetry
politics
pollution control
pottery
product design
product research/
  development
production planning
psychology/mental
  health
public relations/public
  image
public speaking
publishing/printing
quality control
radio
real estate

religion/spirituality	sports	urban planning
renovation/restoration	statistics	veterinary medicine
research	surveying	weather/meteorology
restaurant operation	taxes	well-being/holistic health
retail/wholesale	television	wildlife/nature
sales	textiles/fabric	women's issues/studies
sewing	theater	woodworking
small business	tools/hardware	writing
social issues	tourism	zoology
social work	transportation	

■ **Step 5.** Finally, from all of the knowledge areas you've highlighted in Steps 1, 2, and 4, select up to fifteen areas you'd most want to be involved with in an ideal job. Again, anything goes, no matter how inexperienced you are in the areas you're most drawn to or how varied your list is. List your final selection under Statement J of the "Ideal Job description" ("The areas of knowledge I most want to be involved with").

Exercises 9, 10, and 11 dealt with identifying content-related items you would like to have in an ideal work situation. Look over the content section of your "Ideal Job Description." Add under Statement L any other content items not yet mentioned that might be important to your work satisfaction.

Exercise 12: Summary of Skills I Would Like to Further Develop

---

"The thought of taking even one course scared me. But having a purpose and a desire for learning a new skill made my going back to school at age fifty a very rewarding experience—much better than when I was last there at age eighteen."

Review Exercises 9, 10, and 11, and list in your notebook those qualities, abilities, and knowledge areas you marked with an asterisk to possibly further develop/acquire. Next to each skill, note how you might accomplish this (i.e., by taking courses at local schools or colleges, pursuing an internship, volunteering).

This information does not go onto the "Ideal Job Description", but is for your own use in the job-search process. Use it later in the chapters on planning and networking as you explore how to identify and find work that will fit your current skill level.

Break time again! Nice going. All of your hard work will pay off, so stay with it. You have only one more section, Compensation, to address on your "Ideal Job Description."

Compensation

Exercise 13: Salary and Other Forms of Compensation

"I know that money is a necessity in my life, particularly now that I'm a single parent. Yet, I had a lot of resistance to really thinking about what I need to earn. Putting a budget together and attending a financial workshop for women really helped."

■ **Step 1.** In your notebook, identify the following three income figures. In the immediate future, what do you need to be earning? What would you like to be earning? And what would you love to be earning? The need figure should reflect the salary level that is as low as you'd go. This should be a figure that accurately reflects your bottom line. You wouldn't be willing to take anything less, given your financial and self-esteem needs. From your need figure, calculate what you'd like and what you'd love to earn. All of your figures should be gross earnings (pretax).

■ **Step 2.** Next, list what other benefits you will need: health and dental insurance, disability, profit sharing, retirement. What about child-care and further education subsidies? How much time off a year do you want (holidays, vacation, personal days)?

■ **Step 3.** Write your income figures and benefits under Statement K of the "Ideal Job Description" ("What I need/want for compensation").

Now look over your "Ideal Job Description" and make sure that anything and everything you could possibly want and need in your job is acknowledged here. Make sure that all of your conditions, content, and compensation requirements are acknowledged. If something is missing, add it under Statement L of your "Ideal Job Description" ("Other items I need and/or comments I'd like to make about what the ideal job would look like for me").

Keep in mind that in order to ensure satisfaction in your job, all three C areas must have your basic criteria fulfilled. If you select a job that meets your content and conditions needs, but doesn't allow you to make the kind of money you need, it will most likely not satisfy you (particularly if you're looking for work that may have long-term potential).

On the other hand, if you select a job in which the conditions and the compensation meet your needs, but the content does not, you are probably not going to like what you're doing and may outgrow it very quickly. This is quite common in larger organizations, as one engineer expressed it: "The money is great. I like the corporation. But I'm bored, bored, bored, and I see no room for advancement and growth."

If you take a job that meets your content needs (you like what you're doing) and your compensation needs (you're making the kind of money you need), but you're not happy with the conditions (you don't get along with the people you work with, you don't like the organization, too much travel), that's not going to work for you either. "They've given me a great job, but a lousy boss. I really don't get along with her, and I'm losing my motivation fast!" Make sure, then, that anything you want in your work in order to be satisfied is acknowledged somewhere on your "Ideal Job Description."

Narrowing

At this point, you've got a lot of information to try to assimilate. To help you focus, you need to decide upon the conditions, content, and compensation criteria most critical to your job satisfaction.

> "At first, I felt more confused than ever when I looked over 'My Ideal Job Description.' Reading it over and sharing it with supportive friends helped me to identify common themes running through all of my three C areas... themes like being creative and having my own business."

Exercise 14: My Top Twenty Job-Related Criteria

> "This was the most clarifying exercise—I even prioritized my final list, so I had a solid set of criteria against which I could consider job options. I was somewhat surprised to find that other peoples' criteria are quite different from mine. We're each unique!"

■ **Step 1.** Looking over your "Ideal Job Description," extract the twenty criteria that you feel are most critical for you to have in an ideal job. List them in your notebook. To make the list most helpful in your future decision making, select a minimum of three items from Statement I, four items from Statement J, and one income figure from Statement K that is halfway between your "need" and your "like" figures. The remaining twelve items can be any items you want from anywhere on the job description. The items need not be brief—they can be fairly lengthy. What's important here is that the twenty items be twenty distinctly different items. For example, do not select (1) coaching, (2) giving advice, and (3) consulting as three separate items. If these three are basically addressing the same job component that would be important to you, lump them together and count them as one: (1) coaching/giving advice/consulting.

■ **Step 2.** Once you have extracted your twenty items, write out a few lines explaining what each item means to you in the context of a job. Below is a sample list of twenty job-related criteria and their meanings to give you an idea of how your list might look:

(Three items from Statement I)

1. Coaching/giving advice/consulting: I'd like to be in a position where people seek me out for my wisdom and expertise. I've always enjoyed telling others what to do!

2. Persuading/influencing/selling ideas: I am good at convincing people to take a particular line of action. I would like to be persuasive and have an impact on how people think.

3. Planning activities and events: I would love to be a professional party planner! I love giving dinner parties and planning big events like birthdays and weddings.

(Four items from Statement J)

4. Management/small business/nonprofit administration: Through volunteer work, I've become interested in how organizations work (or don't work!). I would like to be involved in the management of a business or an organization. I don't want to be at the top (too much pressure), but could see myself working up to managing a few people or maybe a whole department.

5. Personnel/human resource development/industrial psychology/counseling: This relates to the above item, because I think that what makes a company successful is its employees. I'd like to help my fellow employees solve work-related issues, so that they can be happier and more motivated in their jobs.

6. Education: I don't want to work in a school system. As much as I love my kids, I want to work with adults who need information and guidance about something meaningful in their lives.

7. Entertainment/hotel-resort work/tourism: A part of me wants to do

something fun like working with people who are on vacation or out to be entertained. This relates to my interest in events planning.

(One item from Statement K)

8. $31,000: This salary would support me and my daughter, plus give us a little left over for savings.

(Twelve items from the entire "Ideal Job Description")

9. Clear separation between work and personal time: I literally (as well as emotionally) do not want to take work home with me at the end of the day. I want to be free to spend quality time with my daughter, plus have a social life for myself.

10. Day care: I would like my employer to either subsidize my child care or provide on-site child care. I don't want half my pay check to have to go toward child care.

11. Minimal commute: This relates to Item 9. I want to work no further than fifteen minutes from my home. Ideally, I'd love to walk to work!

12. Small business: I don't want to work for a large business where I'd end up feeling like a number. I want to know the people I work with and feel connected to them.

13. Respect and recognition: Respect and recognition need to come from my boss and my coworkers. I need positive feedback to let me know I'm doing my job right.

14. Ability utilization/expertise: The ideal job would tap into all of my abilities and allow me to become an expert at something.

15. Honest, reliable, committed, communicative, and fun coworkers: What more can I say? It's important for me to like the people I work with and perhaps become friends with them.

16. People contact/work with adults: Having been a full-time mom and volunteer at my daughter's school, I want a job with lots of contact with the grown-up world!

17. Self-direction/minimal supervision: I want the freedom to do my job as I best see fit. I need a boss who gives me decision-making authority and room to set my own priorities.

18. Creativity: I want to use my imagination and creativity in my work. I'm not an artist, but I am an idea person. I like brainstorming and trying out different ideas.

19. Get out of the office: I can't stand the thought of being in one room all day. I want to be able to get out and interact with people at other places of employment.

20. Fun!: No matter what, I want to have some fun in my job, but also be treated seriously as a professional. I want to enjoy my work and go home at night feeling fulfilled.

Putting the Pieces Together:
Identifying What to Do Next

Exercise 15: Fantasy Want Ads

"I looked in the help wanted section of our newspaper to help me get started. I even cut and pasted some ads together to create a fantasy job. This was a fun exercise!"

What do your criteria mean in terms of actual jobs or fields of work? To help you connect your criteria to the real world of work, you need to visualize how your conditions/content/compensation criteria might combine in a work scenario. In your notebook, generate up to six fantasy want ads. These are want ads that would lead you to go and camp on the doorstep of the advertising employer to ensure you got to the job before anyone else. You're going to make up these ads drawing from the twenty items that you've just generated from your "Ideal Job Description." These can be as outrageous and nonspecific as you want. Each want ad does not have to integrate all twenty of your items – you may decide to use only five or six different items for each of the want ads. Here's a sample fantasy want ad that draws from the twenty criteria listed in the sample under Exercise 14.

Wanted: Individual interested in managing our conference center. Applicant must enjoy planning events and motivating a team of honest, reliable, committed, communicative, and fun coworkers. Must like self-directed work. Job involves traveling to area businesses to coordinate conferences. On-site day care provided. $40,000 to start. No experience necessary. Will train.

Remember, don't be reasonable here. This exercise is designed to get you thinking about how your interests and needs might be put together in an ideal work scenario.

Exercise 16: Identifying New Career Options to Explore

"I had to spend a lot of time in the library and talking with people to get a list together of possible career options worth exploring, but it was worth it. I found out about a lot of jobs I didn't even know existed."

Congratulations! You've just completed a lot of work, some of which may have been very challenging. You have done a lot of soul-searching to piece together what you need in a job to ensure your satisfaction.

And what do the results of your efforts mean? At this point, focus on these three exercises: Exercise 1: My Ideal Job Description, Exercise 14: My Top Twenty Job-Related Criteria, and Exercise 15: Fantasy Want Ads. Look these three exercises over carefully. Brainstorm in your notebook any types of jobs, fields, or industries that might help you identify career areas to explore. If you can't think of a specific job title or field, perhaps you can make up a brief role description like "manager of a department" or "someone who organizes special events within a company." Your list might end up looking something like this:

1. Management
2. Someone who organizes special events within a company
3. Party planning or bridal consulting
4. Business consulting
5. Adult education (like at a college)
6. Hotels
7. State tourism
8. Personnel
9. A place that helps people further their education

Most people who are considering changing careers or entering the work force for the first time feel that this step — identifying what jobs will match their content/conditions/compensation needs and wants — is the most challenging one toward making a job choice. Most of us have a very limited awareness of what types of jobs exist out there in the world of work. There are probably hundreds of jobs that you don't even know about. To help you find out what and where these jobs might be, refer to the chapters on planning and networking. Go to the library and look through career encyclopedias and other publications that can expose you to new jobs that may meet your needs. Share your ideal job description, top twenty job-related criteria, and fantasy want ads with as many people as you can think of who might assist you in coming up with job possibilities. Don't be shy! You may feel vulnerable, but keep in mind that most people you ask will probably welcome the opportunity to help you out. You may even want to consult with a career counselor who has been trained to help you identify suitable careers, given your needs.

Whatever you do, don't give up! There is a job – probably more than one – out there for you that will match up with most of your criteria. You have to be a detective and be willing to search high and low for ideas of job areas that would be right for you!

Exercise 17: Researching New Job Opportunities

"I asked some tough questions about the field of advertising and got some answers that really made me think. I've decided to go for it and feel like I'm going into the field with my eyes open."

Once you've got a list of types of jobs/fields/industries that may be right for you, you are ready to begin researching these areas. A well-made job choice is one that is based on both what you want (Exercises 1-15) and the reality of what certain careers are really like. Sometimes we are drawn to a field, based on false information. For example, many women are drawn to the field of human services because they imagine they will be working with people. Many jobs in human services actually involve working predominantly with data. How worthwhile it is to know just what a job will entail before committing to it! As you research job opportunities, keep your criteria in mind. Find out what you need to know to ensure the job will meet your content/conditions/compensation criteria.

While the research process may seem slow and cumbersome at times, it works. As a young woman looking for her first job out of college commented: "I just got a great job with a nonprofit agency and my nine months of researching and networking has definitely paid off! At least I'm getting off in the right direction rather than falling into something that later I'll feel stuck in."

Exercise 18: Some Suggested Career Growth Alternatives

"When I realized that I could do other things to make a living, I had the courage to confront my boss with some issues that were really

*troubling me. We worked them out and now I really love my job
and don't want to change careers."*

Starting a new career may not necessarily be the only option for you. For those of
you who are already working, there are some other possible options to consider,
given the results of Exercises 1, 14, and 15. Perhaps, instead of leaving your
current work situation, there are changes that could be made that would help
improve your job satisfaction. Generally, it is easier to try to better your current
situation than make a more radical career or job change.

■ **Step 1.** Look through the following list of career growth alternatives and
highlight any that look like they might be steps you could take to improve your
job now.

1. Alternatives within my present job:

   ★ Set new goals and standards

   ★ Tackle a new project; seek trial work on a different project

   ★ Pursue additional education/learning relevant to my job

   ★ Change the emphasis of responsibility; negotiate for added responsibility

   ★ Exchange duties with my coworkers; delegate out some of my work;
   do more of what I like, less of what I don't like

   ★ Rearrange my work environment

   ★ Request acknowledgment

   ★ Job share

   ★ Resolve conflict(s) with my coworker(s) and/or boss(es)

   ★ Other: _____

2. Alternatives outside of my present job:

   ★ Consult with another department or division; work on another team
   or task force

   ★ Propose using my skills in another area, department, or division of
   my company

   ★ Change employers

   ★ Change job within company/organization

   ★ Start my own business

★Other: _____

3. Alternative personal options:

   ★Develop/pursue a hobby outside of my work that will fulfill those needs currently going unmet in my work

   ★Volunteer for community service

   ★Pursue additional education/learning

   ★Participate in professional organizations/clubs/church

   ★Become politically active

   ★Do some creative moonlighting

   ★Other: _____

■ **Step 2.** List the alternatives you've highlighted in your notebook. Brainstorm how these alternatives could be implemented.

Exercise 19: Taking Action!

"I get scared thinking about changing jobs, but I figure if I don't take some action to improve my career, my job will never be satisfying. I don't have much to lose and I've got a lot to gain. I'm ready to go now!"

The time has come to put together a plan of action. What are your next steps?

Look over your list of job areas you'd like to explore (Exercise 16) and job growth alternatives (Exercise 18). List in your notebook those items from either or both of these lists that you intend to take action on. What do you plan to do? Often people find it helpful to give themselves a deadline.

The job-search process involves a lot of self-assessment and research. You can find work that is compatible with your conditions, content, and compensation needs if you give the process the time it deserves. Feel free to return to the work you've completed in this chapter to further reflect on your job-related needs. You may also find the accomplishments and skills exercises useful in putting together your resume and conducting job interviews (covered in later chapters). Most importantly, take what you have learned from this chapter and move on to chapter 4, planning your job search.

The Power
of Planning

Reach high, for stars lie hidden in your soul.
Dream deep, for every dream precedes the goal. – Pamela Vaull Starr

A job search is truly a time to "reach high" and "dream deep." The challenge is to figure out how to stimulate those thoughts and feelings and translate them into action; to clarify what you really want; to define the activities that will get you there; to weigh alternatives and trade-offs; to make the most effective use of your precious time; and to take good care of yourself. That is a major project, but you can succeed if you write a plan to shape the process and keep it going.

Historically, women are excellent planners and organizers. Think of what has been done in the schools – from volunteering as classroom mothers, to building playgrounds, to overseeing internship programs – because mothers have planned, promoted, and organized. Focus on all of the accomplishments women have achieved within their communities – from athletic programs, theater, recycling, zoning, historic preservation, green belts, to safety programs – planned and organized by women who believed in the importance of an issue. Women have organized political movements from temperance to suffrage, antiwar protests, and both sides of the abortion issue. Success in traditional women's professions like teaching and nursing depended, among other things, on good planning skills.

As mothers, daughters, and sisters, we have learned how to plan for the needs of others. We may not, however, always have been great planners for ourselves. While we have been able to do much for others, we may not always have stopped to figure out where we wanted to go or how to get there. If you haven't done it already, this is the perfect time to take your natural planning abilities and use them to get you to where you want to go. If you have been a planner in the past, this is an important time to use those skills.

Why Plan?

If you have a plan, it increases the probability of your success. According to a study of Harvard graduates done ten years after graduation, determining what you want to do and also *writing it down* produces demonstrable results. Robert McGarvey, in his article "Getting Your Goals" cites a study conducted by Forrest H. Patton that found

> 8.3 percent of those surveyed had no goals;
>
> 14 percent had specific but unwritten goals and their average earnings were three times higher than those of the first group;
>
> 3 percent had specific goals that were written down and their average earnings were ten times higher than those of the first group.

Planning works! It makes a measurable, positive difference. If every time you make a decision, you have a written goal to use as a touchstone, you will move closer to that goal. *With a clear plan, you have a much better chance of influencing events.* Because you have thought out what you want to do, the steps needed to get there, and what has to happen, you are in a better position to make it happen. If you believe that a certain person would be helpful to you in your job search, you can develop activities that assure you contact this person. If your goal requires that you refresh a skill, you plan to accomplish that. Plan in advance to make something happen, rather than hoping that luck will strike.

Once you set a goal, you have taken the first step to achieving it. You can begin to see yourself as having accomplished what you set out to do. The often-used phrase "self-fulfilling prophecy" is not an idle cliche. *If you can form an image of yourself as you would like to be, you increase your chances of actually getting there.* Why? Studies indicate that envisioning your goal results in behavioral changes that cause you to begin to act more like you would if you had achieved your goal. As your behavior changes, others begin to perceive you as you want to be, reinforcing the changes. (See chapter 1 for visualization techniques.)

A plan helps you to seize opportunities. How? If you have thought out the process needed to achieve your goal, you know what you must do. If something unexpected happens or when opportunity strikes, you can recognize its relevance to your goals. If you haven't done the planning, you might not even see it as an opportunity! You may even decide to modify your plan to take advantage of an unexpected windfall, because you know the direction in which you are heading. Suppose a friend calls and offers you the chance to attend a day-long workshop on supervisory skills. As a result of the activities you had outlined in your plan, you know that understanding several theories of supervision would be a real asset in the type of work you want. Instead of thinking you are too busy (because you are trying to get a job), you say, "Terrific, it's just what I need. I'll go."

Barriers are those things that make us feel stymied in a job search. In the planning process, you identify potential barriers in advance, and figure out ways to either overcome them or map out alternative routes around them. In planning, you build in reinforcements, which help you feel strong while dealing with problem areas.

One barrier that women are susceptible to in a job search is rejection, because we weave our self-worth into work. When someone says no, we often take it personally. You can combat this by reminding yourself that even though you put forth your best effort, other factors may carry the day. Always evaluate how you have done and improve technique, but remember that the outcome is the result of many factors, not a comment on your self-worth. So, step one in dealing with the "no" barrier is to practice a new attitude; step two is to have a sequence of activities planned so that one negative is balanced by positives; and step three is to give yourself permission to do something that makes you feel good. If you plan all of this in advance, you are much less likely to be caught off guard by rejection and will keep the energy to make progress.

When you have a plan in place, you have a standard against which to measure progress. You can check off the scheduled activities and results as you complete them and see demonstrable accomplishments. Each completed task is a motivator. Without a plan, progress is much more difficult to define, because activities are more random. The distance from the beginning to the end of a job search is long, and you may become discouraged if you cannot tick off the tasks accomplished.

Written plans help prevent procrastination. Without a plan, you may feel that you have nothing to do or that you have run out of ideas, and, therefore, tend to sit around feeling discouraged. *A plan builds a schedule for you, and you always have another step to take.*

When you plan, you have power. You are in charge and can determine, for the most part, the order of events. Without a plan, you are very susceptible to feeling out of control and powerless. If you have a plan, you will gain a sense of control by maximizing your resources. You need to project that image of strength as you go into the marketplace. A written plan gives you the tool you need.

The time that you spend in a job search is an opportunity. It is an opportunity to be creative, to try some things that you may have wanted to do, and to envision some of the things that you would like to learn, practice, and begin. A written plan helps you take advantage of this opportunity whether you have unstructured time or a full schedule of work and other responsibilities. It forces you to think of the steps you need to take. Planning defines the obstacles in advance and figures out strategies to get around them. It helps you visualize the entire job-search process so that your mind is constantly working in that direction. You make the best use of your resources, because you have identified them in advance and figured out how to use them. If planning is already a habit, you can further hone your skills. If you are not a planner, this is the time to learn these new skills and methods, which may even impact on your future job performance.

A Buddy

Did you have the experience as a child of swimming or going for a hike and having a buddy? It was a way of assuring that children didn't get lost or get into trouble in the water. When the whistle blew for a buddy check, you had to grab your buddy's hand and hold it up in the air. If everyone had a buddy, the adults knew that everything was okay. If a buddy came up alone, there was a problem. Your buddy in camp may have been a friend or may have been someone that you didn't know at all. A buddy in the job search process is a lot like that.

The important thing about the buddy system was that you kept each other from getting lost. Your job-search buddy is the person who makes sure that you don't drown in the process, or get in over your head, or wander off in the wrong direction. The difference is that you choose when to blow the whistle. You decide when you and your buddy will get together to do what is needed.

A description of your job-search buddy could be the following: listens well, asks relevant questions, is nonjudgmental, is upbeat, brainstorms well. No formal knowledge of job-search techniques is needed, but common sense helps. This buddy is not there to give advice, but to ask questions that will help you sharpen your plan and to give you a sounding board. When the whistle blows, your buddy listens and asks, helping you to stay on task.

Perhaps you know someone who could be just such a buddy, or perhaps you have no one who could fill that role. The biggest obstacle in finding an appropriate buddy may not be in who should fill the role, but in asking for help. Women are givers, but often not askers. If this is true for you, this is a good time to begin changing this behavior. As a first step, keep in mind that asking for help may benefit both the asker and the giver. The asker gets assistance and the giver gets the satisfaction of helping. The way that you ask is important. Most would-be buddies have many demands in their lives and need to know the parameters of the request. It makes a difference when the buddy clearly understands what is expected.

There are many potential candidates to be your job-search buddy. They include friends and family, all those people who are part of your personal network, a colleague, your clergy, or someone else whom you know in a community organization. It might be a professional career counselor or therapist. One other excellent candidate for buddy is someone else who is looking for a job. You can find another job seeker by checking out who is enrolled in a career course or by asking a job counselor if she would suggest someone. The latter alternative might require a one-time fee. The first step is to identify the person you want.

The next step is to ask that person. It is important to be specific. Jessie asked Mary in a way that made it easy for Mary to respond positively. "I am beginning a job search. From time to time, possibly as often as two or three times a week, I would like to be able to tell you specifically what I am doing. Each time it would probably take about fifteen minutes. What I am asking of you is that you listen to what I have done, ask questions as an objective, commonsense observer, pat me on the back when I have done what I said I would, and encourage me to complete what I have not yet done. In short, I am asking you to be a sounding board to help me clarify my own thinking and stay on track. I do not expect you to give me advice. If I am stuck and you are comfortable in doing so, I might ask you to brainstorm some ideas with me. I expect that this process will be time limited, but I do not know exactly how long it will take."

While there are many things a buddy can do, there are some that should not be expected of a buddy. A buddy is not there to make you do something, to nag you, or to check up on you. If you put a buddy in this role, the result is likely to be resentment on both your parts. You are in charge of what you want to accomplish, and you decide when to ask for a sounding board or a schedule check. You evaluate your progress, determining when or if you want to measure it with your buddy's assistance. Beware of putting your buddy in the policing role, because that sets up a scenario in which you can rebel or be childlike. Your buddy is a colleague, there to assist with the accomplishment of the plan at your request.

Your buddy provides a real service. It is possible, depending on your skills, to barter something in return, such as bookkeeping, painting, car washing, baby-sitting, or home cooking. Bartering is just one kind of exchange. Your buddy is guaranteed to get as much out of the process of helping as you receive. By the time you are done, your buddy will have had the pleasure of helping and will have learned how a good job search is conducted.

Beginning a Plan

A plan is

Written
Shared with a buddy
Flexible
Time consuming to write, but saves time in the long run because it keeps you going
Reworked as you get new ideas and information

Begin immediately by taking the following categories and writing words or phrases – whatever will get your ideas out – under each heading. Simply grab your notebook and start writing. At this point, your plan doesn't even need to be particularly well thought out. You just want to get over the hurdle of beginning. You can go back later and rework any part of it, build, expand, and change. For all the reasons we have listed already now is the time to plan, so get going.

Contents of a Plan

There are many ways of putting a plan together. We've found that the following outline works well. Use it as a starting point, and remember that your plan is flexible. If you need to add other sections, you can certainly do so. You should not, however, leave out any of the sections we have suggested. Some of these sections can seem a little daunting at first, but you will find that the information you develop is indispensable in your job search. The sections in your plan are

1. Your goal

2. Why bother (what will be different when you have achieved your goal)

3. Picture this (envisioning achievement, so you can focus on your goal)

4. Tools for getting the job done

5. Rewards (yes, you get those too!)

6. Barriers (how to overcome them)

7. Objectives and activities

8. Evaluation

We'll help you get going. Enjoy! Planning is one of the most satisfying processes you can undertake. It is a major step toward getting the job done, you can see all the progress you make, and you can write in all those things that you get enthusiastic about.

Your Goal

A plan begins with a succinctly stated goal which encompasses all that you want to accomplish. For example, your goal may be to "define what I want to work at, under what conditions, then find a position at a minimum of $XX,XXX salary." Or, "Get an entry-level accounting job with good potential for upward mobility in a small firm at a minimum of $XX,XXX salary." Your goal serves as a motivator. Remember Dorothy and her friends in the *Wizard of Oz?* She had her goal of returning to Kansas firmly in mind. It helped her to overcome all sorts of obstacles (luckily most of us don't have a wicked witch to deal with), enlist the assistance of very loyal comrades, and keep going even when the next step wasn't very clear or was terribly frightening. We all need to be a lot like Dorothy in a job search.

Define your goal by asking yourself what you truly want and need to do. With a goal firmly in place, you can accomplish more than you ever dreamed was possible. Write down a few ideas about your goal in phrases and refine them as you develop your plan. Don't try for perfection. It is possible that your goal will change, as you go through your job search, and gain new information about yourself and about work. The important thing is that your goal be something that you passionately want.

Why Bother?

Write down how you anticipate your life will be different once you have achieved your goals. What will the changes be in both your professional life and your personal life? Make the list as long and as detailed as you like, and then summarize the most important changes you anticipate. What are the changes you foresee in your work responsibilities, your coworkers, your salary, your recreational activities, your self-esteem and self-image, your family, and your friends. Ask yourself if making these changes is worth the effort? Whenever you feel discouraged or wonder why you started off in this direction in the first place, look at this part of your plan to reinforce the meaning of your efforts.

Picture This

Once you know what it will feel like when you reach your goal, do some creative visualization (see chapter 1 for techniques) to form an image of what you and your new environment will be like. Imagine what an entire day in your new life looks like from the time you get up until you go to bed. Don't leave anything out. Include such details as what you will wear, eat, and read. If you don't know what life with this new job would look like, make up what you would like it to be. Once you have mentally walked through your day, write down enough notes, so that you can recall whenever you want what the day was like. This part of your plan is another motivator, as well as an important step toward getting there.

Have you read about how various sports are "mind games"? If you keep focused on the goal, if you think about yourself as winning, if you concentrate on where you want the ball to land, your playing improves. If you think that a shot isn't going to make it, if you envision yourself losing the game, you usually do. Holding onto the image of yourself having achieved your goal will help you attain it. Recall that image whenever you need motivation, when you talk with someone about what you want to do, and certainly in an interview.

Resources for Getting the Job Done

Your resources are all the tangible and intangible assets in your world that will help you achieve your goal. They are the people you know who will help you, the information sources you can tap, your skills, the activities that give you a positive outlook. Resources are whatever gives you energy and helps you to move forward. List your resources in your notebook, including everything that you think will help you in your job search. If you can't get started, think of the last time you had a problem to solve. What resources did you bring to bear? Were they people who could help you out? Being able to think clearly and analyze the problem accurately? Your courage, humor, ability to research? Someone you knew? Money? Your dog who always makes you cheerful? Your education? The list is unlimited once you begin writing.

There are a lot of ways to create your resource list. If you are visually oriented, try drawing on a large sheet of paper all of those things that cause you to feel positive and get things done. It doesn't need to be a great work of art; you can have fun using symbols. Brainstorm with your buddy or someone else who knows you. That person can either ask you questions or help you remember some of the resources that have helped you in the past. Think of when you felt very good in professional and personal settings. What were you doing? Who was with you? What kind of environment were you in? These are all your tools. Starting a list like this may be slow, but you will gain ideas as you go along. Examples of resources might include

★ You are a great morning person and can get something done before everyone else is up (good time to get tougher tasks done, might prefer morning interviews)

★ You are a good listener (a real asset in interviewing and networking)

★ You had a course in Lotus and like to use it (marketable skill)

★ You just met someone doing something that really interests you (add that person to your network)

★ You usually feel great after an outdoor workout (important for maintaining progress and rewarding yourself)

★ You can organize absolutely anything (a skill that you will use in almost every work setting, not to mention accomplishing your plan)

Create as long a list of resources as you can. Don't be shy about going back and adding to it when something else comes to mind. The more resources you can recall, the more tools you have to work with when you write your plan. If you sense that you have some skills, but don't see how they can be applied, add the practical applications afterward. There is no right or wrong to this resource list.

Rewards

The next step in planning is to make a rewards list. What people, places, and activities make you feel good? Write those things down under rewards. Most of us grew up with the rule that we couldn't have dessert until we had eaten dinner. Stated positively, we might say, "If you eat those pickled parsnips, you can have an extra scoop of ice cream and fresh raspberries." The reward came when we had done what we were supposed to. The rewards in creating and using a plan work the same way. When you've had a long day and have finally finished up your resume or made five tough phone calls or had some interviews, you get to go to a movie, a museum, or the beach – whatever rewards and reinforces you. Those things that help you feel good and are a treat for you need to be part of your plan. When you have finished something tough, give yourself a reward. Actually write it on your calendar. It will certainly help motivate you to get the job done on time. This is your plan; you can choose to reward yourself to keep moving forward at any time. Use this rewards list as you proceed in the planning process. Schedule your first reward for when you finish writing this plan!

Barriers

Barriers come next in your plan. What scares you when you think about doing your job search? What causes your stomach to knot or your neck muscles to tense when you think about getting a job? What is the very worst thing that could happen to you? Let these apprehensions come out. Once out, jot them down. This is a very important step. If you are really denying all fears and cannot think of a small one, give it some time and start with a worry. As the planning process progresses, be very aware of your reactions to what you are doing. Unless you are superwoman, some fears and apprehensions are there. You'll be in a stronger position if you can identify and confront them. Forewarned is forearmed.

It may seem strange to concentrate on your fears in the planning process, but there is a good reason. Denied fears can overwhelm you. When you air some of those fears out in the breeze, they lose a lot of their power. That doesn't mean you need to go around telling everyone what your fears are. What is important is that you take the time to isolate and examine them. Usually a fear is nebulous. It is often a lot of ill-defined issues rolled up into one nasty glob. Fears can be difficult to deal with because you have not sorted out what is real from what is imagined. That is why it is helpful to define them.

An analogy might be the panic you feel when you have so much to do, you are sure you will never get it all done. You have several options in how to handle that type of pressure and time crunch. You can run around in a panic being less efficient because you are not thinking clearly. Or, you can stop and take time to make a list of what has to be done, how long it will take, and the amount of time you have. Often it fits. If it doesn't, you have to delegate or cut. The key is that once you have identified the real elements in your time bind, it can be managed. Fear is very much the same way. If you can unravel the issues causing the fear, then it can be managed. Why talk so much about fears? They are the barriers that each of us potentially faces in a job search.

How do you begin to define the fears involved in the job search? The task is to keep challenging yourself with questions, until you have broken this ill-defined fear down into its component parts. Then you can begin to confront and take action on each aspect of the fear. For example, let's take the fear that you will not get a job. The first question is, "What are you afraid of?" The next question is, "Why won't you get a job?" An answer is, "Because no one will like me." Question: "Why won't they like you?" Answer: "Because I don't know how to do a lot of things." Question: "What particularly don't you know how to do?" At this point, you are getting to a real barrier, and most real barriers can be overcome. If you believe that you lack skills and that is why people won't like you and thus why you won't get a job, then your plan has to include ways that you will acknowledge that you have those skills or learn them, eliminating what may have been a paralyzing fear.

What if you are so depressed that you don't respond with a skill answer, but say that you are basically unlikable? That feeling is also a barrier because at the moment, it is very real to you; these are your legitimate feelings. If you can involve yourself in an activity where you can get a positive response from others, it will help build your self-esteem. It might help to think about past positive experiences in which you interacted with others and choose an activity in a similar environment, using similar skills, or with a similar group of people. If you are feeling too down to even think of any past positive experiences, then one way to overcome this barrier is to seek qualified counseling around this specific problem. If cost is also a barrier, much counseling is covered by health insurance. Alternatively, counseling may be available from clergy who are often thoroughly trained and practiced counselors or through local human service agencies. Once again, the barrier may seem very real, but it can be overcome. The important thing is to include overcoming the fears that create your barriers in your plan objectives and activities.

> *Gretchen was unhappy with her job in the operations department of a bank. She had mastered the tasks, received superior evaluations, but was now tired of the repetitive nature of her daily assignments. She was ready to assume more responsibility and decision making. She talked with her supervisor and with the human resources staff. Due to a hiring freeze, there was no movement between positions and probably would not be for a significant period of time. Given her restlessness, Gretchen knew she should find another position where she could be challenged to use and improve her abilities. But every time she thought of seeking a new job, she became anxious and was unable to move forward. Unexamined, this general anxiety stopped her in her tracks. She could not tell you why she was afraid, but she was immobilized.*

Gretchen was dealing with two negatives: dissatisfaction with her job and fear of changing. She began analyzing her immobility, to discover the component fears. She learned that one of the things stopping her was her fear of separation from the known security of her current job for the uncertainty of a new situation and the resulting loss of control. Recognizing this fear made it possible for Gretchen to deal with it. Since one of the components was fear of the unknown, she had to make the unknown, known. This was the beginning of a job search in which her plan outlined how she would investigate details of other jobs, including content, compensation, and promotion potential, thereby eliminating some of the unknown elements. A second component of the fear was self-esteem. By going to look for a new job, Gretchen felt as if she were putting herself on the line; her low self-confidence would not allow her to do that. Understanding what was really behind the barrier made it possible for her to overcome it. Gretchen defined some of the things that made her lack confidence and wrote activities that would increase her confidence into her plan. She also worked on separating her self-image from the events in the job search. How had Gretchen been able to move from the generalized anxiety and fear to the defined issues of a real barrier? She had followed some of the steps discussed in chapter 1, including examining what the situation was, listening to what she was saying to herself, monitoring her emotional responses, comparing this experience to earlier experiences, and then taking steps toward using more appropriate behaviors.

As you can see from Gretchen's experience, a barrier that can be described can be managed. If your barrier is a lack of confidence in your skills, there are many avenues for addressing this. You might get a volunteer job that would help you prove to yourself that you do have skills, and test out whether those skills are the ones that you enjoy using. Or, you might return to a school that offers a work-study program or internships, taking skill courses like programming. Perhaps, you would decide to work for a temporary service, taking very small steps in unfamiliar territory, gaining confidence at each level before moving on to the next. You can see that with a small degree of determination, you can take nonthreatening steps to help yourself break down the barriers standing in your way.

For each of your barriers, decide what actions to take to break them apart into more manageable segments. How can you defuse those fears so they will not slow or stop you in your job search? Your resource list is a good place to look for ideas. Just thinking about how you have overcome obstacles in the past is a big help. Be sure that you have untangled the barrier as much as possible and isolated all of the issues. Then, the actions to take become more apparent. If overcoming a barrier involves a series of activities, add it to your objectives/actions section as a specific part of your plan, which will have a timetable attached to it. Decide what kind of reward you want for overcoming a barrier and grant it. When struggling with a tough project, knowing that there is a reward at the end can be a sure motivator.

Objectives and Activities

Objectives are the small, clearly defined steps on the way to your goal. When all of your objectives have been accomplished, you will have reached your goal. You determine what your objectives are by asking yourself what you need to do to accomplish your goal. You may not hit all of the objectives with the first try.

Adding and subtracting later is certainly allowed! Each objective should be written with a standard of quality (for example, specifying to what degree, how much, or how many) and with a time frame. When objectives are written, they can be checked off once completed; you have the sense of progress or satisfaction you deserve, which, in turn, acts as a strong motivator to continued progress.

A standard of quality is written into an objective because it forces you to think about the level at which you need to work. It encourages you to acknowledge just how capable you are of doing things well. A standard of quality requires you to decide at what level to function. It really establishes a precedent that will carry over into the quality of your resume and interviews, and thus to the level of professionalism you will communicate throughout your job search.

Choosing a time for completion keeps you honest. It is easy to let something go until the next day when you don't want to do it. With time-limited objectives, procrastination is tougher to get away with. An objective might be to "define the skills I want to use, the environment I want to work in, and the values that are important to me so that they can be stated in a manner that others understand by March 2."

The next step is to decide what activities will accomplish this objective. When you ask yourself the question, "How will I accomplish this objective?" the answers are your activities. Jen's goal was to move to a higher level supervisory position. One of her objectives was to investigate what options existed, would open up, or could be created with her current employer by the first of the calendar year. Her activities included explaining her goal to her supervisor and asking for her assistance in defining a career ladder within the department; interviewing the supervisors of three other related departments about the potential in those areas; discussing her goal with human resources and requesting their advice; reviewing supervisory job descriptions at levels just above her own; and making a written inventory of her skills. Each activity had a written target completion date.

Activities should be manageable bites of effort. It is better to begin with many small steps and feel that you are getting somewhere than to climb a mountain and have so much trouble that you never want to try another. For some, a mountain is a manageable step; for others, a manageable step is a walk to the corner. Respect your beginning ability. That doesn't mean that you won't stretch as time goes on, you just want to start with comfortable steps. As you are writing activities, estimate the amount of time each takes. You need to add a completion date, but may want to wait until you've developed and looked at the priorities in all of your activities.

Personal Objectives

As you write objectives and activities, don't forget about yourself and your personal needs. Yes, you want to find the very best work, but you increase your opportunities to succeed if you remember to take care of yourself in the process. That's one very good reason why personal objectives are so important in your plan. One need is certainly to find work, but another, equally important, is to be a healthy, growing person in the process. If you plan time to grow and expand your horizons during a job search, you will feel more confident, think more clearly, make better choices, and project a healthier image to others.

A job search requires lots of energy, positive energy! Every time we do something new, it takes an extra amount of energy. During the job search, you not only need to feel energized, but you also need to demonstrate that you have a high level of energy in every contact you have with potential employers. Some of the people you talk with during the course of your job search will be very receptive; others will not. Every time someone is not receptive or says, "no," an extra shot of energy is required to get going again.

What does this have to do with planning? You can even plan to get extra energy. What kinds of activities, feelings, and relationships build your energy? Conversely, what saps your energy? Now, as you write your plan, make sure that your activities and your personal objectives include those that build energy. Energy builders vary for each of us. It may be contact with certain people, a balance of quiet and interactive time, exercise, contact with art or nature, giving a party, reading a book, playing with our children, visiting with a favorite elderly person whose life has always been an inspiration, attending a religious gathering, a hobby, or breakfast with a friend. Think about the times when you have felt full of energy, and think too about the times when you have felt exhausted, washed out, or depressed. What were you doing at those times and just before? If you discover activities that are energy sappers, purge them from your list. Then you'll have a high-energy plan.

Common sense tells us to plan to promote a high energy level physically by taking care of our bodies. How much sleep do you require to function at an optimum level? Not getting enough sleep can be the result of having too many other things to do in life, which can easily happen in the job search. If this is happening to you, revise your schedule and adjust your calendar. Your job search will actually progress more smoothly, and you'll feel better too.

You also know the old saying that "what you eat is what you are." Medications, alcohol, drugs, and nicotine all affect our bodies in ways that have been well-documented and publicized. During a job search, anxiety and tension can sometimes leave us vulnerable to abusing these substances. Be wary of these tendencies if you have them. Many of us are less aware of the effects of sugar and caffeine. Both tend to give you an energy surge, but after a period of time, depending on the amount consumed and individual tolerance, result in a real letdown both in energy and, for some people, in emotions. Monitor your intake of sugar and caffeine to achieve a stable energy level. Your energy level is very important during your job search and you can plan to maximize it. This is a part of your life you do control.

Stimulating your mind can also be part of your plan. While looking for new work, you want to be creative and break with stale or rigid thought patterns. What have you always wanted to learn more about, spend more time thinking about, write about, photograph, or see? This is an ideal time to stretch your mind and your understanding of the world around you. You will feel more interesting, more stimulated. Learning something new gives you a sense of accomplishment. It can also be one method of testing out what you would like to do. It shouldn't be a huge new project, and it doesn't have to be expensive. It could be learning more about a kind of music or particular period of art by visiting museums, reading library books, or attending performances. It could be learning more about dreams and what they mean by reading and recording your own. It could be refreshing a foreign language by taking a course, finding a native speaker, or using tapes. It might be learning to cook the foods of a specific country, which might also involve inviting in some friends to enjoy your culinary creations. There are a lot of projects you could undertake; the important thing is to set objectives in this area so that they will be on your calendar.

If you are resisting writing personal objectives, think about how you react when you are overworked. What goes first? For most of us, it is the time we need for ourselves, to collect, to center, and to gather energy to go forth and accomplish. It is the recreational time that keeps us feeling good. Especially if you are balancing work, children, spouse, and home care, it may seem that the only way to get it all done is to give up your own time. Don't. Give yourself equal priority with all of the other demands in your life. Set objectives for personal time, some social and some solitary.

Child Care

Child care can be an overwhelming issue. The importance of caring for our children and meeting their needs in all stages of development cannot be compromised. How do you conduct a job search if you are working full-time and have children to care for, not to mention a home and your finances to manage? After a full day of work, the children are glad to see you and want your undivided attention. When do you have the time to think about or even look for a new job? The answer may simply be that, unless some changes are made, you do not. You may have to plan to do some things differently if you are going to free up time. If you have a partner, is it time to renegotiate your responsibilities? If they are already fairly evenly divided, is your partner willing to pick up extra responsibility for a designated period of time? If you do not have a partner, do you have a friend or friends who would be willing to spend an occasional day with your children for a limited period of time, while you look for a job? Do you know someone who would be willing to exchange watching children, giving each of you a free day? It may not be any more difficult to take twice as many children for a Saturday walk or trip to the beach, especially if the reward is a day for yourself. Is there a college student who would exchange child care for room, board, and a homey environment? Would you consider a roommate or another single parent, if you have space? Do you have enough money to hire someone to do the housework for an interim period of time, thereby lifting one responsibility? Is it possible to take vacation or personal time, while continuing to take the kids to day care, and use the time to search? There are options, many of which will work, if you take the time to plan ahead.

Aside from the time aspect of child care, questions of availability and quality are critical. Whether you are beginning to work for the first time after giving birth or have used child care for some time, it is a continuing issue. By writing child care into your job-search plan, you resolve one of the barriers in advance. One of the best ways to find child care is by talking with others with the same needs. You can find profit and nonprofit child-care referral agencies in most communities. Some colleges have excellent child-care programs, as places for education students to do practicums. Increasingly, employers provide inexpensive day care as a means of attracting and retaining good employees. Get a list of these day-care centers and visit. Spending a morning in day care is one way to assure yourself that the standards of the provider match yours. That will make going off to work a lot easier, especially when your children are getting used to a new setting and fuss about being left. Having chosen day care, the next task is to set up back-up day care for the days when the first string doesn't work. Your back-up is more likely to be friends and relations or individual providers.

The mix of children and work always seems to be with us, whether we are searching for quality care for a six-week-old, trying to get time off to attend a school play or game, working to pay college tuition, or wanting time to spend with grandchildren. As women, we often are or want to be the primary care-givers for our children. This makes having a career much more conflicted and tougher for women than it does for men. Finding the time to spend with our children can make life much more satisfying. But satisfying does not make it easier. Planning ahead will certainly not solve all problems, but it makes life a lot smoother than reacting to a crisis. There will be enough crises, even if you have warded off half of them with a plan!

Evaluation

Lastly, evaluate your plan as you go along. If you have written your objectives with standards and deadlines, you will know if you are on target. What a sense of accomplishment, as you move closer to your goal! What if you have gotten new information that means you need to go in a different direction? Modify the plan. Having a plan keeps you on track; you decide if and when to change the course. If you need to alter your plan, you will understand what you are giving up and gaining as you make that change.

What if you are not meeting deadlines? Take time to figure out why. If your schedule is unrealistically full, then it needs to be modified. You will get discouraged always trying to meet impossible deadlines. If you are procrastinating, check your barriers. What is preventing you from moving forward? How can you overcome it? Would a reward help you get moving again? A plan is flexible; it is evolving, rather than stagnant. You can change it at any time and in any way that meets your needs. Treat your plan as a map, something to guide your progress and to turn to when you feel lost.

Time Lines, Calendars, and Ticklers

These organizational tools are a must if you are to keep the varied details, dates, and appointments organized. If you can, get a big one-month-at-a-glance calendar with a lot of writing space under each day, or make a big calendar for every month of your job search. Write in each objective and activity with its expected completion date. (Work backward to the date you need to start in order to have it completed by the target date.) Make necessary adjustments to even out your schedule. Now, schedule in your rewards, being sure to make time for the rewards to happen. Review your calendar again for flow. Is the schedule logical and reasonable? If it is, you have a schedule to get going on. If not, then revise, until you are comfortable with it.

A calendar is one way of organizing the activities in your plan; a time line is another. Use whichever one you are most comfortable with, as long as you use one of them. If you want to create a time line, use virtually the same process. List the dates along the top and the activities down the side. Then use horizontal lines to indicate when the activity will begin and end. One advantage of a time line is that you can assess the required activity level at any given time.

A tickler file is a helpful tool to use with a calendar or time line. It is a series of file folders arranged by date. You can set it up by days of the week, by week, or by the month, depending on what will be most useful to you. With your folders arranged in chronological order, simply put notes or messages in the file for the date the work should be started and check regularly.

Scheduling activities is an essential part of planning. Until you complete this step, you will have accumulated a lot of incredibly valuable ideas, but you won't know if they can realistically be accomplished. When you put everything on a calendar or time line, you can smooth out the rough edges, and then rely on it to keep you organized and moving forward. If you are not working, you now have a schedule that takes the place of going to work every day and where achieving results is certainly just as important. If you are working, you have made the essential decisions that allow you to get it all done. What if everything does not fit onto the calendar or time line? What can be delegated to your children, a friend, your spouse, or a colleague? Which activities are not essential and can be eliminated? To make this judgment, you may want to look at some of the things you now do on a daily basis that are not in the plan and set priorities. As much as we each are sometimes tempted to be superwoman, we cannot do everything. Taking a good look at your job-search plan and other things in your life means that you take control.

A Sample Plan

For some time, Jane had been restless in her job. She had found it interesting at first, but now her skills were not fully used and there was no challenge. Because of the nature of her job, Jane did not have close working relationships with colleagues. She missed these. It was not possible to increase her responsibilities, nor could she make an internal move, since her company was downsizing. The economy was far from robust, so she merely held on to her job, rather than being involved or creative. Jane began to lose confidence in her own abilities, which in turn made her less enthusiastic about her work. She had not sought a new job because her morale was down and because she was concerned about leaving a secure source of support. Jane is a divorcee with financially independent children, but she is her own sole support. She is also beginning to think more about the money necessary for her retirement. But, as a result of spending a weekend with a friend who was excited by her own work, Jane was reminded of what that feeling was like and inspired to consider a change. Jane knew the importance of strategic planning and how much it could do for her. She began her job search by sitting down at her computer and writing the working draft of a plan.

Jane's Magnificent Plan

Goal: Define a career direction and test its feasibility in this community within the next three months.

Why bother?

1. I could be doing work that really interests me, demands my skills, and challenges me.
2. I could be working in an environment where colleagues stimulate and support each other.
3. I could earn a salary commensurate with my skills.
4. I could be excited about and proud of the work I do.
5. I could be making a real contribution to the world around me.

Jane's Visualization of Her Ideal Lifestyle

Get up, run or row, depending on weather. Shower, dress, prepare a bagel and tea in my travel mug. Drive to commuter lot. Read the *Wall Street Journal,* eat a bagel, and drink tea in the forty-minute ride in the van. Walk five minutes from van to office, a beautiful old restored Victorian on the edge of the downtown area, go in and greet my assistant. Look over my schedule and then review the upcoming week's work with her. Spend the first part of the morning reviewing research. Meet with a client. Write a proposal based on research done this morning and last week, and meetings with client. Eat lunch with Sarah, good friend and energy raiser. Meet with another client. Make marketing calls, both by phone and on site. Review proposal drafted in morning. Meet with partners to critique the proposal. Catch van, read local paper. Drive home. Change clothes and mow part of the lawn, weed until dark. Eat dinner of leftovers and clean up kitchen. Get ready for bed and read before falling asleep.

Tools and Resources

I have listed some of the skills, qualities, people, finances, and rewards that will help me achieve my goals.

■ Skills

Computing

Synthesizing

Reading

Listening

Organizing

Questioning

Evaluating

Motivating

Systematizing

Communicating

Researching

Writing

Promoting or marketing

Presenting information

Planning

Reporting

Summarizing

Teambuilding

Analyzing

Interviewing/Being interviewed

■ Personal Qualities

Curious

Bright

Attractive

Optimistic

Loyal

Quick learner

Self-reliant

Healthy

Interested

Strong values

Articulate

Courageous

Good-natured

Competent

Humorous

Hardworking

Athletic

Energetic

■ People

Sarah, Jen, and Sally, my big morale boosters

Mom and Dad

The kids

Fr. James who'll encourage and help me with contacts

Other people at church

Rob, Ellie, Nancy, Jack, Rachel, Connie, acquaintances with whom I do some fun things

Other members on the zoning board who work in lots of different places

Neighbors and some of their friends

Mark, for whom I used to work

College alum career network

Parents of some of the kids' friends whom I've known well

■ Finances

Mortgage paid off

My current pension plan can be rolled over and I am fully vested

No other real debt except the car

Some savings, which could be used if absolutely necessary even though I wouldn't want to

■ Rewards

I will do one of these things for myself each time that I have accomplished something in the plan or that I have gotten through a really tough spot. I can also use one to keep me going, if I feel that I am slowing down.

A day hike

Tennis lesson

Dinner out with a friend

Buying all the ingredients and preparing a really great gourmet dinner for myself and friends

A movie out

Free Sunday concert at the museum

Long bike ride, two-day would be even better

Day of skiing

Buy and plant a new shrub

Breakfast or lunch with a good friend

A winter vacation with swimming and snorkeling

An unplanned day off

A day of sailing

A long walk

Unlimited time in a bookstore and the money to buy two books

A rainy morning with a new book and nothing else I have to do

A long distance phone call to the kids

Make a beautiful wildflower arrangement

An afternoon at the museum to look

Barriers

■ **Inertia.** I have had a heck of a time getting this far and I don't want to lose any of the motivation that I have gained. *Remedy:* Keep going back and reading the second and third sections of this plan. Schedule a reward on the calendar when I feel myself slowing down. Spend more time with Sarah and get reinspired.

■ **I'll never find anything that I like.** *Remedy:* That is a great example of global thinking when in fact, if I work at it, it would be impossible for me not to find something that I really like. I need to be on guard against this kind of thinking and talk myself out of it when it comes. I also need to go out and do something physical which usually builds up my positive thinking.

I also need to take on a problem and organize it (always possible on the zoning board). This usually make me feel as if I can accomplish anything.

■ **I hate to ask for anything from anybody.** *Remedy:* This is the time to reward myself (bribe?) after I have actually done it. So, as I sit by the phone trying to force myself to call someone, I know that I can have a great walk after I call. Otherwise, I just have to sit here. Also, figure out what the worst thing is that can happen. They say "no" and I have to call someone else. What if the next person says "no"? Then I need to think about what I am asking, try my requests out on Sal or Jen to get their reactions. I need to remember that the "no" is not to me as a person, but to my request.

■ **What if I find something that I really want to do for which I am not qualified?** *Remedy:* Take the challenges one at a time. If I do find something for which I am not qualified, then I can figure out if it is worth it and how to get it.

■ **As I begin asking around about careers, my current employer might find out and that might make my job less secure.** *Remedies:* Talk to George again about possibilities for additional responsibilities or move to another position, so that he understands that I do have some additional goals. Also be very positive about what I am doing at work now, so that he is reminded about how good I am. If he does hear that I am making inquiries, it will be clearly a career-oriented interest and not dissatisfaction with him or the company. Also, I can explain to people I seek information from that I am looking for alternatives, not committed to making a change and ask them to be discreet. Figure exactly how long I could live on my current assets without endangering the house, car, etc.

Objectives and Activities

1. Tap into some of my own creative juices and at the same time do some things that promote my upbeat self on a daily basis for the life of this plan and thereafter!

   a. Go back to writing in my journal on a regular basis.

b. Spend 1/2 hour a day by myself: no compromises, no chores, unless they are relaxing.

c. Pick out some biographies of women and read.

d. Check myself to make sure that I am using all of my senses regularly. What does this sound like? Smell like?

e. Do power walk, exercise bicycle, floor exercises, aerobics, or some other exercise daily.

f. Finally, finally take that water color course that I have been talking about for so many years! Even though I can't draw, it will help me really observe.

g. Spend some time with Judy who does alternative theater and Julie who does massage in an alternative health center to derail my thinking onto a different and possibly more creative track. As long as I'm looking at new possibilities, I want to begin by thinking as broadly as possible.

2. By September 28, find out how some others perceive me.

a. Get together with the people on my people resources list who know me well. Ask them what they think I do best, what my strong points are in presenting myself, and what I need to work on.

b. Ask these friends and relations to brainstorm with me about the kinds of things that I could do. Now, some of these people are going to come up with some pretty funny ideas, some serious but some teasing. I'll consider them all because in some of the wilder ideas could be a germ of inspiration.

3. Complete a preferred skill assessment by October 15.

a. Do an assessment of my "Ideal Job Description."

b. Summarize preferred skills into a "This is what I want to do" statement.

4. Complete preferred workplace environment assessment by October 20.

a. Do an assessment of my ideal work environment.

b. Summarize in a statement of "I want to work in an environment that is ... "

5. Find out more about what is going on "out there" in the community getting initial information by October 30 and continuing the process.

   a. Accept invitations I'd normally ignore for gatherings that put me in contact with new people, beginning with the Beethoven Festival donor recognition reception, which I have been invited to as a result of my $25 contribution.

   b. Check the paper for meetings, lectures, events that interest me and attend, talking to as many people as possible about their interests and what they do. (If we have the same interests in one area, there may be correlations with careers.)

   c. Be really curious, talking to people about what they do.

   d. Ask friends and family to tell me about things that might interest me in the community. Since it is a local election year, more people are involved than usual. It could also mean job openings after the election.

6. Match what I have learned about the skills that I want to use and the environment I want to be in with what is in the job market by December 1.

   a. Use the Career Development Center library at the university beginning with the *Occupational Outlook Handbook* to get an idea of growth in various areas and what people do in different careers. Use other resources as I am interested; look at *Catalyst* for specific and general information. Take index cards and keep a file for job titles and organizations that interest me, listing potential contacts and additional sources of information.

   b. Get information from the Chamber of Commerce on all of the businesses in the area. Request annual reports from those that interest me.

   c. From the United Way and Volunteer Action Center get lists of nonprofits. Also check yellow pages and professional associations for both profit and nonprofit organizations. Some will have marketing material that I can request. It will tell me more about the organization than the annual report. Also get information from umbrella organizations like the Area Office on Aging or the Headmasters' Association.

d. Digest this material to decide which organizations I like and would like to know more about. Call for any information they could send that I do not already have and devour it.

e. Make a list of the five organizations that interest me most and use my people list to identify individuals who could give me more information about each. Read about networking.

f. Having identified a contact, ask whether what I want to do is needed within the organization, what it takes to do that kind of work, what additional qualifications are required, and the frequency of openings.

g. Repeat process until I have at least a half-dozen possibilities with openings that would result in my achieving what I want within a reasonable time frame.

h. If what I want doesn't match anything in existence, what can I create? Is it time for a new plan, prioritizing again what is really important to me and looking at ways of creating a position or a business? Resolve these questions by identifying options within two weeks.

Evaluation

I've been pretty good about setting time frames and specific about what I need to do. That means that I just need to keep track of what I am doing and be sure that I am on schedule. If it isn't working, I need to figure out why and take action. Particularly, I need to look at barriers again.

Writing the plan is the first step; the next is to take my calendar and plan when I need to begin. Then, write in each day's activity, including scheduling on a specific day and time my rewards and all activities including solitary time. But, I'm writing in pencil, because some of those will have to change. When I'm done, all of my objectives, activities, and rewards will be on my calendar.

A Final Word

Many of the issues that concern women can be handled creatively within a plan! Confronting them in the planning process means that you get a jump start, deciding how to work with some of the tough questions before they become obstacles. In other situations, planning is a great antidote to becoming crazy from trying to do everything. You can see in the planning process if the number of things to be done is impossible and then set some priorities. Planning also helps overcome myths that shackle us. If we examine them and plan for them, we can escape them.

It can be tough to contemplate a job search and to make the writing of a plan the first step. Writing a plan is work. But plans are working documents with ideas that help you move forward with purpose and energy to accomplish your goal. While we have outlined a process, don't get stuck in it. Get your ideas down on paper. Do as much as you can and then go back to it, adding and subtracting, as your thinking develops. If you are hesitant to begin, go back and read the reasons why it is important to do a job-search plan. They are convincing. Then do it. Planning is a habit, which once developed will continue to help you professionally. Get ready, plan, and go!

Chapter 5

The Written Word: Resumes, Personal Statements, and Cover Letters

Even the woodpecker owes his success to the fact that he uses his head and keeps pecking away until he finishes the job he starts. – Coleman Cox

In planning this book, we spent a lot of time talking about resumes. The use of a resume is an important and controversial subject and one that touches on some issues unique to women. Debate continues as to how to use a resume, and, in fact, whether you should write one at all! We have a real concern that a standard resume format could be detrimental to women. But, after examining the advantages and disadvantages, we believe that a resume should be a part of your job-search process, and therefore, this chapter is included. There are advantages and some potential pitfalls in resume writing. One way to learn what the pitfalls are and how to avoid them is to look at the reasons for not writing a resume. So, as a positive first step to writing a resume, let's begin with the negative!

Resume Cons

Some of the many books written about the job search have advocated that resumes not be used. Some of the reasons are valid. A resume alone will almost never get a job. While there is always the apocryphal story of the person who sent out tens or hundreds of resumes and received the phone call and ultimately the job, such stories seem to be isolated. Most of us have a myriad of skills that can be used in many places and so the one-chance-in-a-million model is not for us. In fact, using a resume *as your main tool* in a job search is likely to fail to get you a job, and, also, to shortchange you, even if it does result in a job. Most people who use a resume as the primary tool in their job search end up frustrated and discouraged.

One of the very best reasons for not writing a resume is that there are much more important activities to do, including defining what you want to do, researching it thoroughly, and networking. The resume can be a distraction, a beguilingly attractive form of procrastination, taking time and effort that could be devoted to other activities. You feel virtuous while working on your resume because you are doing something about getting a job, but the problem is that in concentrating on your resume, you are neglecting more effective tools. Instead of spending all of your time and energy writing, you need to get out there and let people know who you are, what you want, and what you can do.

Some of these other job-search activities are much more demanding than resume writing. They involve asking yourself tough questions and being very thoughtful about the answers. They require going out and meeting with people. Once begun, this process is wonderful and rewarding, but it can be very difficult to begin. Writing a resume can seem like the easier route to follow. It can be viewed (incorrectly) as a review of past activities, safely done in the comfort of home, and then dropped in the mail. This way no one will have the opportunity to say "no" to your face.

Another reason for not writing a resume is that it does not represent the complete you. How can you, with all you have to offer, be reduced to one to two pages of tightly written phrases? Now that is an undersell! In order to adequately present yourself, you have to do it in a number of ways – most importantly, in person. Personality and energy are very important in deciding who to hire. There is virtually no way to adequately express some qualities on paper.

Resumes screen out job candidates more often than they get someone hired. With only seconds to spend on each resume, most employers are reading not only for what they want, but for a reason to eliminate a candidate. When a resume is your only contact with a potential employer, just one phrase or word can result in it being put in the reject pile. One of the best examples of this happened to a human services manager several years ago, when she was hiring a career counselor. She had a glut of resumes to review. The manager decided that if someone really were going to be dedicated to career counseling, she should state on her resume that she was interested in career counseling, not general counseling. Consequently, the manager eliminated all of the applications that did not specify career counseling. This is what we mean when we say that employers usually are looking at resumes as a way to screen out candidates, and the reasons – as you can see – can be quite arbitrary. Unfortunately, this was not an isolated incident. Often the resume reader cuts a wide swath in a pile of resumes by setting some specific criteria that aspiring candidates might never suspect!

A resume is passive. It doesn't offer any opportunity to explore what an individual's experience really has been or what her goals actually are. Employers often choose a candidate because a rapport is established; the interviewer likes the candidate. Try establishing rapport through a resume! When two people meet, there is an opportunity for a give-and-take, to explore, to see how the candidate expresses herself, and for some insight into how she thinks and certainly how she presents herself. None of this happens with a resume alone.

A standard resume is designed to represent a traditional male career path. A man finishes his education, takes a job, moves through a series of promotions, takes another job, goes through another series of promotions, joins professional organizations, and so on. It all fits very neatly into a standard chronological resume format with one experience building logically on the last. There is no room for the rich patterns of a woman's life, which may have encompassed many activities, lateral moves, time out of the formal job market, challenging volunteer assignments, and travel. There is no category for staying home to raise young children, explaining a series of job changes that were actually made to fit a spouse's moves, significant volunteer responsibilities, and other activities that are characteristic of many women's job experience. (This is true not only of traditional resumes, but also of application forms, so beware!)

Busy employers who need to get someone in the door to do the job often do not have time to properly interpret a more varied pattern of experience from a written resume, but, indeed, they may be interested in the very qualities that result. Some employers will simply reject a candidate who does not present the traditional work pattern on paper, although a personal interview might have produced an entirely different response. *If you have a work history that is different from the traditional male model, you need to construct a resume that will portray the value of your experience. But nothing will do this as well as personal contact.*

These are some of the reasons not to write a resume – and they are good ones. Having aired these drawbacks, we are going to tell you to get busy and start writing. Once you understand the limitations of a resume, you are in a much better position to write an effective resume, and you can – even with experience more typical of a woman's life patterns – use it with maximum impact. So, with the foregoing caveats in mind, it's time to think positively.

Resume Pros

One of the best reasons for writing a resume is that it can be very satisfying. Now, before you groan, please read on. If you have done all the tough thinking necessary to define a direction for yourself and if you have identified the skills you want to use, the environment that you want to be in, the values that are important to you, and all of those other important factors that make up the three Cs discussed in chapter 3, then you deserve to hang out your flag. A resume is one of the ways you can do it. It gives you the opportunity to take all that hard-earned information and put it in a form that the audience you are trying to reach will read. You have the pleasure of looking back over your past accomplishments and choosing those that fit into what you want to do in the future. It is something like putting a tangram together. The many pieces can go together in different ways. But when they fit, you know you have accomplished something.

Is it possible to have those pieces fit if your experience is different from the traditional male career pattern? We believe that you can present your own experiences as valuable and meaningful in a resume, and that doing so will be a very useful part of the job-search process. Your task in writing a resume is to look at your experiences and translate them into the currency of your ideal workplace.

Constructing a resume forces you to take your preferences about what you want to do and match them with your past experiences. In order to successfully explain what you can do for an employer, you have to massage the information you have gathered about yourself. You must clearly understand how your skills relate to the business at hand. Putting together your resume is an essential part of the process of taking that raw data and producing a finished product.

After you have written a resume and cover letter, your answer to questions about what you want to do and why you believe you can do it will be sincere and automatic. It is ready not only in writing, but more importantly, you can express yourself verbally, because you have gone through the necessary thought processes to summarize it in your own mind. Many public and private corporations put a lot of effort into writing a mission statement. They expect that any employee can explain what their organization is going to accomplish. Your resume is a bit like your own personal mission statement. It forces you to do the thinking that enables you to state immediately what you will accomplish and how you know you can do it.

For better or worse, a resume is a required element of most formal hiring processes, especially for large corporations. Even if you have successfully avoided the system, you may still need a resume before the final congratulatory handshake.

Even if you have identified a position and talked with some of the people who have the power to influence your hiring, a resume is still required in most cases. It is a piece of paper that passes through the system. Most corporations of any size have a human resources department whose function is to assist in the hiring of needed staff. These departments usually have a well-described process to which they adhere. Even if the boss wants you for the job, she will usually require that you go through human resources. (That is just good business. Having vested the hiring process in a department, a smart boss does not demoralize her own staff by doing end runs around it.) Most human resource departments will still require that resume. And it had better be good, because you want the people you are going to work with to be as impressed as or more impressed than the boss.

Employers use resumes. They often use them to decide whom to interview. In many cases, screening of resumes is the *only* system employers use to decide whom they will interview because they have no other resources available. Many employers screen hundreds of resumes in relatively brief periods of time. As noted, you cannot always know exactly what they are looking for, but prior research can help you through this cut system.

Resumes are used by many employers as an outline for what to talk about in an interview, a basis for their questions. You and the interviewer, therefore, have a scenario that you share. You can turn this to your advantage in an interview. By reviewing your resume before an interview and developing some strategic points you want to make, you will have some control over the interview. After the interview, an employer will also use a resume to review your credentials again, to compare to others who are being considered, and as a part of the paper trail. Your resume may also be reviewed by others who have a role in the hiring process. In larger corporations, if your resume is impressive, it may be passed along to other, more appropriate departments for review.

Finally, not having a resume in a world that uses them can simply be a liability. It is impossible to overemphasize how important it is to avoid using your resume as your main job-search tool; you don't want to be judged by your resume alone. But, at some point, if a resume is needed to keep the process moving forward, it is certainly common sense to have a good one.

These are compelling reasons to have and use a resume. How is it possible to do so without selling your soul to the standard process?

A New Slant on Resumes

Getting a job is a partnership between job-seeker and employer, both of whom have strengths and weaknesses. You are one-half of this partnership. You are in search of work that will fulfill your needs, values, and interests, and make use of the skills you enjoy most. You have the power to decide what it is you want to do and where you want to do it. The more you follow the rules of a job search, the more options you will have. If you are rejected by an employer who interests you, you can develop other possibilities. You can evaluate potential employers and reject them if they do not meet your needs. Yes, you may have limited money and time, but within your own parameters, if you are willing to work hard, you have a lot of power and control in this partnership.

Employers have the power to choose the candidates they want, but what a risky process! They often base their decisions on little information. They are vulnerable, because if they choose incorrectly, time and money are wasted. The job doesn't get done, the morale of other workers is affected, and the judgment of many people may be questioned. The result can be devastating for the employer and for the individuals who made the decision.

The extent to which you accept your responsibility as a partner in your own job search influences how successful and positive the experience will be. You have to make choices about how to best use your skills and who is the best employer for you. You do not want any job, because any job may not fit. If it doesn't fit, you may end up having your needs unmet and therefore being either unhappy or back in the job market sooner than you would like to be. Therefore, you need to evaluate every potential employer very carefully.

A resume is part of the cooperative process in which you are sharing information and learning through reading and talking with others. You and a potential employer can demonstrate from the beginning that you can work well together. You are the initiator when you express interest. You decide what information you will give and how you will position yourself in your resume and in an interview. Through the process, you are working with a potential organization to determine whether this is the best place for you and you are the best person for it. Either partner in the process can make the decision. If an employer doesn't hire you, that is one option closed for now, but there are others, some of which may be better. If you turn down an employer, the employer can move on to find a candidate who would be a better match for the job description.

Is this realistic? Yes! If you are willing to make the effort to get a job, you are the judge of the opportunities to pursue. What about the job ad with the blind box number and little information; how do you become a partner in that process? You may not. All you can do is submit your resume, and, if you receive a response, then work at becoming a partner in the process. But in that situation, it may not be possible. The question is, do you want to work for an organization that elects to hide instead of making a statement about its identity? This is where your judgment comes in.

A Unique Personal Accomplishment Statement

We have long debated how individualized a resume could be. Some thoughts on that issue follow. In addition, we had difficulty with the term *resume*. It seemed anything but individualized. Since many of us have a richness of experience, creativity, and daring unrelated to anything as traditional as a career ladder, we decided that a resume could be anything from the most traditional to the most individualized, but that it must communicate what you want to accomplish. The word *resume* certainly did not say all that we wanted to. We decided that to us a resume is a unique personal accomplishment statement.

Thinking of a resume this way more accurately reflects what you are about to write. You have a unique set of accomplishments that you are going to compose into an outline to explain to others what you want to do. Only you have this combination of qualities, accomplishments, personality, needs, and goals. It is personal in that you have chosen the particular path that you want to take and, therefore, have decided on a specific method of presenting yourself. It is a statement to share with others, communicating what you expect to accomplish for your new employer. They may call it a resume, but if you think of it as a unique personal accomplishment statement, you will create a tool that works harder for you.

Can a resume written like this be so individualized that it will exclude you from most opportunities? Certainly, but you are the decision maker. Through your research, you learn what the type of employers you are looking for want in a resume. Put yourself in the shoes of the readers at the places you want to work. If you had their responsibility for evaluating resumes for this job, what would you be looking for? How would you want an applicant to present herself? Does it match what you are writing? If it does – good work. You are on the right track in finding the employer you want.

If it does not match, why not? Are you looking at the wrong kind of organizations? Do you need to find out more about them or rethink the way you describe yourself? We believe that your resume should express your values stated in language that is meaningful to your potential employer. Do you want to use your resume to make a statement of your individuality, testing the outlook and flexibility of future employers? What will this accomplish for you? Will it test that potential employer in a way that will tell you if this really is what you want? If so, great! If not, consider a compromise. Compromise is often the nature of work and for that matter, life.

Many of us love our jobs, although they are not perfect. You can choose to have a terrific resume that will limit some job possibilities because you believe that you need to state your experience in a certain way. You may also choose to tailor a unique personal statement to a specific employer whom you know is a good fit for you, and thus choose to present yourself to fit that employer's needs. You decide. You are the boss of your job search. The important thing is that you achieve the goals you have set for yourself.

Writing the Resume

Contents

A basic list of information employers often find helpful includes the items in this list. Of course, not all of this information would be included in every resume. Select those items that suit your needs and personality best.

Objective

Summary of accomplishments

Profile

Skills

Professional experience

Accomplishment detail

Other work experience

Professional certification

Professional affiliations

Education

Community service

Other information that might be relevant to what you want to do

Some items such as personal information are left off this list because we don't believe they are appropriate. "References available on request" is also omitted because this is understood and takes up valuable space that can be used for something else.

You have a lot of choices to make, but some commonsense rules apply for almost every resume.

★ It must be neat with all spelling and punctuation perfect.

★ The organization of the information must be immediately obvious and meaningful.

★ The reader must be able to cover all key points within seconds.

★ When listing responsibilities, accomplishments must be included.

★ Your personality and individuality must shine through.

★ A high energy level and enthusiasm for what you want to do must be conveyed.

★ Use the "I" word only in the profile.

★ Scratch the flowery or overstated adjectives; use straightforward, descriptive words instead.

★ Always have at least two other people (who are prepared to be tough) critique your resume before you give it to a prospective employer.

The organization of a resume is analogous to a pyramid. At the top is an organizing statement that summarizes the essence of the applicant. All other information builds to and supports that statement. This means that the reader knows immediately, in summary form, what you are trying to convey, and then can read on to examine the evidence.

Are there exceptions? Of course! There is the flower designer who sends a smashing arrangement with a list of accolades from clients, the marketing manager whose presentation to the potential employer mirrors the kind of campaign that the employer needs, the producer who presents a video, or the programmer who delivers a unique program that would be useful to the potential employer. We certainly urge you to be creative within the parameters of respect for your own goals and the potential employer's time.

These examples are dramatic. They attract attention, but at the same time clearly demonstrate what you can do to fulfill the employer's needs. These actions stand in contrast to the person who supposedly wore a sandwich board saying "hire me" and walked up and down in front of corporate offices. Some methods of getting attention, unless they are in line with what the potential employer is actually looking for, can backfire. They may indicate that the job candidate is not a team player, may be more interested in her own point of view than that of others, has problems with authority, or may lack business judgment. Your resume should demonstrate how you can accomplish what the potential employer needs; it should not simply be a means of attracting attention. It is a first step in demonstrating how you would work together.

Opening Statements

The Objective Statement

Debate continues over the use of a job objective statement. These statements can range from being so specific that they exclude some excellent job opportunities to being so general as to be meaningless. A job objective states what you want to do. For example, a highly specific objective would be: "To be first line supervisor of a programming group in a defense-related high tech industry." A more general objective would be: "To use proven accounting skills to accomplish corporate objectives."

A good objective statement must describe what the potential employer is looking for. Less effective is the general job objective statement that does not contradict what the employer wants, but also loses some of its punch by hedging the issue. The objective statement on a resume should hit the reader right between the eyes. A job objective can be forceful if you find out exactly what the position entails and then write the objective to meet these needs. How do you do this? When you uncover an opportunity, ask for a job description. If one is not available, ask if you can speak with someone who could give you the information. *Another way of finding out about the job is to arrange an interview before you submit a resume.* This is often possible in places that do not have a formal hiring process. Actually, this may be the ideal way to use a resume anyway, as you have already made a favorable impression, and now your resume will be read more carefully, and if you have done your homework, your resume will reflect those qualifications that best suit the employer's needs.

There are some drawbacks to beginning a resume with a job objective. *Whether specific or more generalized, a job objective statement gives limited information. It tells the reader what you want to do, but usually does not give any substantiating information, and is often written from your perspective as the applicant.* An example of an applicant-centered job objective would be: "Use my marketing skills in a challenging position with opportunity for advancement." The only benefit in that statement for the employer is that the person says she has marketing skills; the rest is what the applicant wants. *Job objective statements should be aimed at what the employer needs.* A better statement is: "Design, produce, and evaluate marketing campaigns that will increase sales to exceed corporate goals." The prospective employer reading this objective learns that the applicant believes that she knows the entire process, including evaluation, and acknowledges the importance of getting results.

Profile and Qualification Statements

Two other alternatives for beginning a resume are a statement of qualifications and a profile statement. These are something like an executive summary of what is to come. A qualification statement does just what the name implies; it is a succinct statement of your qualifications for the position you are seeking. It says what you want to do. It is most effective when you have appropriate job experience. A profile is longer and can contain other types of information, for example, personal qualities. One way to decide between the qualifications statement or the profile is to look at your background and determine which fits your needs and your taste. Another factor to consider is how conservative the reader will be. *A qualification statement is more traditional and is broadly accepted. A profile can be most useful when you are changing fields, need to show personal qualities, and where less formal applications are acceptable.*

Both qualification statements and profiles can include more information than the job objective statement. They provide the opportunity to show your enthusiasm, to summarize accomplishments, and to state a goal. But most importantly, they give you the opportunity to interpret your experience exactly as you want your reader to understand it. If you have had many jobs, you can emphasize your breadth of experience. If you have had a dearth of paid employment, but a lot of responsible volunteer positions, you can tell why your comprehensive understanding of community needs or your developed, proven management techniques will be effective.

How do you write a profile or statement of qualifications? It takes time to hone a lot of words to a few. Our recommendation is that you begin with a rough draft of your opening statement, and then write your complete first draft of your resume, returning to the opening statement to refine it. The process is really circular with each rewrite improving on the last. Remember that the opening statement on your resume – no matter which format you choose to use – not only has to grab the reader's attention, but also has to be the succinct summary of what is to follow. Once you have sorted out your work history, skills, and accomplishments to write the body of the resume, summarizing them for the opening statement is easier. Then, having worked on the beginning statement, go back and reshape the rest of the information to more explicitly support it.

Here are some examples of profiles and qualification statements, juxtaposed so that you can clearly see how differently the same backgrounds and experiences can be expressed in an opening statement.

Qualification statement:

Proven skills in individual counseling, team building, leading group sessions, conflict resolution. Average reduction in absenteeism in client companies of 20 percent.

Profile:

As an employee of a large company, I quickly learned what a detrimental impact employee problems can have on productivity. Unhappy employees not only have impaired work skills, but infect the attitudes of colleagues. A combination of programs successfully treats the problem. I train supervisors to spot problems and refer employees for assessment and treatment. Depending on the employee, individual counseling, referral to a specialized community agency, group meetings with family or others related to the problem, or conflict resolution may be required. I also train supervisors to motivate employees constructively and to work with them to correct poor performance or initiate an orderly termination process. The overwhelmingly positive response of supervisors and employees increases participation in the program. I believe that this expertise is what can get the job done in your employee relations manager position.

Qualification statement:

Reduced time from initial order to delivery in manufacturing plant by an average of two days through the design, management, and revision of systems and computerization records. Systems included conversion of sales to work orders, computerization of routing and billing, numbering of all parts. Supervised up to eight staff. Full-entry bookkeeper.

Profile:

The experience of being half owner of three businesses, managing office personnel, customer service, route accounting, and all bookkeeping taught me quickly how important it is to set up good systems. I took this lesson to a manufacturing plant where I began as a payroll assistant and was promoted to routing supervisor. Since then, I have been setting up systems that have resulted in an average decrease of two days from order placement to delivery. I have designed and managed systems to convert sales to work orders, do computerized billing, and number all parts and continue to upgrade and revise them as necessary and supervise up to eight people to get the job done. I look forward to using this base of management decision-making and systems development experience in a corporate operations position.

Qualification statement:

Directed annual fund-raising and public relations event attracting over 4,000 people. Raised 20 percent of an organizational budget, increasing by 10 percent each year. Supervised 120 volunteers, ten of them half-time for two months. Organized and built high morale team to accomplish preset goals, marketed proposals to a broad spectrum of community.

Profile:

When the Cedar Ridge Environmental Center was on the verge of bankruptcy and had little public visibility, the board asked me to design a last ditch plan to raise money and attract attention. The fall fair and subsequent activities did it! The Center now has a secure budget and serves school and college students and more than 10,000 adults from the community each year. The events that I have developed and directed each year have brought in over 3,000 adults and 20 percent of the budget. This required setting very high goals, building a team of over 120 volunteers, selling the ideas to corporations and organizations to gain their support, working with the press and designing publicity, scheduling and setting up events and assuring that they ran smoothly and being attuned to community interests so that our fund-raisers remained popular. I believe that I can put these skills and energy to work as a development director for your organization.

The Body of the Resume

Chronological versus Functional Formats

Although these terms sound dull, we use them because they are descriptive. Don't let their pedantic sound quash the enthusiasm in your resume. A chronological format is the most traditional, with work experience listed beginning with the most recent. In a functional format, information is organized by skills with a brief chronological listing of job history. It sorts and prioritizes the information for the reader and is most useful if you have an unusual pattern of experience or if you are about to change fields. However, this format is less acceptable in some of the more conservative professions. Human resource people with whom we spoke favored the traditional, one-page, chronological format, because it was familiar and resumes could be easily compared. Most said, however, that other styles, *as long as they were superbly done with the information immediately comprehensible,* were certainly acceptable.

Sample Chronological Format

Name
Address
Telephone number

Opening statement (job objective, qualification statement, or profile)

Professional experience

Title, employer, dates (most recent)
- Responsibility/accomplishment
- Responsibility/accomplishment
- Responsibility/accomplishment

Title, employer, dates
- Responsibility/accomplishment
- Responsibility/accomplishment
- Responsibility/accomplishment

Professional activities

Community responsibilities (relevant leadership positions)

Education

Institution, degree

A chronological resume simply lists your experience, most recent first. Each listing should have your title, the employer, and the dates of your employment (years only). If you have had more than one position with a given employer, each position should be listed separately (to the extent that the accomplishments differ), repeating the title and dates, but not the employer. For each position, select responsibilities and accomplishments that support what you plan to do in the future. All information should be in brief phrases, beginning with action verbs. Each verb should describe a specific action. For example, it sounds strong to say "supervised," but weak to say "responsible for." (Use the list of action verbs found in the chapter 3 section on abilities to get ideas.) Accomplishments can be grouped in very short paragraphs of four or five lines or bulleted. The advantage of bullets is that they are easier to read; the disadvantage is that line listings use a lot of space. Your objective is to organize the information so that the reader will immediately understand how it is organized and be able to locate the most important information.

In either a chronological or functional resume, education would be listed first if it is the most recent experience that you have had to qualify you for what you want to do. Otherwise, it comes after all professional experience if your professional experience is a better recommendation for what you want to do. You should list your last degree first, your grade point average (if it is recent and would be to your advantage), and with honors, magna, summa, or Phi Beta Kappa, even if your degree is ancient history! If your degree is recent and you took leadership roles in relevant activities, list these also.

Sample Functional Format

Name
Address
Telephone number

Opening statement (job objective, qualification statement, or profile)

Proven abilities (skills, accomplishments)

Ability

- Responsibility/accomplishment
- Responsibility/accomplishment
- Responsibility/accomplishment

Ability

- Responsibility/accomplishment
- Responsibility/accomplishment

Ability

- Responsibility/accomplishment
- Responsibility/accomplishment
- Responsibility/accomplishment

Professional experience

Title, employer, date

Title, employer, date

Title, employer, date

Title, employer, date

Professional activities

Community responsibilities (relevant leadership positions)

Education

Demonstrated abilities are those skills that you most want to use in your next position. List the ones you feel strongest about first. The skill can be as specific as fund-raising, data entry, or product management, or it can be as general as organization, management, or motivation. If the skill is very general, be sure that your accomplishments are specific, so that the reader knows what kind of organization or management you are talking about. Use action verbs to begin each accomplishment; make sure the accomplishment states results. Use quantitative or qualitative information whenever possible. Professional experience is simply a reverse chronological list of the work you have done. You have already grouped the accomplishments above for the reader.

Advantages and Drawbacks

A chronological format emphasizes the growth and progression in your career. It is an excellent choice if you have a very traditional work history and want to continue in the same field. The format highlights continuity and your most recent experience. Potential employers are comfortable with this format and some, who are conservative, do not want to deal with unfamiliar formats. One of the people we interviewed referred to corporate human resource professionals as "risk adverse," which would indicate that the more traditional approaches are certainly the safest.

The chronological format may be easier to write. You can be creative in the opening statement and in how you state your accomplishments. The drawback is that the chronological format highlights the progression of what you have done, instead of your strong points. Frequent job changes, employment gaps, lateral career moves, and unrelated experience become very apparent, and it is more difficult to show the importance of volunteer experience. For these reasons, women often find the chronological format less advantageous than other formats. It is clearly the format designed to display the assets of the traditional male career path. Use it if it works for you; otherwise consider the functional format.

The functional format is an excellent choice if you are changing fields and want to emphasize your transferable skills, if you have had a lot of valuable volunteer experience, or if you have changed jobs frequently and want to emphasize the value of your breadth of experience. *The functional format allows you to tell your story in exactly the way you want the reader to understand it.* You explain to the reader what skills you possess to accomplish what is needed. It is the second most familiar format to human resource people. The functional format allows you to downplay all of the things that a chronological format emphasizes, because here the reader is focusing on your skills and not on your employment history. The disadvantages of a functional approach are that some employers may not see the link between the skill and the specific job, or they may be suspicious that a listing of skills may be used to hide information. A functional format is more difficult to put together because it takes time to massage your information into a meaningful whole. Yet, it can also be more creative, because you are free to work outside of the framework of the straight, chronological listing. It may be easier to get excited about your abilities and use wording that expresses this enthusiasm.

In summary, some of the pros and cons of these two resume formats are

Chronological	Functional
· Most accepted	· Also accepted in most fields
· Emphasizes traditional career path	· Emphasizes skill groups
· Gaps, lateral moves, frequent changes, unrelated experiences highlighted	· Downplays less traditional career path; can be arranged in priority you want reader to follow
· Not very flexible	· Flexible
· Creativity limited	· Can be very creative
· Easier to write	· More work to write
· Easier to limit length	· More difficult to limit length

Choose the format that best fits your needs. Or, write a functional *and* a chronological resume, using whichever is best suited to the position you are interested in.

How long should your resume be? This question is sort of like the old term paper question. Remember how someone always asked the teacher how long the paper should be? Well, the answer is pretty much the same. Only as long as it needs to be to get the information across. The difference is that on term papers, some of us added words or ideas that were nonessential. That isn't acceptable on a resume. Most of the human resource people we spoke with expressed a preference for a one-page resume, never more than two pages. The private business sector is more likely to want a single page. The challenge in resume writing is to say what you want powerfully, but ever so succinctly. It is tough to do, but with thoughtful decisions and revisions, you can distill the information to the essence of who you are and what you can do.

The dictates on length do not include necessary addenda such as a list of publications or presentations which will be integral to the reader's decision making. The addendum is written on a separate piece of paper as a separate document. Don't forget that you also have a cover letter and can put more information in that.

Sticky Issues

Do you have nontraditional information to put in your resume? Welcome to the club! You are in the very good company of creative women who have done a number of things with their time. You can state this information in ways that will be an asset depending on what you want to do. (An exception would be if you are trying to make a very large leap into a conservative field, say from potter to investment banking. If this is what you are contemplating, you will need to take some intermediate steps.) Generally, lots of different experiences can be favorably presented in a resume.

Age

You decide whether or not to reveal your age on your resume. Age is never directly listed on a resume, and depending on whether your age is an advantage or not, you can choose what to do with that information. You certainly do not want to be screened out of a job that you can do well because someone assumes that because you are under or over a certain age, you cannot do the work. On the other hand, you need to carefully consider whether you want to fight a potential employer on issues of age discrimination. (Often this battle is more likely to be won, if you can show discrimination by your present employer rather than when applying for a position.) If you think that your age will be a negative factor, it is better to do as much research as possible beforehand to find out what the attitudes of that workplace really are. You should be able to learn a lot about age prejudices from an interview.

One way to indicate your age is to list the dates that degrees were awarded. If your employment experience has been continuous since graduation, that information will obviously reveal your age. If you have taken time out to raise children or pursue other interests, your employment history may be fairly recent. For example, with ten years of employment listed, an employer could expect to see a thirty-five-year-old woman walk in for the interview, when actually you may have spent an additional ten years as a full-time mother. It may not be a good idea to totally surprise an interviewer; you avoid that by listing other accomplishments in a cover letter or by indicating what you did during those intervening years. One way of indicating that you are older than your resume states without giving an exact age is to say in your profile that "after raising a family," or "after leading the capital fund drive for X." Conversely, you can indicate that you are younger by saying that you "took responsibility quickly" or that you were "successful at work in X, beginning as a student."

Your ability to get the work done is more important than how old you are. Not only is the law on your side, but so are the majority of employers who want to find the best person for the job. You control the information and can choose to handle it on your resume in the manner that best fits your needs.

Who Me?

The last time someone complimented you, did you give them a big smile, look them in the eyes, and say thank you, or did you say something about it being really nothing or someone else should get the credit? Many of us tend to do the latter. We were brought up to be modest, and it is hard to take the credit for doing something. Well, in writing a resume, it is very important to overcome this modesty. You have accomplishments. You are not going to brag about them, but you must acknowledge what you have done. It helps to be aware of any tendencies to deny accomplishments and to think of this modesty as counterproductive. We live in a very straightforward world where accomplishments matter. Putting those accomplishments on a resume is simply a professional way to behave. If employers don't know what you have accomplished, what grounds do they have for hiring you?

Gaps

What do you do with the gaps in your employment history? For one thing, avoid thinking of them as gaps, but as periods of time when you did something else. Many times, what you did during the gap can be a strong statement of accomplishment. If you took time out for children, say so. There are several ways to handle this. In a chronological listing, simply put the years and state that you raised your children. Most employers are fathers and mothers. They certainly won't promote you for having done it, but most will not hold it against you. If you use a functional format, some of the things you did may show up in your accomplishments supporting your skills. Most women who stay at home when children are young also do some other things. What did you do and what skills and accomplishments can you extract from those activities?

If there is a gap because you pursued some other interests seemingly unrelated to your future goals, it can be treated simply as an entry with dates in a chronological or functional format. Actually, there are very few life experiences that we can't apply to new situations, but if you are uncomfortable with certain time periods, use the functional format.

What if the gap is caused by something that you do not want a potential employer to know about before you are hired or at least not until you have had the chance to meet? Perhaps you have undergone treatment for alcoholism, drug addiction, or a mental breakdown. If you have had enough work experience since the gap to demonstrate that you are fully functional and achieving, then simply leave the gap and, if asked, explain it in the interview. This approach works best if you know your previous employer will give you a good reference, and you can say so in the interview.

If this is your first iob since the event and you do not have a track record, handling the information is more difficult. If you are applying for positions to work with others with similar experiences or if you are part of a recovery job placement program, this belongs in your resume. If this is not the case, you need to consider carefully whether the work environment you are pursuing will be supportive of what you are trying to accomplish. If this looks positive, then use a functional format, which is less apt to reveal this gap and answer questions truthfully if asked.

Frequent Moves

Sometimes job changes happened for reasons over which you had little control. For example, you may have followed your spouse who was transferred or made a career change. Do not dismay! Your background may actually be an asset. Multiple job changes can be turned into a real plus in the profile or the cover letter by emphasizing what you gained from the experience. For example, the development of your management style may have been greatly helped and refined by observing and evaluating the management styles of others in a variety of settings. Or, you may be flexible and better able to problem solve as a result of having experienced several different work environments. If you wish to camouflage some of these moves, the functional format may be a good choice.

Volunteer Experience

Volunteer work is valuable in your job search skills repertoire, from gaining challenging experience to pure satisfaction, or from testing out potential career interests to learning and validating skills that can be transferred from one position to another. Volunteer work is a valuable method for moving into the job market, to boost your self-confidence and to meet people who can help in the job search. If your volunteer experiences are stronger than your paid experiences, consider a functional format to emphasize skills and accomplishments. The rapidly growing movement from volunteer to paid positions at all levels is impressive. Finally, the private sector is acknowledging the wealth and diversity of experiences gleaned from volunteer work. Emphasize your level of responsibility, your impact on the community, and similarities to the position you are applying for in the cover letter. If you use a functional format, list your volunteer positions under "Community Responsibilities." If you use a chronological format, consider beginning with "Volunteer Work Experience" or "Professional Volunteer Experience."

Techniques

Now it is time to put pen to paper. How do you start? The first step is to gather information. The second is to poke and prod your memory a bit for some of the things that you would like to say. Use the following suggested categories to gather all the information you need in one place and list it in your notebook. At this point, you do not need to be selective; that will be the next step. While you are gathering information, also jot down the names, addresses, and phone numbers of people you will use as references. This doesn't go on your resume, but it is a good time to solidify that list.

For each job you have had, list

Title
Dates you worked at that place
Name of the organization
Responsibilities
Results (quantify when possible)

For each other professional activity you have participated in, list

Name of professional organization
Activity
Role
Leadership position (if applicable)
Results of your participation (quantify when possible)

For each other volunteer responsibility you have had, list

Name of the organization
Activity
Role

Leadership position (if applicable)
Results (quantify when possible)

For each educational degree you have, list

Name of college (if did not attend, list any special
training or vocational education)
Degree
Date (optional)
Honors
Leadership positions held
GPA (optional)

Skills you most want to use (from your work in chapter 3 or from your head, if you
already know them)

Personal qualities that are most important to you (see notes from chapter 3)

That takes care of the factual information. Now it is all in one place and you can go to work to make sense out of it. Begin by listing the skills that you want to use and your favorite personal qualities (all in your chapter 3 notes) at the top of the page. Everything else you write should substantiate what you have just written. If you are writing a chronological resume, choose those responsibilities and results within each job that best support these skills and personality traits. You cannot list everything you do in a job. This is an exercise in selecting the most significant, either because it is a skill you have used or an accomplishment that cannot be overlooked. If you are using the functional format, then list the skills you most want to use and begin combing back through all of your experience for substantiation. Any kind of activity and accomplishment counts!

Take every point you want to make and reduce it to a phrase beginning with an action verb. (See the list of abilities in chapter 3.) Action verbs allow the reader to skim for the most important actions you have already taken. Organized, directed, coordinated, maintained, built, painted, constructed, and all of the other verbs on that list create an image of you as a talented, high-energy person. Whether you do it chronologically with the phrases under each job or volunteer activity or functionally with the phrases under a skill, use those verbs! Again, do not use "responsible for," because it does not tell what you actually did. What were you responsible for? Writing these phrases isn't as easy as it looks, but keep at it. When you've got them the way you want — congratulations! You have completed a big piece of work.

Now, back to that opening statement: job objective, qualifications statement, or profile. Think energy, think essence. What is it that you really want to do that you have substantiated in the rest of your resume? Boil it down to a brief, dynamic set of words. If you get stuck on this, or any other part of the resume, go talk with your buddy or someone else. It is easier for some of us to get blocked when we write than it is when talking. So, get someone to ask you questions and prod you a bit until you say what you want. Then get the words on paper and work with them until they feel right. Now you have accomplished another important piece of work!

With your draft opening statement in hand, review your skills and accomplishments, revising as necessary, so that they support your opening statement. Remember, this is a circular process and you may need to work back and forth, making changes in the opening statement and the rest of your resume until it becomes cohesive.

What if the skills you want to use that are listed at the top of the paper are not really substantiated by what you have done? First, look again. Sometimes it is hard to think of what you have accomplished in a different light. Try to free up your thinking and take a new look at your activities. If that doesn't work, ask someone else to go over it with you and see if they have a different view. Suppose it still doesn't fit? Then you have some soul-searching to do. Is it possible that you are taking too big a step from what you have done to what you want to do? Check it out with someone in the field. If necessary, you can take a different route to reach your goal, or perhaps you can get additional training or experience.

What if your job titles do not accurately reflect what you did? Your real talent could be hidden. One possibility is to change the job title, but do this only if the person who will be called as a reference would support that change and you let that person know. Another option is to omit the title and just list the employer. This makes the resume a little harder to read, but it is better than a misleading job title.

When you have a draft you are pleased with, show it to several people. They don't have to be experts, but they must be willing to read it critically. Evaluate their comments, and where you agree, revise. The reason for having several people comment is that everyone who reads anything will suggest changes, because we all have our personal style. You don't want to revise your resume to reflect another individual's sense of style. Your resume should be yours, but others can confirm that you have communicated your message clearly. There is a lot of common sense in the resume process, and most people can tell you if your resume is dynamic, easy to read, and logical.

Jess spent three years working for a manufacturing company that undervalued her skills. When she took the job, she was coming out of a difficult period in her life, lacked confidence, and was grateful for the offer. During the next couple of years, she worked hard, but was often taken advantage of by being given a lot more work without recognition or recompense. The owner hired, used, and then lost employees, apparently believing that the cost of turnover was less than the cost of treating employees well. She found that she was no exception. Over time, however, Jess learned just how good she was and decided she could get another job. Her total job experience was with this manufacturing company and two other businesses in which she had been a co-owner with her former husband.

Jess wrote two resumes: a chronological version for potential manufacturing or small business employers who would appreciate her experience in those fields and a functional one that emphasized her skills for those who might think that the particular fields Jess had gained her experience in were less appropriate to their needs.

JESSICA RUTH JACOBS
341 Mayflower Road
Baltimore, Maryland 84536
(213) 845-6302

PROFILE: Creative team member; motivate those who report to me. Problem solver who designs or revises systems to improve work flow with quantifiable results. Independent self-starter who welcomes increasing responsibility. Thoughtful decision maker.

SKILLS:

SYSTEMS DEVELOPMENT AND MAINTENANCE

- Designed and implemented parts numbering system resulting in 15 percent decreased time for placing each order

- Computerized (with consultant) manufacturing, resulting in 10 percent decreased time from order placement to finished product

- Converted factory sales to work orders

- Estimated cost of all manufacturing raw materials for purchasing and finance departments

- Coordinated work flow through manufacturing

- Managed accounts receivable/payable, general ledger, franchise reports, taxes, state reports, route accounting

- Developed and managed payroll systems

PERSONNEL SUPERVISION

- Hired, trained, and evaluated office staff and temporary employees

- Supervised data entry, processing, and sales personnel

- Motivated and held sales staff accountable

CUSTOMER SERVICE

- Addressed customer concerns and resolved problems

- Trained employees to work with customers

- Coached sales personnel for improved performance

DECISION MAKING

Shared in all corporate decision making as half owner of two small businesses

WORK EXPERIENCE

XY Furniture Company, Baltimore
- Manufacturing Process Coordinator, 1987 to present
- Payroll Assistant, 1986-1987

Office Manager/Half owner
- Jacob's Produce Company, Inc., Baltimore, 1977-1987
- House of Jacob's, Baltimore, 1970-1977

EDUCATION

Sienna College, AB, 1970

COMMUNITY LEADERSHIP

- Secretary, Bears Auxiliary, 1989 to present
- Nominating Committee, Acton Parent Teachers Organization, 1990
- Member, Voters Service Committee, League of Women Voters, 1990

The advantage of this resume is that Jess was able to succinctly summarize both her personal qualities and her skills. The reader then is encouraged to consider what Jess has done and her working style rather than the particular field she has been working in. For jobs in a different field or which have a different title but use similar skills, this resume style can be a real advantage. Jess also wrote a resume for manufacturing jobs that were similar to those she had direct experience in.

JESSICA RUTH JACOBS
341 Mayflower Road
Baltimore, Maryland 84536
(213) 845-6302

QUALIFICATIONS: Self-starter with proven skills in developing and managing systems to improve work flow, office management, and supervision

PROFESSIONAL EXPERIENCE

MANUFACTURING PROCESS COORDINATOR, XY Furniture Company, Baltimore, 1987 to present

- Design and implement parts numbering system resulting in 15 percent decreased time for filling each order
- Computerize (with consultant) manufacturing systems resulting in 10 percent decreased time from order to finished product
- Convert factory sales orders to work orders
- Estimate cost of all manufacturing raw materials for purchasing and finance departments
- Create routings for new products
- Create and enter materials billing

PAYROLL ASSISTANT, XY Furniture Company, 1986-1987

- Calculated and entered piece-work rates and hourly wages on computerized payroll system
- Assumed payroll supervisor's responsibilities in her absence
- Assisted in the development of new system to record hourly charges

OFFICE MANAGER, HALF-OWNER, Jacobs Produce Company, Inc., Baltimore, 1977-1987. House of Jacobs, 1970-1977

- Maintained all accounts receivable, accounts payable, payroll general ledger, franchise reports, state reports, and taxes
- Hired, trained, and supervised office personnel
- Managed customer service
- Supervised on-site data processing and worked with programmers to develop new systems to meet changing needs

- Supervised sales representatives

EDUCATION

- Sienna College, AB, 1970

COMMUNITY LEADERSHIP

- Secretary, Bears Auxiliary, 1989 to present
- Nominating Committee, Acton Parent Teachers Organization, 1990
- Member, Voters Service Committee, League of Women Voters, 1990

After graduation, Sarah worked for two years as a teacher in the public school system. When her children were born, she left teaching and stayed home with them. She returned to teaching when her youngest started school, as well as continuing her strong volunteer commitment to a local nature center during the summer months. While teaching was stimulating initially, after five years she realized that she was dreading returning to school in the fall because she loved her volunteer work with the nature center. The volunteer work has involved many things, but what Sarah really liked was planning and putting on events to raise both money and visibility for the center. After talking with many people in her community, which was heavily white collar corporate, Sarah decided that she would like to try to get a job as an events manager for a large corporation or as a development director of a nonprofit organization. In order to best approach these two alternatives, Sarah tailored one resume on her home computer for each constituency.

SARAH LEE ADAMS
14 West 184th Street
Sandstone, Iowa 65492

PROFILE: Designed and conducted annual fund-raising programs, each of which exceeded its goal, for five years. Recruited and supervised volunteers, the majority of whom returned to work the following year. Developed low budget public relations campaign to support fund-raising.

SKILLS:

FUND-RAISING

- Designed annual summer fund-raising program which included a major event, member renewal, and new member solicitation
- Developed all membership renewal materials and worked closely with staff through production
- Organized a member-get-a-member campaign
- Managed the annual fund-raising event from initial planning through putting it on and evaluation. Participation has increased each year by at least 7 percent.
- Exceeded all fund-raising goals by 5-10 percent annually

VOLUNTEER MANAGEMENT

- Recruited volunteers and wrote job descriptions for each position
- Set up a system of volunteer supervisors and trained them; evaluated our performance with each supervisor
- Computerized volunteer records to track hours served and performance evaluation
- Planned and put on with staff a volunteer recognition celebration at the end of each summer
- Filled volunteer quota and had a 62 percent return rate for a second project

PUBLIC RELATIONS

- Solicited service-in-kind contributions of graphic design and printing of fund-raising materials and programs

- Met with electronic and print media reporters and obtained coverage in every media outlet in the county, including a Sunday supplement and television PSAs on each channel

ORGANIZATION

- Planned a full schedule of individually tailored learning activities for 25 to 30 children
- Created an environment in which children were creative and enthusiastic, found it was okay to make mistakes, worked hard, and exceeded learning goals
- Involved parents in supporting the learning of their children
- Developed curriculum on special topics and produced learning materials

EXPERIENCE

DEVELOPMENT DIRECTOR (Volunteer), Prairie Nature Center, Little Creek, Iowa, 1893 through present

CLASSROOM TEACHER, Sandstone Public Schools, 1973-1978; 1987-1990

PARENT/COMMUNITY VOLUNTEER, 1978-1987
Raised my children until the youngest entered school and worked as a volunteer with such organizations as the Parent Teachers Organization, Girl Scouts, and the Prairie Nature Center

COMMUNITY SERVICE

Volunteer of the Year of Greater Sandstone, 1989

EDUCATION

Mountain Rock College, AB, 1972

Central State University, MEd, 1973

Since Sarah was using this resume for a development position with nonprofit organizations and because she wanted to highlight her volunteer skills, she chose to do a resume organized around her skills, showing her natural energy and enthusiasm. For the resume to be used for a position as event coordinator with corporations, Sarah chose to be more traditional.

SARAH LEE ADAMS

14 West 184th Street

Sandstone, Iowa 65492

QUALIFICATIONS: Demonstrated skills and success in designing and producing events, organizing tasks, supervision, and teambuilding. Proven ability to develop public relations support for events.

EVENT AND FUND-RAISING COORDINATOR, Prairie Nature Center, Little Creek, Iowa, 1985 to present

- Developed and produced a major public event each summer designed to meet the strategic goals of the center
- Coordinated all details, logistics, and schedules with center staff and the ongoing program
- Recruited people, set up, and managed a supervision system for 250 volunteers
- Trained and motivated volunteers to achieve a 62 percent return rate
- This was a volunteer position requiring independent work and close coordination with paid staff. There was no paid support staff

TEACHER, Sandstone Public School System, 1973-1978; 1987-1990

- Organized schedules and all activities for 25-30 students
- Designed and taught curriculum to meet individual and group needs
- Maintained an environment which maximized learning, resulting in students surpassing goals every year
- Involved parents in supporting their children's education

EDUCATION

Mountain Rock College, AB, 1972

Central State University, MEd, 1973

COMMUNITY SERVICE

Volunteer of the Year of Greater Sandstone, 1989

If, after reading this, you are a bit overwhelmed and are considering a resume preparation service, think very carefully. If you are so pressed for time, or there is some other reason that you believe you cannot do the rest of a job search without having someone else write your resume, then please consider the following factors before choosing a resume service.

★ What is their track record? What percentage of their clients have gotten jobs with which they are satisfied?

★ How much experience do they have in the hiring world? Have they been in human resource or other positions that would assure they know what the marketplace wants?

★ Does the person know about the field you are interested in and its particular culture?

★ Is that person familiar with the level you are interested in?

★ Is that person willing to take the time to understand how you wish to position yourself, so that your resume will be unique and personal?

★ After taking the time to gather the information the writer requires, is this a cost-effective way of doing it?

The answers to these questions will help you evaluate a service. If you can find a service that meets your needs, and it can do something you cannot, there may be reasons to use it. As you can tell, however, we are skeptical.

One of the reasons for writing your own resume is that *it helps you* to summarize and put your own information into a usable form. If you have someone else write for you, you are losing the benefit of that synthesizing process. You have not taken your own background, evaluated what is most important to you, acknowledged it, and put it into words which are meaningful to someone else. In other words, writing a resume serves at least two purposes. It produces an end product that is sometimes a requirement in your job search and equally important, prepares you to take the next step in your job search.

If someone else prepares your resume, you have lost the advantage of your individuality. One of the human resource managers we interviewed does not pay much attention to resumes because she finds so many have the tone of a professional preparer. If an applicant has not done her own resume, many human resource professionals are not interested in it. If you use a preparation service, be sure that it is one that will not force-fit your background into a preset mold. If you are considering a resume preparation service, does that mean you are unwilling to take charge of your own job search? If that is the message, then roll up your sleeves and start writing!

Additional excellent sources of information can help you write your own resume. An abundance of good books with many sample resumes is available. Looking at examples of other resumes can give you ideas. If you want additional assistance, visit your local bookstore or library and look through the job-search section. By simply browsing through resume preparation books, you can review a myriad of styles and make some decisions about what you like and don't like. The big step is just to sit down with a pad of paper or your computer and start writing. Thinking about writing a resume can be tough; actually sitting down to do it is a lot easier.

Production

The most effective way to produce a resume is to use a computer and a laser printer. You can choose from a range of type styles, boldface or underline to highlight, and have flexibility in layout. The result is that you can design and produce a good basic resume and then tailor it to a particular job opportunity whenever you want. The finished quality must be excellent, and it will be if you use good paper and a laser printer. If you do not have a computer or a laser quality printer, do you know someone who would let you use theirs, either at their place or yours? If not, look for a business that rents computer and printer time, billable by the hour or partial hour.

The layout should make it easy for the reader to find all key information within seconds. Again, it is helpful to ask others to look at your layout to test whether it really is user friendly. Evaluate their comments, revise as necessary, print, and go.

Cover Letters and Correspondence

A job search is the time to write letters. The more letters you write, the more frequently your name and your needs come to someone's attention. Your written communication is the place to be succinct and creative. These are *not* contradictory terms! There are cover letters, thank you letters, and acknowledgment letters. If you think kind thoughts about someone, write to tell her. If someone has helped you, write to tell her. If contacts have not helped you, but spent some time trying to do so, write to thank them. If they have given you a good idea, write to tell them. We all like to receive personal mail, and we all like to be appreciated for our efforts on behalf of someone else.

The Cover Letter

Many of those things that you wanted to say, but didn't dare to or have room for in your resume can be written in your cover letter. Wait, that needs qualification! Add only those things that you can say in three paragraphs and fit on one page. For readability, you can break the middle paragraph in half for a fourth paragraph, but in most circumstances, you should honor the one-page rule. Get your message across in a manner that expresses what you want, but at the same time respects the reader's time. Most ideas can be expressed briefly and with personality, but it takes discipline and effort on your part.

What are those three paragraphs?

★ Why you are writing

★ What you can do for them and how you know you can do it

★ How you will be in touch with them again

A potential employer receives a lot of mail. The first paragraph is where you focus on what you want to say. Why are you writing? Are you interested in a specific position or in this employer for a particular reason? If you are responding to an ad, say so and name the position. Hopefully, you have already spoken with someone who has told you about the position or the employer, or called and requested the full job description. Tell them what has piqued your interest, using words that will encourage their confidence in your candidacy, so that they will read on. Avoid saying that you "wish to apply." Obviously you do, but position yourself as a candidate for the job, which subtly assumes that you qualify, moving you out of the resume pile and into the callback pile. Be positive about the skills you have and how they will help their organization. "I have written X and would like to write Y for you." "I have supervised or managed, and I know these are qualities you are looking for." Always identify what the position is and the key element that attracts you to it.

In the second paragraph, take advantage of the fact that this is a letter, breaking out of the format that a resume imposes. Show how you can write, demonstrate how you link ideas and synthesize information, and be enthusiastic. Sell yourself! Connect your accomplishments and experience to their expressed needs, if you know them, or begin with your strongest qualifications. "I have motivated people to get the job done," and then give examples. "I have managed and constantly improved systems." "I have designed programs which . . . " "For ten years, I have written newsletters . . . "

You can mix volunteer and employment experiences, always demonstrating that you can do what is needed. If you are moving into a new field, make the link between what you were doing and what it is you hope to do by emphasizing your transferable skills. Tell the person clearly why she should seriously consider you for the job.

The third paragraph tells the potential employer how you will be in touch again. Certainly say that you would like the opportunity to talk about the position. Specify a time that you will contact her to schedule an interview and answer any questions about your candidacy. Then, be sure to call. (It is good to have some questions, perhaps about the timing of the search process or some additional specifics about the position, but the questions should be genuine. Again, respect the employer's time.) End the paragraph on a positive note, mentioning your excitement about the potential match of your skills with her needs.

What if you really want to take a different approach from the one described here? Do it! As long as you have imagined yourself in the position of the potential employer and believe that what you want to do would be useful and respectful, be original.

Other Letters

If in doubt, write. After an interview, certainly send a letter immediately! Decide what points you want the interviewer to remember and specify them. If you had one of those brilliant flashes of hindsight after leaving the interview, be sure to write it in the letter. If you said something in the interview that you don't think was well received, you can recast it in the letter. (If it cannot be recast, don't remind the interviewer.) You also know a lot more about the job than you did when you first went for the interview, and thus you have an opportunity to mention more specifically what you can accomplish, based on the employer's description of what is wanted. Reiterate what you understand the timing of the process to be and note when you will call. Thank the interviewer for time and interest, and if that person was particularly good at something or you found something in common, mention it. "You really gave me excellent insight into the challenges of this particular position." Or, "I very much enjoyed comparing kayaking experiences. I am looking forward to trying the North River."

Letters should also be sent thanking anyone who has given you information. You still want them to keep an ear to the ground, listening for opportunities that might fit. Tell them how they have helped you. It is important for people to feel they have been useful. Repeat what it is you are looking for, so they have it in writing and can refer back to it. If you have been given the name of someone else to contact, be sure to send a note after you have made that contact, thanking them for the referral and mentioning how useful it was.

Another kind of letter to write goes to people you haven't had time to write to for awhile. Catch up on the news and then tell them that you are looking for a job. The encouragement and suggestions of old friends can be helpful. You also never know who they will know — and thus the network spreads ever wider.

We all respond to being treated well. As a job seeker, you can make a lot of people feel good by letting them know how helpful they have been to you. If you do it in writing, they have a piece of paper to remind them of you and what you are looking for. All of those people going to all those workplaces feeling good about you will certainly uncover something helpful to you and feel good about themselves, too.

Chapter 6

Networking: Making
It Work for You

People are lonely because they build walls instead of bridges. — *Joseph Fort Newton*

Networking. The consensus is, do it! If you do nothing else, network! Every woman we interviewed repeated this message again and again. Why? Very simply, because it works! Networking has lots of other benefits, too. It can even be fun. Thoughtful, consistent, effective networking opens the necessary doors for you. How can we say this with such certainty? Over 60 percent of people who have found jobs say that it was due to networking. Women who network attribute their success in *finding satisfying work* to the networking they did.

What Is Networking?

It is a series of one-on-one contacts that branch out to an everwidening circle, giving you advice, guidance, tips, hints, bona fide leads, introductions, informational interviews, and support. Sometimes a network serves as a security blanket; other times, it's a kick in the pants to get you going again, and sometimes it's the fairy godmother who makes an ideal connection for you. Networking is a concept that gained momentum in the 1980s, but it had been around for many, many years before then. It is not a new fad. Use it to your advantage.

Webster's defines a network as "a fabric or structure of threads or wires that cross each other at regular intervals and are knotted or secured at the crossings." We like this description, particularly the "regular intervals," "knots," and "secure crossings." In essence, to network in the job search is to build a series of contacts that are used for mutual benefit and enjoyment, becoming stronger with every appropriate use. The analogy becomes more meaningful when you think about the support that a fabric can give, particularly when well cared for. It is this supportive structure that is important to build and maintain, before, during, and after a job search. Most of us already have all different kinds of networks; we simply aren't aware of them as such.

So, how does networking specifically help? A lot! Begin with personal support. Your personal network is the group you turn to when the search gets discouraging and you need help to pick yourself up, dust yourself off, and start again. This same network is there when you have a great victory and want to tell someone about it or celebrate. A network is where you go to find new ideas to test; to talk about a strategy and find out if others think it will work; to find out who does what, where, and how; to make other contacts and learn about job openings; and to assess what it is like to be in a particular job. Your job-search plan is interwoven and enriched with network leads and activities. Your network will help sustain you, help you think strategically, and keep you in touch with other segments of the community, even after you have the job. In short, *networking is one of the essential activities of the working world.*

Why is networking effective? Human nature! Here is just one illustration of how networking works. Put yourself in the position of the person doing the hiring. Suppose you had a leak in your roof and needed someone to fix it. What would you do first? Call up someone you know who has information about good roofers! Suppose you don't know anyone who knows about roofers? What would you do then? Call up a person who knows someone who knows about roofers. Feel stumped? Don't. Think of how many people you are somewhat acquainted with who live in neighborhoods; call to ask them which of their neighbors has had a roof repaired in the last few years. Then call the person who had the roof work done. Several calls and you should have recommendations with a list of the strengths and weaknesses of each. Not only that, you've added a new contact to your home repair network.

As you see, you already network. It may have been your roof that needed fixing, the need for a good baby-sitter, or buying a stereo, but you have gone to other people for information to help you make decisions. You already know how. Networking is the most natural thing in the world to do. Now, it is time to use networking to help you focus on your goals and to get you into that job.

Just as personal recommendations are much more reliable than the yellow pages when it comes to home repair, so, too, are personal recommendations much more reliable than the brief impression made by reading a resume or conducting an interview. Experience has taught potential employers that a personal recommendation is more effective than a superficial impression. *Reliable first-hand information about an applicant from a colleague is a better indication of future success than a resume or interview.*

Another reason why networking works is the flip side of the picture; if you make a good, qualified recommendation to a colleague, it is a credit to you. You, as the recommender, have done the employer a big favor. We all like to do something for someone else. In this case, two people (the employer and employee) have been helped. It is a very good feeling all around. *Networking works because it is a balanced equation in which all of the participants win.*

> *Trudie is head of human resources for a medium-sized human service agency. She was looking for a public relations manager to replace a mediocre employee. She wanted a high-energy spark plug. After interviewing the five most promising applicants (all of whom had good qualifications and references), she had not found anyone exciting. At this point, Trudie's friend Sam called. He had worked with Martha on a charity fund-raiser and thought she was terrific, particularly in promotional skills. Martha had applied for the public relations manager's job, but had not been one of the five selected for interviews, because she had so much less experience than the five who were invited. On the basis of Sam's recommendation, Martha was interviewed and made a tremendous impression. Even though Martha had less experience, Trudie trusted her own hiring judgment, Sam's perception, and recommended her. Martha was hired and is doing a dynamic job for the organization. Trudie says she "owes" Sam, and she has even called him once to find out who else he knows.*

If you are reading this and saying to yourself, "Oh great, this sounds good, but I don't have a network, and I don't even think I know how to be part of one," don't despair. You probably do have the seeds of a network, although at this point you may not be thinking about them this way.

The Old Boy Network

Back in the days when schools and colleges were the bastions of a privileged upper class, there was an old boy network from which women were excluded. The old boy network was based solidly on shared experiences. Boys who grew up attending school together, participating in clubs and fraternities together, playing on teams together, sharing the passages of adolescence, formed strong bonds. These friendships did not end with school but continued by tradition and example into the workplace.

Most men, upon graduating from school were helped into their first jobs by family or alumni contacts. For example, when Sandra was graduating from college and struggling with how to find her first job, she asked her father how he had gotten his. He told her that his uncle was on the board of directors of a company that asked her father to work for them after graduation. There was no interview; his education and his uncle qualified him for the job. Whether a boy entered his profession through an apprenticeship, an entry-level position, or with an advanced degree, a family or school contact usually paved the way. Fathers and uncles helped their sons and sons of friends.

As an employee advanced in his chosen profession, he, in turn, was able to help others. *The male network succeeded because men had strong bonds built on shared experience, and they knew how to use them.* In the process of growing up, men learned how to support one another while competing. These skills stayed with them and became the basis of a lifelong network.

Women did not go to school with the old boys nor did they experience all of the related activities. After graduation, most women stayed home to raise families. Those who entered the working world did so in positions that were considered acceptable, such as nursing, teaching, and some kinds of manufacturing. A network was not needed to get into these traditional female career areas because there usually were no promotions from these positions. The rare woman who dared to enter one of the professions often did so without encouragement, and indeed, with harassment.

As women began to seek both higher education and full professional careers, they were hampered by not being part of the old boy network. While the old boy network continued to work for men, many women and other minorities who were now attending college and expecting full careers did not have similar access to the working world. This created a problem for the colleges confronted with graduates deprived of equal access to the career market. Career development offices sprang up on college campuses as one way of helping women and other minorities into the job market. The staff of these offices taught job-search techniques and established a formal career network, dependent on alumni sharing knowledge of their career fields with undergraduates.

Today, the old school bonds may not be as strong because more of us go to school, diluting some of the exclusivity. However, there is evidence that men are still much less hesitant than women about depending on networks. Men understand the power of calling an acquaintance and asking for information or help. Whether the bonds were formed in school, the locker room, at work, or through volunteer responsibilities, many men use them. It is ironic that women – for whom personal relationships may be more important – have not networked as effectively. But women are learning; more of us do call, ask, and share information and influence.

Male networks remain very strong; they do have opportunities that are closed to women. Male bonds are formed and strengthened by the few clubs that are still all-male, the schools whose graduates before the mid-1970s were all-male, labor unions in trades that have been all-male, boards of directors that are predominantly male, and senior executive associations that are mostly male. True, women are making inroads. Important groups like Rotary and Kiwanis now have open membership, and women who have made it above middle management levels have become more visible in professional associations. As more women join the work force, we are in a position to help each other into jobs. As more of us are promoted into management and senior positions, we are able to help each other move forward. As we realize the power of networking, we are able to rely on both men and women to help us get in and get ahead.

What can you do to fully utilize networking as a tool? To begin with, you need to recognize that you cannot directly change the behavior of others. You can only change your behavior and hope those changes can affect the environment. You have to begin with yourself. First, accept yourself as an individual who has a tremendous amount to offer, no matter what your background or work history. You have much to offer to family, friends, colleagues, and other working people. You must believe in your own self-worth if you want others to believe in you. An offshoot of this is to begin trusting your own judgment. One of the biggest challenges in networking is to take yourself seriously, which can be difficult to do. Once you do that, then you have a chance of opening doors.

How you perceive yourself has a tremendous impact on how others perceive you. Your behavior influences their behaviors toward you. This has tremendous impact on how you function in a network and how you function on the job. Judy relates an experience that confirmed this.

> "One day when I was Christmas shopping, I had purchased some gifts I was very excited about, and as I walked down the street, I found all these strangers smiling at me and many saying, 'Hello.' My first reaction was to think that they, too, were pleased with their shopping. It was when I passed a friend who said, 'Do you ever look happy!' that I realized what was happening. The people on the street were reflecting what I was projecting about myself. To test my observation, I played Scrooge for a block, and sure enough— what a bunch of grumpy shoppers!"

If we want others to regard us as valuable to their networks, we have to believe in ourselves. Others reflect back what we project about ourselves.

Women need to work together. We have a lot of shared experiences and goals.

We can talk to each other about issues that others may not understand. We can gather strength from each other through mutual encouragement. We can share knowledge, contacts, and influence, whether it is how to find good day care, get a neighborhood zoning law changed, or find the best person to fill a key position in a company. We can improve our networking by searching out other women whom we find interesting and taking the initiative to get together. No agenda is needed; it will evolve.

Women also need to network with men. Often, we, as women, will have to be the initiators; offer and ask in a way that is clearly of value to us and to the men we would like to have in our networks. Why do we need men? Men are in places that we need to have represented in our networks. One example is senior management, another is trade unions. Why would men in senior positions want to network or mentor? Women and men can help each other.

> *Connie, a teacher, volunteered with Jethro, a senior officer in a bank, on a nonprofit project to build a community youth center. Over the course of the project, Jethro grew to respect Connie's ability to plan and to enlist the cooperation of various segments of the community. After the project was over, Jethro sought Connie's advice on community projects that the bank was undertaking. Connie asked for and got some advice from Jethro on how to involve representatives of local corporations in the classroom. When Connie decided to leave teaching, she requested and got both enthusiastic introductions and recommendations from Jethro. They continue to be a part of each other's network.*

Two of the lessons from Connie's experience are that she acknowledged the importance of networking and that she was willing to take the risk of not only giving, but asking.

The room at the top is limited; women who want to get there need to apply many tools and strategies to keep moving forward. Networking is one of those strategies. You must be willing to look for and connect with women and men who can help you. You must be willing to ask as well as to give. You must be willing to take risks. You can find potential networkers in professional organizations, service clubs, volunteer projects, church, the office, and the gym. Your attitude makes a difference in forming these relationships. It is worth the effort.

Women's Issues

We discussed many of the myths you will run into in the world of the job search in chapter 2. The slow but steady progress of women into management positions has uncovered the fallacy of the stereotypes that are based on male models of development. As female models emerge, so, too, will important lessons about women's strengths and value systems. We'll find that these values impact on networking and the job search.

Relationships: Helping and Asking

Women interpret life and work through relationships. Ask most of us how the work day went and the answers will often involve other people. Ask us what we did on the weekend and our responses will often include what we did with others. We're a little like Rabbit in *Winnie the Pooh* who is always mentioned in the same breath with "friends and relations."

Whether life is solitary or crowded with people around us, relationships help us shape our identity. We express ourselves and find the meaning in what we do through our relationships. In studies reported by Josselson in *Finding Herself,* young girls showed an overwhelming focus on relationships, in sharp contrast to boys for whom goals were the primary basis of self-definition. These tendencies continue throughout our lives. The goal for men is some form of achievement; for women, the goal is successful relationships. Women's sense of themselves is influenced by their ability to build and maintain relationships. It has even been suggested that one role a mentor plays for women is to demonstrate the interaction of work and relationships.

The instinctive primacy of relationships for women means that we are naturally adept at networking; in fact, we may feel more content in our work if we do form and maintain networks. Networking does not begin or end with a job search.

Women have communication skills and attitudes that foster good networking. We like to share ideas with people we trust. We often make decisions by bouncing ideas off others. We can talk about personal issues that matter to us. Columnist Niki Scott says, "We, women, were fortunate to have grown up with permission to form close, emotionally intimate relationships with one another. We don't have to spend time talking about golf or Monday night football." Many of us are good listeners and know how to ask questions that draw others out. These qualities mean that we have a natural advantage because we have learned and practiced some of the skills that make forming a network easier.

While helping others may come naturally, many of us need to work on asking for help for ourselves. Part of the problem may be that we have not fully made the distinction nor the maturational move from pleasing people to helping people. Until we can help without needing to please, it remains difficult to ask others for assistance. Some of us were taught as children to be good girls, to figure out what behavior was expected and to give it. If we spent childhood years trying to please others by our behavior instead of setting our own priorities and determining how to achieve them, asking for help can be difficult. Some of us also learned to please others to get attention and reinforcement. The problem is that simply pleasing others may not achieve what we want nor will it satisfy us. Conversely, if we can be genuinely helpful, the result will be a healthier relationship from which we can derive great pleasure. As adult women, we can recognize behaviors that do not work, choose to change, define what we want and need, and enlist the support of others in making those changes.

> *Joan, who was applying for a position at a local university, had heard mixed reviews on the working environment. Since she was coming out of a nonsupportive office situation, a positive environment was one of her top priorities. Joan contacted Sally whom she knew slightly through an informal women's lunch group. Sally worked in a different, but related, department. Joan's question was easy: What is it like to work where you do and how do you think it is different in the other departments? Sally happened to like where she worked and the telling reaffirmed this, plus she helped Joan. An additional benefit of the conversation for Joan was that Sally became her advocate, on the alert for openings at the university.*

A reluctance to ask for help for fear of losing control or owing someone something can be countered by the fact that a team effort makes many things work better. You have something to contribute and can expect to receive something in return. Whether you ask for or give help, all partners are stronger for it.

Shyness

Do you feel too shy to ask? Shyness sometimes becomes much less of an issue when you are genuinely curious and interested. Try to remember a time when you surprised yourself by speaking out about something you believed in deeply. Think of what you really want to know about the job market and go forth. If asking still seems overwhelming, maybe you are not confident about whether or not you know enough about the kind of information you want. If not, work on defining what you want to know, so that you can increase your ease and confidence in asking. When you know what you want, it is a lot easier to ask. Also, verbalize what you are asking to yourself or your buddy to make sure that what you want is readily understandable and succinctly stated.

It is important to take small, steady, significant steps in overcoming shyness. Start by asking an easy question of a person who is certain to know the answer. Remember Joan's question for Sally. It was a question Sally would definitely know the answer to. When you sense the pleasure someone feels in being able to respond to your questions, it will reinforce your ability to ask. The more you ask, the more you'll receive this positive feedback, and the easier asking will become.

If you have tried all of these measures and still feel too shy to act, you may want to seek counseling for this specific reason. Some of us were raised in families of genuinely shy people where shyness was our only model. In other situations, you may have been discouraged any time you asked for something or been generally put down by significant people in your life. This kind of background is a barrier, but like most barriers, it can be overcome. You can choose to think differently. In an age of aggression, shyness can be a rare and appreciated commodity. The key is not to let your shyness restrict your actions.

Most of us believe that we are alone in our personal struggles. Certainly, no one else could have the same problems! Fortunately, it is no longer possible to believe that any of us are unique in our shyness since public radio star Garrison Keilor brought shyness to national attention with his powdermilk biscuit song. When you are feeling shy, try listening to one of the old tapes of his broadcasts, available in public libraries. You'll know that you have lots of company.

Some women are shy about networking with men, because they do not want their intentions to be misinterpreted. There will always be some female/male issues in the workplace. If you are very clear with yourself about what you want, if you are asking an appropriate person and your behavior is completely professional, you can expect to receive an appropriate, professional response. Most men want professional women in their networks, as much as women want professional men in theirs. The occasional male who may have an inappropriate agenda is probably not someone you want in your network. If he is an influential person in an organization that you are trying to approach, question whether you want to be part of that organization.

A Sisterhood?

The first interview we did for this book was with a woman who had known professional women throughout her community for twenty-five years. She is perceptive and eloquent in her ideas about the job market and women working. One of her first statements was provocative and angry. She said that women do not stick together to get ahead. In fact, they often undermine each other. We couldn't contradict her because we, too, have seen or experienced turf battles and competitive situations in which women are actually more judgmental and harder on each other than on their male coworkers.

It is almost as if there is a backlash from the decades when women were not permitted to compete with men. Now that women are assuming more leadership positions, some don't know how to handle the power and responsibility. It has been a fight to get in and remains a fight. Instead of building bridges, we erect barriers and even set land mines. Some of the attitudes are unconscious, built on a reality that no longer exists, a situation we discussed in chapter 1. We must question, examine, change attitudes, and try to build together, all the while learning new, more appropriate behaviors. We must recognize that it is possible to compete and cooperate.

At the same time, we also know many women who really do support each other in their work. As we form and nurture our networks, we will find men and women with whom we can form working bonds. We cannot assume that a sisterhood of women exists presently, but we can strive toward establishing one and can set an example that builds on our strength in relationships.

Types of Networks

We recommend two main networks: personal and career information. Many of the techniques of the career information network are the same as those of effective informational interviewing, which is popularly recommended now, but we suggest that your objective be a long-term network instead of a single informational meeting. A network continues to function with many value-added benefits during and after the job search.

Personal Support Network

A personal support network is a friend, family, or group of friends with whom you share support, companionship, fun, intellectual stimulation, and a whole range of other necessities of life. You may turn to siblings or other relatives, childhood or school friends, neighbors, or colleagues at work. Your network may be one person or several. Whatever the combination, these are the people you can tell about the good things, and these are the people who will help you pick yourself up after the bad. In a job search, this personal support network can be the source of information, motivation, guidance, creative ideas, laughs, other contacts, emotional support, and much more.

At times in our lives our network of supportive people may seem quite thin – when living in a new community, when we feel overwhelmed by life, or when we have a feeling of isolation during transitions. Your network may still exist and be accessible, but you may find it hard to take the necessary initiative to reach out. Sometimes a small gesture or single word ("help") will activate your personal network. If you have tried and are unable to take this step, try smaller steps, perhaps asking one person you know well to do something recreational with you. If you are still stymied, then it may be time to consider some personal counseling for help in this area.

Some of us find ourselves in the job market because of divorce or death. Even if we are already working, such a tragedy makes career decisions much more overwhelming. Loss can make you feel terribly isolated and unable to reach out. It can be difficult to connect with others even though those connections may be even more important than usual. It is usually a time of great emotional pain. Josselson, in *Finding Herself,* says that the loss of a loved one who had soothed in times of distress, been someone to structure time around, stabilized and reassured you, and helped you feel worthwhile is often the beginning of a period of real growth. It is clearly difficult if loss is the cause of a period of personal redefinition, but it can be a time to learn that you can stand alone and that you can set your own goals. Take courage that something positive can evolve from loss. During these times, a network is a key ingredient to personal and professional progress. Many women who have suffered loss can speak from personal experience about how important that network can be.

"When my husband and parents died within a two-year period, my children were all living in other communities or countries and my siblings were a day's plane ride away. My networks were there for me and have been ever since. There were times right after my husband's death when I could not reach out, because I was trying so hard to hold onto myself and to get through each day. But people waited and supported, and as I became more centered, I was able to respond. My husband and I had been in a new community for only a year, but I had gotten to know a small group of professional women well. We had lunched together, gone out to relax for a couple of hours after work on occasional Fridays, talked about forming a defined group including other professional women, and occasionally gotten together with spouses. These new friends

hung in. Good old friends from our previous community, an hour away, called and came. The network helped me journey back to life.

In this personal network, we laugh a lot and talk about professional and personal issues and occasionally try to influence something that is happening in the community. I thought we must be unique, but my college-age daughter, after joining one of our Friday night gatherings, expressed surprise that many of the issues and much of the humor were similar to what she shared with her friends. This kind of network helps sustain through all kinds of transitions, including a job search. When it was time to change jobs, I bounced ideas off this group and made a final decision with their help."

A personal network can also function as a job-search resource. The people in your network know you, your strengths, and your weaknesses better than most. These are the people who want what is best for you, and who care about your contentment in all areas of your life. They are in a better position to know what you might like and what would be a good fit. Tell them what you want. Ask some of them to critique your job objective, your resume, help you maintain your motivation, and, above all, keep their ears to the ground. Do your remember the Sorcerer's Apprentice? He cut a broom into pieces, so that each piece did what the broom had done. That is a little like a personal support network turned loose on a job search. Your efforts are multiplied many times. To summarize, some of the ways your personal network can help you are:

★ Suggest contacts

★ Critique a job search plan

★ Help you to remember resources

★ Ask questions to keep you on track

★ Cheer you on when you have an obstacle to overcome

★ Keep ears to the ground for potential openings

★ Help figure out whether it is time for a new job

★ Let you know about their work environment

★ Praise you when you've completed a tough task

★ Help you figure out where your skills fit

Career Information Network (CIN)

A career information network is the tool to find the kinds of information and assistance you need to get the job you want. It is an ever-enlarging group of people who help you define what you want to do, where you want to do it, and how you will actually get the job. A career information network is where you take your job description from chapter 3 to figure out where it can fit. Yes, reading and research are important first steps, but people still provide the best information. More importantly, they become part of your job-search team. When you are in the process of doing the exercises in chapter 3 to decide what you want to do and you need a little help, this network is a great place to go. Once you have your ideal job description, pass it around and ask the people in your network if they know where this type of job is available.

Use a career information network to get general information on a career field or geographic area, find out about a type of organization, uncover the jobs in a field that you have chosen, investigate a specific employer, and talk with the decision-maker in an organization that you have targeted. The CIN differs from your personal network in the types of issues you'll bring to these people and the kinds of information you'll be seeking. The CIN is more job specific and less motivational in nature.

Faced with a move to another state, Peg, who was working as a career counselor at a university, asked her boss to write letters of introduction to the college career development directors in her new location. The contacted directors graciously met with her, told her about their campuses, and gave her other names to contact. As she went along, Peg gathered promising information to follow up on. On one campus visit, a stand-in showed up for the director. Alice was not in career development, but was directing a volunteer program similar to the one Peg worked on earlier in her career. They had a great time comparing notes and continued to get together once Peg had actually moved to the area. Some time later, Peg received a call from a wonderful foundation requesting her application for a position based on her volunteer program experience. Peg had been recommended by Alice. Peg applied, was offered the position, took it, and the work was terrific. What happened to all of those other contacts? They certainly gave her some ideas, but Peg chose not to pursue her contact with them. They did not stay on Peg's career network nor she on theirs. Could Peg have remedied that? Probably, but she chose to develop other contacts in her newly chosen field.

Some of the many things that the people in your career information network can do for you are:

★ Tell you about working environments

★ Suggest contacts

★ Tell you what kinds of jobs match your ideal job description

★ Challenge you to think more creatively

★ Keep ears to the ground for potential openings

★ Give you information about a geographic area

★ Tell you what their jobs and work environments are like

★ Give you the inside scoop on their own organizations

★ Uncover different fields and jobs you never dreamed of

★ Suggest that someone interview you for a job

★ Pass your resume on to someone else

★ Tell you about the value system in an organization or field

★ Tell you how realistic/unrealistic your goals are in their field

★ Let you know about salary and benefits in the places they work

★ Explain how hiring actually works in their organization

★ Tell you how the organization, job, or field is expected to change

★ Explain what their field's career ladder would be like

★ Recommend additional training/education to strengthen credentials

★ Define what skills are needed for a particular job or field

★ Describe the pros and cons of their job, organization, or field

Creating Your Career Information Network

The first step is to go forth acknowledging what you have to offer. You are a woman of worth who has definable experience, skills, and values. You are ready to work hard. You are smart and enthusiastic about getting into or moving up in your chosen field. You have something to offer that makes it worthwhile for others to talk to you. While you are networking, you, in effect, become a communication link between the people in your network, sharing nonconfidential ideas and happenings. And all of these things that you have to offer are the building blocks of a job search; imagine how helpful you'll be when you land the job! This is just the beginning!

Will people speak with you? They certainly will – if you have done your part of the work. First of all, you must have defined what you are looking for. Remember Alice and the Cheshire Cat? When Alice was wandering in Wonderland, she came to a fork in the road and happened on the Cheshire Cat's grin and then the cat. Being lost, she asked him which way to go. Logically, he asked her where she wanted to get to. When she responded that she didn't know, he gave her the only advice he could. It really didn't matter which route she chose.

Beware of putting the people in your network in the same position as the Cheshire Cat. If you cannot tell them where you want to go, all they can do is tell you that it doesn't matter what you do. They end up feeling useless and you don't receive the information you want. So, define those questions beforehand. Work on the exercises in chapter 3. Have a job-search plan in place beforehand. Grapple with your personal issues, barriers, blocks, and myths beforehand. Then, onward!

At the outset, the questions may be somewhat general, such as "Describe the environment of a high tech manufacturing plant (or the headquarters of an insurance company)" or "What are the advantages and disadvantages of living in Columbus, Ohio?" These would be level one type questions, and you wouldn't, quite obviously, be bothering someone high up on the career ladder with these basic, but often necessary, questions. At the other end of the spectrum is an interview with someone in your target organization. A logical question might be one about what that person sees happening in his or her career area or to the company over the next five years, what will be the advantages and barriers in pursing a chosen direction. More specifically by stating your work objective, you can ask how those goals would fit a specific position.

Whatever the level of information, the people you network with must know what you want. When you contact someone tell her what you are trying to do, a bit about why you are doing it, and specifically what you need from her. For example, "I feel as if I am at a dead end in what I am doing. I would like to move into research. I've had a lot of software experience, and I would like to talk with someone who can tell me what is happening with software marketing in this community." If you are reentering the formal job market, you might say, "I have volunteer experience managing events and want to talk to a person in X Corp who would know who manages the corporate and community events for them." Or, with a major in history, "I've done a lot of research and writing. I've gone through the *Job Bank Book* and made a list of companies that have entry level analyst positions. I've also read the annual reports of companies of interest to me.

Now I need to learn more about what working for one is really like. Do you know anyone who works at X, Y, or Z company with whom I could speak?" To be successful in building a career network, you must clearly express what you need and make it easy for your contact to respond. After an initial visit, keep in contact. Meanwhile, don't overlook the basics. Writing to say thank you is an absolute, but calling or writing to report progress, to respond to a mutual interest identified during the conversation, or to give pertinent information all help build a relationship.

When you go to someone else with questions, be sure you are prepared. For example, if you are trying to find out about Columbus, be sure that you have gotten all of the information from the Chamber of Commerce and directories of the area. Then you not only know enough to ask questions that get at the deeper information you want, but you also demonstrate that you have done your research. People provide the insights; the books provide the basic information.

Annual reports are an excellent source of information. They are required of publicly held for-profit companies, and are put out voluntarily by many nonprofit corporations. They are a gold mine of information about the organization and, in combination with others, of the world of work. They not only reveal the financial picture, but usually the major officers. They describe the goals of the corporation and whether and why the goals were met. Studying annual reports is a requirement before contacting anyone in an organization. The reports are free; many career development libraries maintain a collection.

Who should be part of your career information network? Everyone who can help. Each will offer different resources, so don't leave anyone out. Most of us are at least acquainted with or know of someone who has access to the information we need. It could be a friend of your parents, or the parents or children of a friend, a sibling or colleague of a member of your religious organization, an old school friend, a former boss, a neighbor, the colleague of a neighbor, or your dentist, haircutter, or real estate broker. Don't forget the people you exercise with and all the people you have ever worked with in volunteer or paid positions and their spouses or contacts. What about the parents of all the children yours have been with in school? A teacher who wanted to change careers might say that she had been in a school for so long that she had no contacts in the outside world. Wrong! What about the hundreds of grateful parents of her past students who would be pleased to be included in her career network. What organizations, including condo associations, professional groups, and social clubs, do you belong to? When you start thinking about it, the list is endless. Best of all, people – even people in high places – generally want to help!

Think of people you have met through community or religious activities whom you have always thought that you would like to get to know better. Ask them to lunch. At parties, make the extra effort to talk to people you don't know or you want to know better. Join organizations that have a broad-based membership of both men and women. Rotary and Kiwanis are good examples of such groups where membership is by invitation, but you can let members know you would like to join. Other community groups like the PTA are open to any interested community member. *Your natural curiosity and interests are both guideposts and assets in adding to your career informational network.*

Suppose that you have just moved to a new community, are looking for a job, and have not made any friends. Now, how do you go about putting together a career information network? Ask old friends who are in other locations for contacts in this new community and keep in touch weekly by phone (if resources permit) or letter. It will also give you a source of encouragement. Check with your school or college alumnae office. Fellow graduates would be pleased to give you an initial helping hand. Through people you have known, find a friend of a friend in the community. Join a local religious group and talk to the spiritual leader (many today actually receive training in career counseling), join a health club and get to know some of the people you work out with, join an interest group like a reading group or hiking club and you will meet people of similar interests quickly. When asked to network in an area in which we feel we have something to offer, most if us are happy to pitch in.

Should your list include men as well as women? Yes! If you do not include men in your network, you will be leaving out a lot of people who are in positions to influence what happens to you. You would also be omitting people who may have a different perspective and a lot of experience. People with varying points of view enrich you and your network.

The nurturing that can take place in an all-female network is essential, but some all-female networks have a downside. The members can spend a lot of time talking about men. This type of network can be a place for anger and frustration to be vented. While venting in itself is not bad, getting stuck in anger is certainly counterproductive. An effective network moves from the negative (What is wrong?) to the positive (What do we want to do now?).

Involving men in one of your networks may yield additional influence, a different point of view, and a preventative from concentrating on the unfairness of the "system." Both mixed and all-female networks work. Try to cultivate both.

Formalizing a Group

So far, we have been talking about a group of people who you are in close contact with concerning career issues. Do such groups ever get together or become more formalized? Yes, they do, and the outcome can be very positive. The personal support network mentioned earlier is a good example of one that became a professional network as well. A group of five women in leadership positions in the community got together occasionally for lunch. They discussed both personal and professional issues. They began to invite other women to their occasional Friday night gatherings, and at one point, frustrated by the local women's exclusion from all-male lunch clubs, they began an informal monthly luncheon group with a speaker. There was tremendous interest, and they had no difficulty finding fifteen to twenty interested women who welcomed the opportunity.

From their members' various perspectives within the small community, the group had some clout as well as the potential for a creative exchange of ideas. The experience of organizing and managing the formalized group was important for some members who needed to acquire these skills. A formalized group requires delegation, something that many women need to practice because it involves asking for something. Through the group, members could find out more about what others did and exchange business leads. Did the group survive and prosper? No. About this time, Rotary, Kiwanis, and other service groups opened their doors to women and most of the group's members opted to join. Now, the merits of this move can be long debated, but one thing is very clear – professional networks can be formalized, offering members many benefits.

Establishing the Network

Remember, your objective is to enlist long-term support, so be flexible and courteous in all of your contacts to keep the door open. Write or call the person you want to add to your network and arrange to see her at her convenience. You will obviously be most successful if the person already knows you, as she is much more likely to want to meet with you. If you give the name of a mutual acquaintance or colleague your contact is likely to be similarly receptive. Contacting someone "cold" is tougher, but depending on that person's schedule and how you appeal to her interest, she may very likely listen. With cold calls, if you are asked the subject of your call, respond in general terms in a straightforward, nonapologetic way. You are most likely to add someone to your network who has some mutual interest, such as being part of the same industry, professional, interest, or social group.

Some people prefer to write and then follow up with a call. That way, your contact has time to consider your request and expects your call. There is no confusion about the purpose of your contact. A potential downside is that a contact who does not want to talk with you also has ample opportunity to decide to turn down your request. If you write, mention who has given you her name and why, a very brief overview of your background, what you want to discuss, and an indication that you are not going to take up a lot of time. This should all be said in less than a page.

It is preferable to meet face to face with the person you want to add to your network because you have the opportunity to establish a firmer, better impression. If you do not know the person, meeting is really the only way to establish the kind of rapport that makes someone a part of your team. Be sure to read chapter 7 on interviewing. Many of the points made there also apply to your networking meetings. Sometimes it is not possible for someone to meet you in person. If a telephone conversation will accomplish part of your purpose, call. Your good judgment will dictate what works best and what keeps the door open.

If you know a potential networker in one role, but are trying to establish yourself in another, a formalized meeting is very important.

> Lisa got to know Bob when they both coached Little League teams. Because Bob worked for the Chamber of Commerce, he could be a big help to her in making contacts. The problem was that Lisa knew that Bob would think of her in jeans and a sweatshirt surrounded by kids, not as the professional woman she was. So, instead of talking to him on the ball field, she made an appointment with him at his office. Dressed in her business suit and in a work setting, Lisa was viewed in a context compatible with her goals.

The Informational Interview

Richard Bolles and other leaders in the field of career development advocate the informational interview as a way of defining what you want to do and reaching the person in a position to hire. This idea made sense when it was first presented, and many people in the job market set up informational interviews. The problem was that too many of these same people did not do their homework and used the interview as the only way of getting information, much of which was readily available in print. Too many people with too little time were asked too many questions about things that could have been looked up. Some used informational interviews as a pretext for asking for a job, creating awkward and irritating situations. A lot of valuable work time was lost. Information of merit was not exchanged, and informational interviewing got a bad name. Now, some of these problems have been addressed. The concept of informational interviewing is excellent and, as you can tell, we advocate it, with the caveats that you prepare thoroughly, present your purpose honestly, follow up, and only add appropriate people to your career information network.

Techniques

The first few minutes of a meeting are important. Our brains naturally grasp for some kind of order or meaning. Whether you are meeting with someone for the first time or presenting yourself to an old acquaintance in a new context, you need to help that person see you as you want to be seen. Set the stage: decide what you want to wear (both comfortable and appropriate), what kind of initial light conversation you can begin with, what you want to say about the person who suggested this contact, and exactly how to state your mission. Outline beforehand both the questions that you want to have answered and what you want the person to know about you. Remember to ask for suggestions for additional contacts. Be sensitive to cues that it is time to end the meeting and act on them promptly.

You are really in charge of this meeting. You have requested it and, therefore, are responsible for conducting it. Create a balance between information given and information requested. The ideal informational interview is a dialogue because that is the best way to establish mutual respect.

Two recent experiences with job seekers have left us wanting to stress a couple of points. In one meeting, the woman had a good list of questions to ask about the community and work environments, but she never made her goals clear to us. We were unable to grasp a sense of who she was, where she was going, and what she wanted. Although we answered her questions, we were left wondering if our responses were at all helpful. This woman was doing a good job with some career-search techniques, but she had not taken enough time to define what she wanted to do with her skills and interests. It would have helped us if she had either said that her purpose in meeting with us was to help her define a direction or expressed what her goal was.

The second interview represented the opposite extreme. This woman gave a clear impression of her interests because she never stopped talking about her current job, how much she loved what she did, and then, how she hated leaving it to accompany her husband to this new community. She was very vague about why she had requested this meeting except that we might know of job openings.

Because there were none, and she had no other substantive questions, she lost a valuable source of other information, and frankly, left us feeling deflated. She talked incessantly while she should have been asking about other organizations and opportunities in town.

Meetings such as these can be very productive. The job-seeker explains enough about herself so that some of her background and current direction are understood. The woman is relaxed and natural so that her enthusiasm and energy are communicated. She smoothly demonstrates her knowledge and preparation for the meeting. There is no confusion about the kinds of information being sought. The result is that the woman is helped and all participants feel good about having been a positive force in the job search.

As you leave your meeting, be sure to summarize exactly what has been helpful. This provides positive reinforcement right on the spot! Then send a thank-you note that evening. It should be specific, reiterating what you learned from the interview, something about what your next steps will be and when you will be back in touch. If you want this person to be part of your career network, maintaining contact is very important.

The type of continuing contact depends on your sense of the situation. You should maintain contact in the way that is most comfortable and convenient for the other person. If you are not sure what is appropriate, ask. Simply say that you have appreciated the encouragement and would like to let her know what is happening. Would she be willing to get together for lunch on a specific date or would a note or phone call be more convenient? Seniority will be a factor, as a senior executive is less likely to be a lunch partner unless you have other things in common. Then, get back to your network on a regular basis. Your goal is to remain in touch with this person without becoming annoying or needy.

One of the key tasks in a successful career information network is record keeping. It may sound funny when you are starting out and have talked with just a few individuals, but you will find that as your network grows, remembering just what you said to whom becomes a lot harder. So, begin with a good-sized package of 5×7 cards or use your computer. Use one card or page per person, beginning with name, address, phone number, and the person who referred you. Then list each conversation by date, key points you want to remember from that meeting or phone conversation, date you sent a thank-you note, and anything that you need to remember to follow up on. Then enter key dates on your calendar or tickler file.

When do you call back? Certainly when you have followed through on a suggestion someone made, that person should be the first to know. It is motivating to have someone take your advice and give you a prompt response. Even if a specific suggestion was not offered, write or call periodically with a progress report or touch base on a mutual interest. Again, you have to use your own common sense about how often is flattering rather than bothersome.

Words to the Wise

Some issues require patience. It is important to have realistic expectations. Networks work, but not always immediately. It usually takes three to six months to find a new job, sometimes longer. Your network will work and may well produce a burst of information when you begin, but key information and meaningful leads will probably come along more slowly. So, get it going and give it time, all the while nurturing it.

Don't be reluctant to involve your strongest network opportunities early in your job search; do not put this off for fear of using up all of their insights and information. That fear presumes that your network is like a bowl of apples, which once eaten, is gone. In reality, the network is more like a well that is constantly refilling. The workplace is continually changing. A network is a dynamic group with renewing ideas and information.

Your network can accomplish tremendous things for you, but you still need to do the research, follow-up, and leg work. If you make the effort, your network will be one of the most productive and enjoyable aspects of your job search!

What happens if people you want to have in your network won't see you, or you have the meeting and there really is no chemistry? If it happens once, review what you did, and make changes where your techniques need improving. Don't forget that there are people who are too busy or are not interested, and there are also well-intentioned people who simply do not make a great impression on each other. Or, a single meeting may go well, but the contact may have so many higher priorities that keeping the job seeker in mind is difficult.

If a mismatch happens multiple times, stop and trouble shoot. Go over the techniques we have stressed and think about what you are doing. Ask someone to listen to what you say and review what you do. If you seem to be on target, then think about who you are asking to be part of your network. Are you asking the right people? Maybe you are asking people who will be too busy, or at a level where they are simply not interested. Are you talking with people about subjects appropriate to them? Make sure that your questions match the expertise of the person you are talking with. Are you specific enough in what you ask, so that the person can respond and know what is expected? If not, work on refining your meeting objectives. You should be able to relate exactly what your goal is and exactly how your contact can help you. The exception is when you are in the early stages of defining a direction. Then you need to say that is what you are doing.

Remember that a good meeting is a dialogue with each person enjoying some benefits. It is not unusual to deal with nervousness by overtalking. Beware! Keep your purpose and plan for the meeting firmly in mind, and then you will not overtalk.

Mixed motives and insincere questions make bad impressions. Don't say that you are looking for information when the only question you really have is, "Do you have a job here for me?" The problem with that kind of question is that the answer has to be yes or no. There is little to say after that. The information you might have gained, if you were genuinely curious, is lost, and the door to a continuing relationship may be closed. The person feels that you are there under false pretenses, which may eventually make it more difficult to meet with others if word gets around. Your objective and your words must match!

The power and rewards of networking are demonstrated every day in personal life and work life. All of the women and men we informally talked with or formally interviewed for this book identified networking as the key part of the process of finding satisfactory work, progressing in the workplace, and maintaining personal strength and direction. Most talked about their networks as one of the most satisfying parts of their professional lives. There are many people out there with much to offer. You have much to give. This is the time to activate and build your network and watch it enrich every part of your life.

Chapter 7

Interviewing:
Lasting Impressions

Give what you have. To some one, it may be better than you dare to think.
— Henry Wadsworth Longfellow

Okay, everything has moved forward, and now you have been invited for an interview. This is a critical part of the process of landing a job. Before your interview, you will have already done your mental and physical homework, so that you have the necessary mind-set; you understand and practice the basics of communication, know the importance of dressing and behaving appropriately, and have already researched the company or position. In addition, it is helpful to know what interviewers are likely to ask. Your goal is to be relaxed, confident, smart-looking, knowledgeable, and ready to conduct the interview. Yes, that's correct; *you* need to be ready to *conduct* the interview. Why? Because many interviewers are not trained and may be as uncomfortable as you, so you might have to take the lead (very subtly!) if you want to make sure that you get to stress the points that are important to you.

A business woman we know sometimes wears a button that says, "Uncertainty is not Chaos." Being uncertain can be a marvelous incentive in the discovery of new directions or new methods for doing things. When you feel uncertain about interviewing, it is time to put on the "work clothes" and master as much of the process as possible.

What You See Is What You Get

How you choose to perceive the interview will have as much impact on the interviewer as what you actually say. Interviewing is another one of those situations in life with a tendency to release the contents of your anxiety closet. But the more you understand about interviewing, the more you can keep the closet gremlins at bay. Remember that the way in which you see or perceive your world has a direct bearing on how you feel or behave. Then, you create behaviors to support your perceptions. So, if you choose to see all interviewers as potentially devious and out to get you, and the interview process as a necessary evil, your behaviors supportive of this view are likely to be defensive, closed, and nontrusting. A woman who appears to have a chip on her shoulder is not likely to be hired. Even though you may dress appropriately, your appearance may well be tight, tense, and gloomy.

On the other hand, if you perceive the interview to be an opportunity to learn something about the company, meet an interesting person, see if you are up to the challenge, and hone up on your interviewing skills, then your behaviors that support this perception are likely to be energetic, personable, enthusiastic, open, and thoughtful. Your appearance is likely to be relaxed and your face bright. You might even put the interviewer at ease.

Demystifying the Interviewer

Most interviewers are decent folks who are simply trying to fill a job opening with the candidate who is best qualified and who will best fit in with the company or work group. They are courteous as they go about the task of finding out if you are that "best" person. In the process, interviewers may ask tough questions. They want to see if you are up to the challenge of the job. Some interviewers, on the other hand, can be difficult, unpleasant, and insulting. What you need to do is to distinguish between the challenging interviewer and the rude interviewer; then, know how to handle each.

Be very astute about assessing your interviewer, first, because you want this job, and, second, because everyone needs practice in handling a difficult person without collapsing into a heap of emotionalism. Do not jump to conclusions too quickly. Remember, your worldview is only half of the equation.

The challenging interviewer is looking for a person with energy, stamina, commitment, and the ability to get along with others. She wants someone who can function as part of a team, or conversely, be able to work alone, if required. The challenger is really looking for adaptability, strength, and the ability to handle various situations. These interviewers are apt to ask you what you would do in difficult, but plausible, circumstances. They will give you a hypothetical example to react to and come up with some possible solutions. Perhaps, the interviewer likes power and control. So what! You do also. Let us not deny in others that which we would like to possess ourselves. *Accept and respect the interviewer as she presents herself. Try not to spend a lot of time wishing she were different.*

The difficult, rude interviewer, on the other hand, also likes power and control, but uses it abusively and destructively. This person can be insulting and intimidating, and no matter how you respond will never seem to be satisfied. Nevertheless, reply to the best of your ability – sharp, clear, firm, and with total commitment. If the interviewer persists in unacceptable behavior, you need to distance yourself from her behavior. Under no circumstances should you blame yourself or own her obnoxious behavior. You might also want to distance yourself from the company. You could choose to look upon this kind of interview as just an exercise in handling difficult people. Understanding the basic rules of interview communication are a must for bringing a clear focus to the positive as well as the (hopefully rare) unpleasant moments in the interview process.

Some Basic Rules of Communication

■ **Rule 1.** *When a person talks, she is really talking about herself.* After all, who else can she be talking about other than the collection of her own life experiences and resultant attitudes? An interviewer's style, attitude, and demeanor are telling us a lot about herself, her interests, and even what is going on for her in her own life. Try not to own the interviewer's behavior if it seems unpleasant to you. She is just showing you who she is. Respond to the content of what she is asking you. Her style is only useful to you in that it tells you something about her.

■ **Rule 2.** *Maintain your personal integrity and honesty.* You will not get tongue-tied if you respond to questions honestly. In other words, be you! Be your usual, wonderful self.

■ **Rule 3.** *Listen! You can't talk and listen at the same time.* You can discover what the interviewer is looking for in a prospective candidate by listening attentively to the questions that are asked. Make eye contact in a comfortable manner. React to the content of what is being said and try not to be judgmental. Focus and be motivated to listen. Remember that by listening you are showing respect and interest in the interviewer. It is very important to respond to the questions the interviewer asks. Do not interrupt. If you do not understand the question, ask for a clarification, or repeat the question in your own words by starting with, "Do you mean ... ?"

Answering the following questions can help you define and hone up on your listening skills. Write out your responses in your notebook.

1. Under what conditions do I listen most effectively? (In the morning, when I am truly interested, etc.)

2. Under what circumstances do I have difficulty being a good listener?

(When I'm unhappy, when I'm worried about my kids, when I'm bored, etc.)

3. Define any listening problems that you have that need improvement, and write out a short and reasonable action plan to overcome the problem.

■ **Rule 4.** *Focus on what the person is saying; clear your mind of your own distractions.* Sometimes it is hard to listen because you become nervous and begin forming answers in your mind while the interviewer is still talking. It is important to stay focused and be aware of forming judgments that may not reflect what is really being asked, but are more related to your own past experiences.

Try this! Pick a day, perhaps tomorrow, and in every conversation you have with friends, coworkers, or family do some highly focused, concentrated listening. When they are talking to you, listen as if your life depended on not missing any word, concept, or idea being expressed. Don't allow any of your own thoughts to creep in, stealing away your concentration.

■ **Rule 5.** *Value and respect the interviewer as you would yourself.* Be sincere and committed to the interview. If you can get the interviewer to be comfortable and like you, then you have achieved a lot. Generally speaking, a person is hired because she is liked, and it appears that she will fit in well with the work group. Even if you are not serious about the job, it is still important to be your best, courteous, and professional self. You never know when you might cross that person's path again, or if she knows someone in another company in which you hope to interview. This scenario is more common than you would expect.

> *Two interviewers are having lunch at a personnel association conference. Interviewer A, from Energy Associates Inc., is complaining to Interviewer B, from Advanced Strategies Corporation, about how difficult it is to find committed candidates. "Why just yesterday," says A, "I interviewed this woman from Macrosound Corp. She was so casual, she wasn't even listening to most of what I said to her." "Oh," says B, "I've got a woman on my schedule from Macrosound tomorrow. What's her name?" You can imagine the rest. The worst part is that this woman really wants the job at Advanced Strategies and plans to be sharp for the interview. Even if she does interview well with B tomorrow, B is already negatively predisposed to this candidate and has information on her that would make him question her consistency, sincerity, honesty, and commitment. This is also an example of how networking can backfire if you don't pay attention to your professional presentation.*

First Impressions

Most of the time interviewers will make up their minds about you within the first one to five minutes of the interview. "Not fair," you say. We agree, but then we also know the realities of human behavior, particularly when interviewers have full work days and do not have the luxury of extending the hand of human kindness if they have a poor initial impression. If you take the care and forethought to make the initial impression a good one, the interviewer will be hooked early on. The stage will be set for the important part of the conversation (displaying your talents and depth) to be warmly received.

What many people don't realize is that the most important part of making that initial impression is not what you say. How you say something and what you look like are far more important than the words you speak. This is not to downplay the content of what you say, but rather to upgrade the important initial impression that reveals your energy, confidence, interest, and commitment to the job for which you are interviewing. In the book, *First Impression, Best Impression,* Janet Elsea says, "What you look like constitutes more than half the total message. An astonishing 55 percent of the meaning is conveyed by facial expressions and body language alone. And you haven't yet opened your mouth. Next, people focus on what they can hear. When you speak, out comes a voice with additional characteristics, among them rate of speech, loudness, pitch, tone, and articulation. These give the other person more information about you. Your voice, not including your actual words, may transmit as much as 38 percent of the meaning in face-to-face conversations; it conveys a great deal more information on the telephone, because the other person is deprived of your body language, facial expressions, gestures, eye contact, and the rest. Last, and certainly least in terms of those first few moments, the other person gets around to your words, which contribute a mere 7 percent to the meaning. It's not that your words are unimportant. But if others do not like what they see, or if they get past your body language only to be stopped by something in your voice, they may not care at all about what you say. Their minds already may be made up, their first impressions indelibly formed." (Makes you think you should have gone to charm school or majored in theater, rather than networking and studying for the interview, doesn't it!)

Professional presentation is a composite of many things. Yes, it is important to dress appropriately and be well groomed for the type of work and job setting. Your dress, posture, facial expressions, and gestures are all part of the impression you make. Your voice, including how fast you talk, the tone and pitch, softness or loudness, help determine what you sound like. But equally important is the attitude about life, people, and work that you convey, the amount of self-esteem that you project with what you say. It is essential to communicate consistency, sincerity, and integrity in order to project your image as a solid person. And again, listen, listen, listen, demonstrating to your interviewer, your ability to be a good listener. Practice different presentation components with a friend. There is no question that practice helps us to gain confidence and the ability to project and feel comfortable with ourselves.

Some General Ideas for Dress

The most important issue about proper attire is to wear something that makes you feel terrific and comfortable. If you like what you are wearing, you will project that in your posture and ease with yourself. If possible, try to get a sense of what the standard attire is in the company in which you will interview. That may mean a casual visit to the company to see for yourself or a chat with an employee. You want to give the appearance of belonging, ready to be a member of the team. Within that framework, when you look in the mirror at your chosen outfit, you need to feel very positive and confident with what you are wearing. If you have the slightest doubt, go back to your closet or your favorite clothing shop, and start over.

Basically, it is best to dress conservatively. As a woman you want to project a solid, professional, and "in control" image. Neutrality is important. You are trying to land a job, not a date. The workplace is never the place to be sexy. Jewelry should be simple, makeup as natural as possible. Do not wear perfume as its scent rarely has neutral appeal. Your hair and nails should be clean and neat. Your shoes should be polished and the heels low enough that there is no chance of tripping. Have everything ready the night before so there is no last minute anxiety about neatly pressed clothes or what accessories to wear. Any purse or handbag should be such that there is no major fumbling around to find a pen, notebook, or address book. It also should not be large or detract from your appearance. Do not let your handbag be the albatross of the interview. Many women find it easier, for organization purposes, to bring a small briefcase – one that does not require lap balancing, lock combinations, or noisy, awkward clicking of opening mechanisms.

What to Bring to the Interview

Some women question whether it is appropriate to bring a portfolio or a notebook to the interview. An interview portfolio consists of examples of your past work that you are proud of or publications or achievements that can demonstrate your skills. For some kinds of employment a portfolio is a must: any work requiring artistic abilities, drawing, photographic talents, graphic design or layout skills; employment where the company must have a sense of your creative abilities; or any work requiring writing skills, such as academic positions or law. If you are applying for a position that requires typing or computer skills, you can also bring samples of your work, particularly pieces that were challenging. Make sure that these pieces are not confidential.

During the course of your detailed research of the company, you may get some helpful clues as to what would be appropriate in a portfolio. If you are not sure what the company is looking for, it may not be a good idea to leave your whole portfolio. If, during the course of the interview, you feel that some of your portfolio is appropriate, you can choose selected items. Make sure to organize your portfolio ahead of time so items can be pulled selectively without leaving a disorganized impression.

It is important to carry a small notebook with a pen inserted in your briefcase or handbag. Women often ask whether they should take notes during the interview or wait until afterwards. Items requiring action should be jotted down quickly during the interview. The basic rule of thumb is take notes when necessary, but don't let the notetaking distract from the purpose of the interview. If a woman is constantly writing down everything the interviewer is saying, it may interfere with her ability to listen actively, prepare appropriate responses, and give an accurate impression of what she is really like. You can always sit quietly immediately afterward to write down notes about the interview, what went right or wrong, and things to include in a thank-you letter.

The day before the interview is important. It helps to eat properly, so that you will have energy and not be dragging from alcohol, too much sugar, or caffeine that could lead to sleeplessness. Some reasonable exercise or a healthy walk is helpful in reducing tension. You should try to get a good night's sleep. If you should experience some nervousness or sleeplessness, don't fret. Your body systems seem to mobilize and rarely will you feel tired during the interview.

Obstacles in Interviews

A woman we interviewed, who is an astute and successful owner of her company, has interviewed many women for positions. She shared her insights and con-cerns about women in interviews with us.

About comanaging professional and home responsibilities, she said, "Frankly, I appreciated the candidates (male and female) who made it clear that they had their personal lives and their children under control. We didn't ask them, but when they offered in conversation, 'I really feel great about where my kids go for child care. I never have to worry about them and I can concentrate fully on my work,' that was a real plus. It told us a lot about the person – her values (her children obviously come first) and her ability to manage her life. On the other hand, we interviewed a very capable person – in this case a male – who hinted that his personal life was unsettled. Though he never said so, we concluded that he didn't seem very committed to remaining in our geographic area. Needless to say, despite his qualifications, we didn't hire him."

One of the most difficult issues that women have to deal with is the bias that they won't be reliable because of allegiances to children and other day-care issues. Many employers worry that female employees will frequently be absent without warning because their children are sick, leaving the work undone and customers complaining. Even though questions regarding children are illegal before hiring (if you have them, are planning to have them, their ages, who cares for them), there are interviewers who will take a chance and ask anyway, just to make sure they hire people who will be there for them. That is a reality for employers. Make sure your child-care and other personal issues are well in hand. This is one of the important planning aspects discussed in chapter 4. A good child-care plan with a contingency plan for sickness is essential for your and your child's well-being. If you are forced to address issues about children during the interview, you can respond by saying, "It sounds like you are concerned about my being able to meet the attendance needs of the position. I can assure you that I plan my family care well and I am thoroughly committed to doing an excellent job." You may wish to slip in this point even if not asked.

"Women tend to undersell themselves. They don't know how to exude confidence and show a seriousness about the challenges of the position at the same time." Historically women do not have a strong sense of how to present themselves with confidence because the messages that women have been given until recently have been to be demure, modest, and nonassertive. If they did otherwise, it was considered unfeminine. However, it is essential that women learn to distance themselves from these messages and practice how to present and answer questions that display both confidence and a thoughtfulness about the challenges of the position. If this is difficult for you to do, it would be helpful to ask the interviewer to identify and break down the tasks of the position, showing that your interest is sincere. You can make appropriate comments about the specific aspects of the job and past experiences that show your familiarity in dealing with its components.

"Women often fumble over why they have left a former position or have had multiple job changes." If you have gaps in your employment history, anticipate a question concerning this and be prepared with an answer. At times, the explanations for these happenings can make the interview come to a dead halt. Have a well-practiced, clear explanation for these events. It helps to have written it out ahead of time and practiced with a friend or career professional. What should you

say? By all means, be honest and maintain your integrity. Under no circum-stances should you bad-mouth the company you left or fumble around so that you are perceived as disloyal, telling confidential secrets, or making blanket judgments. The company owner put it well, "We were turned off by all those who explained the inner turmoil and financial precariousness of their present employer."

If you left your previous position because you wished a specific kind of working environment, be prepared to define what that environment is. Or, if you are relatively new in the job world, and have had four different jobs in the last four years because you have been trying to find a niche for yourself where the skills you possess and the job you are in match, say so. Or, if you have done some soul-searching and career examination and you feel this is the job where your skills and the tasks required come together, say so. However, if you have been fired from four jobs in the last six years, it is time to examine (perhaps with a career or personal counselor) what is going on *before* you interview for another position. What you learn about yourself can be translated into positive language in a job interview where you convince the interviewer that, indeed, you have a very positive handle on your past mistakes or job mismatches. Be honest, firm, and prepared!

"It is amazing how many candidates failed to ask to see our product line or showed little interest in our catalog." This is basic interview preparation! It's simply good business and polite behavior (no matter what kind of interaction you have with other people) to show interest and curiosity in the other person or company, but it is especially important in an interview. Here's a chance for you to show you know something about the company, to compliment something, and to show enthusiasm and curiosity. Again, know as much as possible about the person or company with whom you are interacting. It will help you feel more in control, less scared, and definitely smarter.

"Poorly prepared resumes or cover letters with typographical errors were the kiss of death to us." Can you imagine applying for a position and not even taking the time to make sure you are handling the written word or spelling correctly? It happens all the time. This is, in many cases, your very first impression. Make it shine.

"Promptness, flexibility in arranging an interview, appearance, demeanor, and energy level are so important to us. Why are so many women candidates unaware of these essentials, and why do so many of them seem depressed?" Promptness and the courtesy of arranging a time convenient to the interviewer are essential. Why they don't happen can be ignorance, nonchalance, or just poor planning. Oftentimes, poor appearance and energy level are indeed connected to depression. Depression can hit any one of us at any time. It can be caused by any

number of events from PMS (premenstrual syndrome) to going through a divorce or the loss of a job, close friend, or family member. Some career counselors report that up to 75 percent of their clients are experiencing some stress-related event that is affecting their careers. Some people suffer depression chronically because of biochemical factors, others because of difficult present situations such as the loss of a loved one. For still others, events that happened early in life that are not yet resolved can cause depression.

In an ideal world, you would avoid interviewing at a time in your life when you are depressed or feeling down. If you are feeling very down and have absolutely no choice but to interview, try to see a professional counselor who can help you deal with your depression and assist you in being more positive. Unfortunately, you cannot expect an interviewer to have sympathy for your personal problems. Personal problems do not belong in an interview or in the workplace. If you are experiencing problems that are affecting your work or your capacity to present yourself well in the job market, get professional help! It can make a world of difference. Find a qualified counselor and be committed to the counseling process as well as to the changes you need to make.

"The whole issue of women and commitment was an underlying theme in our interviews, because frankly, we had been 'burned' twice by women who left prematurely, due to their husbands' career choices. The sense is (and I'm flabbergasted to say that our experience has been) that men at least have a choice about leaving. Women seem to be, more often, pulled (or pushed) by external circumstances. Sexist, yes, but a reality that small- to medium-sized companies can't afford to ignore. How can an equally qualified woman overcome this unspoken obstacle to landing a job where the employer will be investing time and money in her extensive training?"

The issue of the dual career couple and which job takes precedence is a relatively new one for our culture. It used to be that a woman always deferred to a man's career. Next, there was recognition that it was all right for a woman to have a career. Then, the goal was for her spouse to also value her career and respect her for her goals and accomplishments. Next, the spouse began to help with the household chores. It became more practical to defer to the mate who was producing the most income. But income is not the total answer, as many women have some enormously satisfying careers, although their salaries may never match their spouse's. So how do couples make the decision? This is still very individual among couples. Indeed, some women are pushed by their spouses to leave their careers, or they choose to defer to their spouse. Other couples take turns at having the job of their choice in the location of their choice. Still other couples combine child-rearing and work in five- to ten-year blocks, so that one spouse can get established in a career, and then the other spouse takes his or her turn.

This is not a simple issue, yet it is one that women should consider when taking a job because employers are certainly thinking about it. If the issue is presented in an interview, most potential employers simply want an honest, but reassuring response. They are not looking for lifelong commitments or crystal ball predictions. They are looking for a sense that you understand the upheaval your leaving would produce. A good response is, "In the event that I ever had to leave, it would be important to me to train my successor, and give ample notice. I care a lot about my work." If premature departure does come to pass, remember these words and make good on them.

"Many women we have interviewed had no idea how to end the interview positively with firm expectations that they will hear from us. The last impression as they leave is second only to the first impression when they arrive. Women, especially, seem to lose it here. I'm not sure why, but it's almost like they deflate before getting out the door." This is a very important comment and an essential one for women to address. We talk a lot about preparing for the interview and taking steps to assure that the initial impression is a good one. But then the energy level dissipates when the interviewee feels that the formal interview is over. You have heard the expression that the "show must go on." The interview is a performance that goes on with total energy and professionalism from the beginning to the final exit. This means a planned wrap-up of no more than a couple of minutes on your part, including the business details of finding out what the hiring schedule is, when you will hear from them, and a firm handshake while thanking them by name and with eye contact for their time.

A Sample Interview Dialogue

Sam Parker, Moose Environmental Products Inc., is interviewing Kay Gordon for a position as a manager overseeing a group of people working on the development of a product that has great promise in decomposing landfill refuse with a resulting major impact on waste management. Kay has checked in a few minutes early with Cindy Lassem, Sam's administrative assistant. Kay is careful to be polite, sincere, and friendly, knowing full well that Cindy's impression of her will probably be passed on to Sam Parker. After a few moments, Sam emerges from his office, greets Kay and has her take a seat in the middle of his office in a chair that is facing his. Kay sits down, placing her small briefcase against the chair.

Sam: *"I hope you enjoyed the ride up here on this lovely fall day."*

Standard small talk that interviewers engage in at the beginning of the interview helps both parties feel more comfortable with each other.

Kay: *"Thank you, Mr. Parker, the ride was wonderful. The hues on the trees are exceptionally brilliant in this neck of the woods. More so than my trip here three years ago."*

Kay gets a chance to slip in her knowledge of the area and the fact that she has been here before.

Sam: *"You were here three years ago?"*

Sam's interest is piqued.

Kay: *"Yes, I was involved in some research for my present company with chemicals that Moose Environmental has had extensive experience with. I met with Lisa Welling and Michael Burns who supplied some information on how they were using the chemicals. I, in turn, gave them the results of the research so that they could see if the chemicals would have greater applicability."*

Kay is using this opportunity to give Sam a couple of names within his company to check for a reference. She knows that she, Lisa, and Michael got along very well. She is also showing Sam that she knows how to collaborate for results – an important managerial skill.

Sam: *"So, you already know something about Moose Environmental?"*

Sam is checking to see what kind of research Kay has done on the company, knowing that this is the mark of a good potential employee. He makes a mental note to talk to Lisa and Michael about Kay.

Kay: *"Yes. Mr. Parker, I have done a lot of reading and talking with people in the industry and within the company. This is important to me, because I am looking for work that is challenging and can make an important social contribution. Moose has an impeccable reputation, and it meets both of my requirements."*

Kay speaks with confidence. She shows that she is a serious candidate for the job with her understanding of managerial values (corporate culture) at Moose Environmental. It is obvious to Sam that she is looking for a position with a good fit for her. She has made her own needs known early in the interview, and Sam senses that she is a determined and focused woman.

Sam: *"How would you manage a group of people to develop a product that has a deadline?"*

He needs to know whether she can lead a team under pressure.

Kay: *"The important thing is that my employees have a sense of the team. One of my strengths is to inspire people and sustain that inspiration throughout the project. To get people to produce, it is important that they feel encouraged, valued, appreciated, and rewarded for their work. That is as important as a plan with clear goals and objectives. At the very beginning of the project, I lead my team, and together we create a strategic plan. Goals, objectives, time lines, responsibilities, and methods of implementation are carefully spelled out. The team members have optimum involvement in the planning process, because they are the ones who will carry out the plan and are more invested in the project that way. During crunch time, my team meets for fifteen minutes at the beginning of every day to review and outline our goals for the day. I believe that good planning and time management reduce a lot of the panic people feel about deadline problems. I have found that pressure can be stimulating, and can actually pull the team closer together."*

Kay has given an answer that spells out her philosophy of management, as well as how she would lead under pressure. It is a question she anticipated when she did her research and found out that the manager they hired would be leading the development of a product under a deadline. She had rehearsed both parts of her answer well. She answered succinctly, in an organized manner, showing that she is a good planner, as well as a person who really cares about the people she manages.

Sam: *"Kay, what would you do, if you had an employee who suddenly became troublesome, unproductive, and was holding up the whole team because he wasn't pulling his weight?"*

Sam knows full well that, occasionally, there can be a troubled employee who can bring things to a grinding halt. He wants to see what Kay, as a manager, would do to handle the situation.

Kay: *"The first thing I would do is to schedule a private appointment with the employee away from our work area and point out to him very clearly the specifics of his declining job performance. We would talk about what he needs to do to improve and what help he would need from me or the team to get back on track again. I would give him a specific time frame in which to improve and schedule another meeting within two weeks. If he points out that he or his family are experiencing* personal problems, I would suggest to him the company's Employee Assistance Program (EAP) for assessment, counseling, or referral. I would document this or any other meeting, and what we agreed upon with the hope that would take care of the situation."

Kay can tell from Sam's question that he is concerned about both the employee and his impact on the workplace with a deadline. She tries to be specific, keeping in mind the deadlines, about how she would handle the problem. She also shows her knowledge of the company's EAP and the troubled employee procedure.

Sam: *"But Kay, what if the employee's troubled behavior continued?"*

Sam expects that this employee's behavior will continue to decline; he may even have a specific employee in mind.

Kay: *"If after the second meeting he shows no improvement and refuses to go to the Employee Assistance Program, then I would have to tell him his job is on the line. Again, I would document any meetings I have with the employee. I would have given him every chance to improve. My focus would be on his job performance, leaving any personal problems to the professionals at the EAP. If he doesn't improve, then I may very well have to fire him."*

This is a difficult situation, but Kay knows that there are times when an employee will not improve. She shows Sam that she is up to the task of firing an employee. She also shows him that she knows how to follow procedures, so that the company would not be liable.

Sam: *"Kay, I noticed from your resume that in the early part of your career you had four jobs in six years."*

Sam is concerned about her record and wonders whether she would really have the commitment to the company.

Kay: *"When I first got out of school and was young, I wasn't as sure as I am now about what I wanted to do. I see those years as invaluable for gaining experience about what kind of workplace I ultimately wanted to be in. Those four jobs were all different and gave me some good insights and a base for where I am heading now. I chose those changes for reasons of interest, not any personnel or personal issues. Three of those companies wanted me to continue with them and the fourth went out of business. And as you can see, in the last two jobs, I have stayed for five years, and four and a half years."*

Kay has given a reasonable answer here, pinning her early changes on youth and wanting to further define what she really wanted to do.

Sam: *"Kay, if you join the company, what do you see yourself doing in five to ten years from now?"*

This can be a difficult question, because Kay needs to strike a balance between sounding too modest or too ambitious. Specificity about a particular job may actually be seen as limiting. In addition, she needs to demonstrate that she has thought about the future. Sam asks this question because he feels that a good manager thinks and plans ahead for herself as well as for work-related projects.

Kay: *"I am very excited about the prospect of working at Moose Environmental. I would like to be part of the challenges and the products the company will be developing over the next five years. I feel I can bring a lot of expertise to this job, as well as derive a great deal of professional and personal growth. Ultimately, I would like to gain enough knowledge and experience to be regarded as a top professional in the industry."*

Kay has given an honest answer. She states her desire to be with Moose Environmental for the next five years. She cannot say what kind of job she would like in ten years from now, but she is clear about the level of expertise she would like to attain.

The rest of the interview proceeds well. Kay asks a few questions about the product and deadlines to be developed. Because so many of Sam's questions were directed toward problem employee and management issues, she asks whether there have been production or personnel problems. In addition, she asks whether a new manager coming in might have to resolve past problems. Kay also checks with Sam to find out when she can expect to hear back and whether there will be further interviews.

Sam Parker has a good impression of Kay. She is forthright and knowledgeable about the company and its needs for this position. She has demonstrated a management style totally compatible with the company and a sensitive, realistic picture of deadlines and stress. Although he has a couple of other good candidates, Kay will definitely be called back for a second interview to meet others in the company.

Call-Back or Second Interviews

Some companies will contact you for a second interview. Usually this means that there has been some weeding out of the group of candidates, and you have made it successfully through the selection process. Here are some things to keep in mind when you are called back for a second interview.

★ Review your notes to determine your strong and weak areas.

★ Find out who will conduct the second interview, what that person's position is, and what the format will be.

★ Research the second interviewer's areas of concentration relative to the position you are seeking.

★ Be aware that the questions will be more detailed and more specific. Anticipate these questions and rehearse your answers.

★ Write a thank-you note to the people who interviewed you.

Kay finds out before leaving Sam Parker's office that there will most likely be a call-back interview. When she leaves the interview, she sits in her car with her notebook and writes down every question she can remember. She jots down what she feels went well and what she might have done better. She analyzes what she felt Sam Parker's interests were and also notes what answers she would address with more depth in a second interview. When she returns home, she immediately writes a thank-you note to Parker. When he calls her to set up an appointment, she plans to ask who will interview her (and what the interviewer's position is). Once she gets the names, she will try to determine what the interviewer's interest is in her position. She can ask Sam Parker directly, or if he is vague, she might ask people she knows in the company. Most likely, Sam will provide that information for her and admire her again for her thoroughness.

Kay can expect more detailed, in-depth questions. The interviewers will take her from the general questions of her first interview with Parker to more specific responses, while they try to get a picture of how she would actually do the job and work with her staff. They might ask her the specifics of her plan to get the product developed as well as her priorities for doing so. Kay will have to listen carefully to their questions, pause, and try to determine their interests, so that she can address those as well as the content of their questions. There is the likelihood of meeting with more individuals or groups of people. Certainly, she would be interviewed by others who would interface with her department. As part of her plan to prepare for the second interview, she arranges to spend time with her friend, Barbara, an experienced manager, to develop more detailed responses to questions she anticipates as well as ones that Barbara will pose to her.

During the second interview, Kay met with a number of different people in the company. She did a fine job of understanding the interests of each person or group of people she talked with. Most of their questions were directed toward the details of developing the product, her planning abilities, and how she would motivate the team to produce. She had anticipated this emphasis because in her scouting for information, she had discovered that the previous manager was not a good planner or motivator. She was able to find out the specifics of the dissatisfaction. She felt strongly that she had the skills to correct this situation, and she was sure to emphasize them. The end result was that Sam Parker called Kay and offered her the job. They set up a meeting to talk about salary issues. (We will catch up with Kay and Sam again in their negotiations in chapter 8.)

Interview Formats

The One-Person Interview

For the most part, expect an interview with just one person if you are going to be working exclusively with that person, if you are going to be paid on an hourly basis, or if you are a salaried nonmanagerial or nonsupervisory employee, such as a clerk or secretary. Most of the time you will be interviewed directly by the person with whom you will work most closely. However, you may be interviewed by a human resource or personnel specialist, or your potential boss may delegate hiring responsibilities to another person in the company whose judgment she respects.

The human resource/personnel specialist may actually do what is known as a screening interview to pare down the number of candidates appropriate for the position. At this level, candidates without the necessary skills or experience for a particular position are eliminated. Sometimes this may be done by telephone.

Unfortunately, if your strong suit is personal appearance, and your weak one a telephone conversation, you could be weeded out over the phone. Sometimes there are ways to avoid the telephone screening. If the telephoner calls you at the office, you can say that you are not in a position to discuss another job from your work site. If she says she can speak to you in the evening, you can try to explain why this would not work and tell her it would be best if you met with her personally, and that you would be glad to arrange your schedule to suit hers at her place of work.

In the case of the boss who assigns someone else to do the interviewing, you again may find yourself in a screening interview. If not, you are in an awkward position. After all, you need to know whether or not you are going to feel comfortable or "click" with the person you'll be working for. Many times, the boss only meets the final two or three candidates. You can ask at what point in the interview process you can expect to speak with your potential boss. You have every right to meet your boss and you can diplomatically tell the stand-in interviewer something like, "Obviously Mr. Elusive has great faith in your ability to hire for him and I respect that, but it is very important for me to have a sense of the person I will work for." If the stand-in interviewer refuses, it is usually because those are the directions that have been given. Then you have to ask yourself, "What does this tell me about this potential boss?" It may mean that he likes a lot of distance between himself and his employees. It might mean that you would be free to do your work quite independently, or it may also mean that your boss would be the unavailable type, frequently unclear about assignments and expectations. You could do a lot of guessing or get right to the point and ask the stand-in interviewer what the boss is like, what kind of work or assignment style the potential boss has, or even why the boss does not interview his employees himself. The trick here, though, is not to sound as if you need to have the boss around all the time in order to function on the job. Assess what information you have been given, and trust your feelings as to whether this boss is for you.

The Group Interview

If you will be working for many people, crossing different department lines, or are at the managerial or professional level, you will often be interviewed in a group format or by a team. You may be interviewed individually for the first hour and then speak with a larger group at other times during the day or over a period of a few days. A client once experienced an interview for a position that in essence serviced the whole company. Her interview schedule started at 8:00 A.M. The first three hours were individual interviews from three different people representing different areas of the company. Lunch was with the personnel director of the company. Two people representative of employee groups followed. Then, a group interview with the professionals and staff of the office in which her program would be located took place. The day ended with two interviews with upper management officers. Each member of the day's interviewing team submitted a written evaluation, and a smaller committee from the interview team made the final decision.

This was a standard group interview. These interviews provide for a very long day. It is very important to be well rested and as relaxed as possible. There is a tendency as the day wears on to let down on your listening and questioning skills. If you recognize this tendency, you can remind yourself throughout the day to remain focused. It also helps to eat a light lunch devoid of sweets and alcohol to avoid the sleepiness that is common after a heavy meal.

Other Formats

It is not unusual to be asked to submit to some psychological, career interest, or aptitude tests. The employer is looking for additional information beyond the interview to determine whether the candidate's personal characteristics meet the requirements of the job. These tests can be used to determine attitudes, temperament, values, interests, or ability. Unfortunately, they tend to measure a narrow range of a person and, hopefully, would never be used in place of an interview, but only as a vehicle for additional information. It is best to respond to these inventories truthfully rather than how you think you ought to respond. Some people feel it is possible to "psych" them out, but why try when what you want from a job is the best possible match. Always try to take these tests when you are alert and well-rested. If you are asked to take them at the end of the interview day, say that you have other obligations, but would be happy to return first thing in the morning.

You may also be asked to perform an actual job task that would be required if you got the job. You would then be rated individually or by a team. In these situations, the employer is looking for such skills as reasoning ability, accuracy, how you approach and conceptualize a problem, how you interface with other people, and your ability to verbalize and accurately describe the process.

What Do You Know about the Company?

One of the best tools you bring to the interview is well-researched information on the company or type of work. Gathering information is always a creative and inventive process. Start with the most obvious method: speaking with someone who works there. Obtain any descriptive brochures, financial reports, or advertising material that the company produces. Check in with the nearest public or university library and ask the reference librarian what kinds of material would be available on Company Z and how you go about finding it. Treat this person well as she or he is an invaluable resource. Read local business magazines and check the local newspaper in the library or on microfiche for recent articles pertaining to that particular company or industry.

For each company that you plan to interview, make a large index card to record pertinent data. That card should contain the company name, street address and mailing address, telephone number, type of business, contact person, CEO, names and titles of people in leadership positions in departments you are interested in, general business data such as earnings, profit and loss statements, stock price (particularly important if the company has an employee stock purchase plan), the market area the company covers, Dunn and Bradstreet reports on the company's credit, and finally, names of people in the company you know.

Typical Interview Questions

Typically two different categories of questions are presented to women candidates. In the first category are the typical questions used by the interviewer to acquire basic knowledge about you, your qualifications, and how you and the company might interact. In the second category are the illegal, discriminatory questions which, unfortunately, are still asked all too often.

The usual questions:

★ Why are you interested in working for this company?

★ What can you contribute to this company?

★ What are your strengths?

★ What are your weaknesses?

★ What limitations do you have that would impact on this job?

★ What have been three career accomplishments to date?

★ Why should I hire you?

★ Have you ever been fired or forced to resign?

★ Why did you leave your last job?

★ What do you think of the company you are working for now?

- ★ What do you think of your boss?

- ★ Why have you been unemployed for so long?

- ★ Why do you change jobs so often?

- ★ What kind of supervisor do you like best? Why?

- ★ How do you get along with people?

- ★ How do you handle anger?

- ★ How do you handle stress?

- ★ Are you willing to take on assignments requiring travel?

- ★ Are you willing to be transferred?

- ★ How long will you stay with this job?

- ★ What are your long-term goals?

- ★ What are your salary requirements?

The second category, the illegal or discriminatory questions, present some difficult choices. The law protects you from having to answer them, but you may choose to offer some response, particularly if you feel that the interviewer is naive rather than malicious. You can take the opportunity to turn a difficult situation into a more positive and creative one by addressing the legitimate concerns of the employer even if you have not been correctly questioned.

If, however, you feel that the questions are being presented by a difficult, unpleasant interviewer, you may not want to answer or even continue the interview. You can take legal action against a company if you are angry and insulted by what has happened. It is important to weigh the benefits for you. You should consult a lawyer who can advise you whether your action has merit or can be successful. You also have the option of making the interviewer aware of what he is doing either directly or subtly. You can say, "I don't believe that question is relevant to my ability to do the job." You could ask for his card and tell him that you are going to report him to the Equal Employment Opportunity Commission (EEOC). The following are some typical illegal questions and some suggested responses. Please notice that the answers turn the focus toward the way the question pertains to the job.

Theoretically, an interviewer cannot ask questions based on

Sex: marital status, the presence of children, their ages, child-care arrangements, what you will do if your husband is transferred

Possible response: "I am very committed to my work, being there at all times, and completing my tasks with the highest quality. If something comes up in my home life, I have contingency plans which will not interfere with my work."

Age: how old you are, your birth date, your feelings about working for a younger or older person (unless it is critical to the job, i.e., adolescent to model teenage sportswear)

Possible response: "I have a wealth of experience, enjoy working with all kinds and ages of people, and I get along with everybody."

Religion: Church or synagogue membership, work that might be missed due to religious holidays

Possible response: "My religious preference has no relationship or any bearing on my ability to complete my work."

Race or skin color: questions pertaining to your heritage

Possible response: "I don't think race has anything to do with a person's job. That has been my experience since I've frequently worked with people from varied backgrounds."

National origin: what country you were born in, where your parents or siblings were born, what your citizenship is

Possible response: "I don't know what that question could possibly have to do with my extensive work experience, unless you've heard that I make a great *arroz con pollo.*"

Disabilities: whether you have any and to what degree of severity, what kind of special assistance you might need to do your job

Possible response: "I am very well-trained and an excellent employee. Any adaptations I might need are minor and I can work them out with my manager."

The Interviewee as the Interviewer

All right, the interviewer has had his time with you; now it is your turn. This is the point where you can take some control and ask questions that will help you in making a decision about the appropriateness of this job for you, while displaying your intelligence and commitment to the job. Do not be afraid to ask questions; after all, this employer is fortunate to get such a talented person as yourself. Frequently women feel subservient to employers and are afraid to make their case or project their career talents. No longer! Women are as vital in the American work force as are men.

Try to envision a work setting that you would like to be in and think about the kinds of information you would need to know before accepting that job. What is important is that you have some pertinent questions to ask that do two things: get you information that you need (remember you have to decide if this is the right job for you) and display your perceptiveness and awareness about the field and your areas of expertise. The latter is especially important if the interview has not yet provided an opportunity for you to strut your stuff. Take the time right now to write out ten sample questions that would allow you to accomplish these two things.

Some sample questions you might ask:

★ Can I answer any questions for you regarding my resume?

★ Can you describe the duties and the responsibilities of the job for me?

★ What kind of characteristics are you looking for in the candidate?

★ Is this a new position?

★ Why was it created?

★ Have there been any personnel or production problems in this department?

★ What are the department's strengths and weaknesses?

★ Have there been problems between employees and the past manager in the job that might impact and need to be resolved?

★ What are your company's plans for expansion?

★ What kind of career path is typical for your employees?

★ How is performance measured?

★ Is there a consistent management style that the company endorses?

★ Could you please describe this style?

★ What type of training or orientation do you offer for new employees?

★ It is important to be on time and give a firm, dry handshake (wipe palms with handkerchief before going into the interview).

★ Generally speaking, it is best not to ask questions about salary until you receive the job offer. However, if the interviewer wants to discuss salary, then be prepared to do so. You can find out about benefits separately by phoning the personnel department. (Salary and benefits issues will be covered in chapter 8.)

★ Never appear to be a complainer, particularly about your present or past jobs or bosses. Never bring up personal problems or let the interviewer trap you into that discussion by bringing up his own personal issues. Just listen, but don't try to make the interviewer feel comfortable by bringing up problems of your own.

★ Before the interview, prepare a list of your strongest qualifications for this job. If the interviewer does not ask you questions that allow you to make the points that are important to you, find tactful ways to insert these points into the interview.

★ Don't be overly friendly with the interviewer or joke when she is being serious.

★ Try not to fill silences with nervous responses. There is no crime in pausing for a well-planned response to a question.

★ After the interview is over, write a thank-you note to the interviewer. You also might want to write a note to a secretary if you have had meaningful contact with that person.

We were fortunate to interview a top female executive, who is extremely successful in the placement or "head-hunting" field. She has held top level positions herself in both the banking and political fields. Her main focus is to place upper level human resource executives in national and international companies. We asked her to comment on interviews from the point of view of the business arena. We are grateful for her wise comments which follow.

"You have approximately sixty seconds to make an initial impression, and, if an interviewer is a poor one, that impression may be the only one she takes away with her. What you wear, how you shake hands, your eye contact, and your first few sentences are crucial, especially if your interviewer is inexperienced.

"A good interviewer will start off the interview with some small talk to warm you up and to relax you. You should, in fact, try to relax and talk informally with her for the first few minutes. This is the time to talk about the person who referred you, if such is the case, or about the weather, or about the helpfulness of her assistant or the attractiveness of the company's building . . . or whatever. You are pretty much on your own for these first two minutes. Your cocktail party small talk training should get you through.

"If the interviewer wants to plunge right in, plunge with her. Do not try to take over the interview. Exerting some control is all right to get some points across, but again do not take over. Even if this is the job of your dreams, and the interviewer is warm and wonderful, do not get carried away with your enthusiasm. Interviewers become very angry when the interview is taken away from them.

"Answer all questions concisely using anecdotes or examples whenever you can. This is not the time to philosophize. This is the time to discuss with some specificity what you've accomplished in your previous jobs. Of course, all this gets thrown out the window if the interviewer wants to talk about football, or children, or the state of public education in the United States. But no matter how the interview is going, be aware of the cues that tell you it is over (shuffling of papers on the desk, looking at a watch, eyes that start to wander and perhaps even the odd yawn, all let you know that it is time to wrap up).

"Do not overstay your welcome. Many jobs have been lost because the person being interviewed misread all the cues and continued on with her story or asked two or three questions too many, when the time had come to leave. If the interviewer is bad, however, and never gets to who you are and why your skills are perfect for the available job, you must look for an opening to give what I call a closing statement — one that sums up for her who you are, what your skills are, and why the company should hire you. You will almost always get to insert this closing statement because at the end of the interview, even the worst interviewers will ask if you have any questions or anything else you want to say. That's your moment to tell him or her everything or almost everything he or she forgot to ask. The closing statement, however, should take no longer than two minutes to deliver!

"Try to avoid talking about money at the first interview. You don't want to screen yourself out at this point by asking for a salary figure that may be too high, and you certainly do not want to ask for a figure that may be way too low. If the interviewer insists on talking about salary at this point, turn the question around and ask him or her what range the company has in mind; in short, do anything you can to avoid this topic until after the company has decided it can't live without you and you know more about the job and the people you'll be working with.

"Things to remember are: firm handshake, strong eye contact, no nervous mannerisms (foot shaking, hair stroking, chin rubbing, etc.), a little elegant small talk, promptness, and conservative use of make-up and perfume. In addition, be sure to send a short, one-page thank-you note when you return home after the interview. Send it off immediately while the interview is fresh in your mind."

Chapter 8

Negotiating:

Asking for What You

Want, Need, and Deserve

Once you say you're going to settle for second, that's what happens to you in life— John F. Kennedy

We knew that we were going to be explorers looking for new lands when we asked one of the successful women we interviewed to tell us all she knew about women in the negotiation process. Her response was to back away from the issue, saying, "The truth is that I could never do that for myself; let me know what you find out." Yet, here was an eminently successful woman in her field – bright, charming, assertive, and attractive, having "all the right stuff." It was obvious that she had been doing a lot of negotiating for her corporation and for herself to have achieved what she had. So why did she, like many women, identify negotiation as an unknown area in her experience?

From what we know and have observed, it isn't that women cannot, or even have not, been negotiating, but rather that they do not think of themselves as negotiators. Actually, women negotiate their way through much of what they do, but since they do not think of it in terms of negotiation, the idea seems foreign, intimidating, and outside their realm of experience when they are confronted with a formalized salary or benefits negotiation. The tendency, then, "because we've never done this before," is to let the other party provide the negotiation's structure and guidelines, thereby relinquishing our share of the control from the outset. "Leaving it to others" – now that is a familiar role! Leaving what appears to be the "business stuff" to the "experts" is something many women automatically do, believing that the expertise resides somewhere "out there."

In the book, *Women's Ways of Knowing,* the authors discuss the concept of "received knowledge," which is the idea that many women learn by listening. They point out that for these women, words are central to the knowing process. "While received knowers can be very open to take in what others have to offer, they have little confidence in their own ability to speak. Believing that truth comes from others, they still their own voices to hear the voices of others." These women frequently bypass their own perfectly good judgment in a negotiation session because they are inexperienced in using or trusting their own voices or belief systems.

Sally was told by Josh Stager, personnel director of the Playful Creations Corporation, that there would be a position available for her. Their initial interview had been pleasant, and she felt she had good rapport with him. They were due to meet in two days to make the final decision which would be based partially on nego- tiations about salary and benefits. Sally was a diligent woman and she really wanted this position, so she decided to try to find someone who knew Stager to give her some tips on what he would be like in the salary negotiation process. An acquaintance gave her the name of a former employee, Vivian. Vivian told Sally over the phone that Josh did not like assertive women who were direct in their requests. She suggested that Sally be "demure," letting Stager take the lead. This was of concern to Sally, because she had always been straightforward about her salary and benefit needs with her past employers.

When Sally sat down with Stager, she was confused about how to act, but tried to heed Vivian's advice. Josh took the lead and asked Sally what her needs were. Sally, untypically quiet, responded by asking what the company had in mind. Josh immediately became confused by her reply and thought, "Wow, this is not what I expected her to say. She is acting differently than when she was here two days ago. I offered her the position because her potential boss is looking for an assertive, straightforward person to deal with some difficult clients. She seemed to be that kind of person, but now I'm not sure. I'll come in low and see what she does with it." He offered Sally a starting salary of $28,000 plus the standard benefits package. She then asked him whether he could do better. He said, "not really," giving her a slight opening to come back. Sally didn't know what to do and told him she would think about it. It was too late. Josh had already decided that he had misjudged her and that he would try to discourage her from the position.

When she called back a day later, he jumped right into the conver- sation and told her that after reassessing her candidacy, he had realized that she did not fit the position. He said that she had initially made a wonderful impression, and that she possessed a *lot of talents, but needed to work on her assertiveness for this kind of position. Sally thanked him, hung up, and felt betrayed and foolish. It didn't take her more than two minutes to realize that she had taken the word of a stranger over the phone to assess Josh. And the worst part of it was that she had already developed a good rapport with him. "Why, oh why, didn't I trust my own judgement and be myself, or at least do my homework on Vivian?" Sally learned a good lesson from all of this—that her own judgment and inner voice had been holding her in good stead to this point. She realized the need to affirm that.*

A theme running through this book is that the process of the job search and work for women takes a lot of forethought. It requires some honest soul searching about the perceptions women bring to any situation. In the process, women need to acknowledge and rely upon their vast inner wells of experience and knowledge.

Remember Kay's interview in chapter 7? Let's rejoin Kay as she sits with Sam Parker of the Moose Environmental Products Company.

Kay is thrilled. The day before Sam had called her and offered her a job as a manager overseeing a group of people working on the production of a product with great promise in decomposing land-fill refuse and a resultant major impact on waste management. The job matched her desire to work for a company that could offer her a challenge, as well as involve her in socially responsible tasks and issues. The purpose of the meeting was to discuss salary.

Sam offered her a $35,000 starting salary, $1,000 more than her current job. Kay was disappointed. She had researched the industry and talked with people who had previously worked for Moose Environmental, and the starting salary for two others hired nine months ago was in the range of $40,000-$45,000.

Kay: *"Mr. Parker, it is my understanding that people hired here in the last year as managers have started at $45,000."*

Sam: *"That is true, Kay, but we have had to cut back because of competition and the need to pour more of our resources into product development. There have been a lot of layoffs in the industry and we know that we can hire people at a lower starting salary now."*

Kay, thinking about what Sam said, agreed with his analysis and was about to capitulate, when she remembered the advice of one of her savvy friends:

Buy some time to think if you do not like the way the negotiation is going.

Kay: *"Mr. Parker, I'd like to think your offer over."*

Sam: *"Sure, Kay, but I need to know your answer by the end of the day tomorrow."*

Later, sitting with her sage friend, Barbara, Kay bemoaned, "Darn it, Barb, I can't afford to take that job with such a small increase. I'm so upset because it is the perfect situation for me, and I know I have ideas that could make a smashing success out of that product. I've had a lot of experience with the chemical composition required for that type of product. As a matter of fact, I was involved with some experiments a few years ago and I know from what I learned then that I could get my team to produce that product in far less time than they think and beat out their competition."

Barb: *"Kay, do you realize how valuable you would be to that company? Come on, Kay, use your creativity. You ought to be able to sell yourself at a whopping salary for what you could deliver."*

Kay: *"But, Barb, Parker said they could hire any number of people at the lower figure."*

Barb: *"Kay, listen to yourself. You already sold me on why they should hire you. Why don't you sit down tonight and put a proposal together for Parker. You have nothing to lose and everything to gain. Make him an offer where you both come out winners and see what happens."*

The next day Kay walked into Sam Parker's office.

Sam: *"Well, Kay, what have you decided?"*

Kay: *"Hear me out, Mr. Parker. I have a terrific proposal for you. I feel strongly from my knowledge and past experiences that I can bring the landfill product to market within eight months. I know that your marketing department is planning an announcement in a year. I also know that Chase Ecological Systems is trying to develop something similar. This is my proposal. If I meet my self-imposed deadline, you stand to gain some valuable contracts that will double your corporate earnings from last year. My salary needs are at the $55,000 level. It would be too costly for me to consider changing jobs and moving for anything less. I* want you to guarantee me that you will give me a salary of $55,000 retroactive to my starting date, if I can get that product developed in this time frame. If we don't meet the deadline, then I will accept a salary of $37,000 for this first year."

Sam: *"Well, Kay, you've put together quite a proposal, but I can't do it because it would be unfair to the other managers."*

Kay: *"Mr. Parker, if I meet that deadline, the other managers would love it, because it would mean an unexpected increase for them and perhaps everyone else in the company." And in a tone of voice meant not to be threatening, she continued, "And you know what, Mr. Parker? How can you afford not to hire me? If I look for a job elsewhere, another company would have my expertise. Look, Mr. Parker, you can't lose. I'm creative, I can motivate people, and I'm a great worker. And, in addition, the company really stands to benefit. How about it?"*

Sam: *"Well, Kay, you really do have guts. I admire that. Look, I can't promise you anything, but I'm going to go to the president and really push for you. Call me in two days."*

Kay got the job on her terms. She and her team produced the product in six months instead of eight and her first year salary was $55,000 plus a $7,000 bonus.

As the authors of Women's Ways of Knowing stated so well, to learn to speak in a unique and authentic voice, women must "jump outside the frames and systems authorities provide and create their own frame." Kay did create her own frame. For the first time in her career, she jumped out of the system, listened to her own voice and judgment within, and began to see herself as an authority. Once this happened, Kay could negotiate with confidence.

False Messages

When considering how you handle negotiating, it is important again to recall those early influences. How did your family handle their issues, arguments, or disagreements as individuals or with other family members? Did people sit down and talk things through when someone wanted something or was there a lot of yelling, screaming, and accusing? Or did family members choose to "clam up," ignore requests, and refuse to talk at all? If we learned early that it was permissible to ask for things and that our requests were respected (even though not necessarily granted), or conversely that it was hopeless to try, then we are apt to carry over those messages, allowing them to influence how we deal with negotiation today.

Many of us feel like running in the other direction when we think of being involved in a negotiation. The idea of "working through" a negotiation process or asking for what we want often feels like a hopeless task that will only exacerbate existing tension. On some level, we tend to equate negotiation with conflict, especially if we learned at a young age that asking for something for ourselves actually led to conflict. How we view and deal with negotiating is often an "historical" issue with us. It is deeply rooted in our exposure to similar issues by significant people in our lives such as parents, brothers and sisters, teachers, and friends.

The truth is that many women by nature, by experience, or through roles that have been thrust on them by society, possess tremendous skills that are transferable into the negotiation arena. We have continually negotiated within our families, communities, and jobs for what we believe our children, spouses, community agencies, or workplaces have needed. Many of us, however, are less used to negotiating for ourselves. We are terrific listeners; we are very intuitive about what others are feeling and are sensitive to their needs and wants. Women tend to be flexible in their thinking with a willingness to see and examine both sides of an issue. We have the natural intuitive skills to excel at negotiation. All we are lacking is the belief in ourselves as well as the models to set positive examples of those skills in action.

In order to feel comfortable in the negotiation process, a woman must first define her needs, whether they be salary, benefits, or job responsibilities. But the modeling for most women over thirty-five, and many younger women, too, is that their primary role is to take care of others' needs first. Women frequently have stifled their own needs to the point where they do not even know what it is they want, let alone how to ask for it. If you have had trouble focusing and feeling comfortable about meeting your own needs, it is very important to acknowledge that, come to terms with it, and do whatever is necessary to reverse the process. For you to be successful in any negotiation process, or indeed in the workplace itself, many times it just takes acknowledging that you need to be clear and well-defined about what you want. This isn't selfish or self-centered; rather it is appropriate, honest, and in your best interest. There is no need to give up the role of looking out for others, but when you have your own best interest at heart, the people around you usually fare better because they know where you stand. The stronger you are, the stronger they can be, and the more honest the relationship can be.

Women find very few models for acceptable negotiation behaviors in the media. Books, articles, movies, newspapers, television, and radio often convey mixed messages to women. One day the message seems to be that women are not assertive enough. Another day they hear that they are too aggressive or too set in their ways or too quick to change. It's no wonder that confusion sets in, followed by the tendency to participate in a "paralysis of action." Yes, it is important to examine what is being said about women, but don't get confused by always trying to please. Instead, be yourself, develop your own sense of integrity, and determine what your needs are. Again, it is important to develop your own voice and be at peace with your own style of behavior. When you can do this, then you can enter any negotiation – formal or informal, in your personal life or your work life – and get what you need and still feel very good about yourself.

It is important to realize that negotiating for your needs and wants is a natural aspect of human behavior. You are doing it all the time. Familiarizing yourself with the process in a more defined and formal way will result in a more satisfying work experience. However, to make this happen, both parties need to be willing and committed to resolving the issues before them. It also means that all parties need to recognize that they each will have differing interests, issues, and points of view.

Defining Your Negotiating Self

Fortunately, women are more apt than men to explore their personal dynamics. Self-knowledge about certain personal characteristics is a necessity during any negotiation process. This willingness to examine their own strengths and weaknesses is a special strength that many women possess. In order to negotiate effectively, it helps to understand what you bring to the table. To define this in advance will make you a more skillful negotiator. The following list of questions is a solid step in the process of defining your attributes and eliminating those qualities that can hinder you. Grab your notebooks and fill in your answers to these questions.

How do you feel about asking for something for yourself?

Would you describe yourself as an aggressive or an assertive woman?

When are you aggressive?
When are you assertive?

Are you an ambitious person?
What are your ambitions?

Are you an angry person?
What triggers your anger?
How do you display your anger?

Are you a fair person?

What happens to you when you don't get your way?
What is your attitude toward compromise?

Do you consider yourself a good communicator?
What are your communicating strengths?
What are your communicating weaknesses?

Are you a good listener?
How could you improve your listening skills?

Do you feel that people listen to you when you speak to them?
If so, what are some of the characteristics you possess that allow people to hear what you say?
If people do not generally listen to you, why do you think this is so?

How do people react to you?
Under what circumstances do you react defensively?

Are you known to have a good sense of humor?
How does your humor help you?
How does your humor hinder you?

Carefully considering the answers to these questions will make you more acutely aware of your positive attributes, as well as the pitfalls you'll want to avoid. Spending the time defining yourself will help you to enhance your position during negotiation because you will have a clear sense of how much you have to offer. And, too, you will be reminded of behaviors that are unproductive for you and that you will want to avoid during the negotiation process.

More Than Salary

Frequently when women think of landing a job and negotiating, the issue of salary is the only one they focus upon. Consider the importance of some of these other issues before you enter a negotiating session so that you will know what it is you need to ask for.

★ Medical and dental insurance for you and your family or membership in an HMO (health maintenance organization)

★ Pension or retirement plan

★ Accidental death insurance

★ Travel insurance

- ★ Disability insurance
- ★ Life insurance
- ★ Paid membership in professional associations
- ★ Annuity bonuses
- ★ Vacations and holiday schedules
- ★ Sick leave
- ★ Sick child leave
- ★ Bereavement leave
- ★ Educational assistance
- ★ Dependent scholarships
- ★ Maternity benefits (don't negotiate this, but know what the company policy is)
- ★ Use of company car
- ★ Job description – your responsibilities and tasks

For executive or managerial positions, you may be negotiating for the following:

- ★ Severance pay (sometimes known as "the golden handshake")
- ★ Stock options
- ★ Relocation costs; moving, housing, real estate costs, problem of not being able to sell your house in order to move, payments for temporary housing and meals while looking for new housing
- ★ Assistance for spouse who has to find a new job

Benefits and perks have a dollar value in the range of 10 to 30 percent of your salary and are often negotiable when the salary isn't because of company limits. The key to getting the salary, benefits, and perks you would like and need lies in your advance investigation of what is possible. To get the best idea of salaries in your field consult *The Occupational Outlook Handbook,* which can be found in the reference section of most libraries. This book describes occupations and their typical salaries. It also lists other sources of salary surveys for various positions. The magazine, *Working Woman,* publishes an annual survey of many fields and also has many helpful articles and hints on the job climate and search process. Of course, it is essential that you find out specific salary ranges in the company with which you have an interview or job offer.

Determine your needs very carefully so that you don't get caught accepting a salary that is too low or an inadequate benefits package. If you feel inexperienced in making that determination, consult an accountant, banker, or financial planner. Most of the time there is a suggested cost of living range for geographic area and family size. Please remember that if you are relocating you will have to gather information for moving expenses and cost of living estimates for such things as housing, food, child care, transportation, and parking in your new community. Your local bookstore has many resources to help you figure your living expenses and calculate your needs. Author Richard Bolles in *What Color Is Your Parachute?* suggests that you investigate the salaries of the persons above and below you in the organizational chart to see what your salary range would be.

Sometimes you will be negotiating for specific items such as a salary figure, benefits, or educational support. Other times you will be negotiating areas that actually involve what the tasks of your job might be as compared to those of your coworkers or even your manager. Or even how involved you will be in managerial or agency board meetings.

At The Negotiating Table

★ Listen. It is essential that you utilize the principals of good listening discussed in chapter 7. This will enable you to go beyond just hearing the words to appreciating what is being said on a deeper level.

★ Be honest and open. Maintaining your integrity is the only way you will respect yourself and not get fouled up trying to dance around an issue.

★ Focus on issues, not on personalities. Staying focused on the task before you and getting what you want is primary. Never slip into a mode of blaming the other person or commenting on personalities if things are not going your way.

★ Compromise. The most successful negotiation is one in which both sides feel they have won. Bad feelings can be engendered if you are so unyielding that you go beyond "strong" and into "impossible."

★ Define agreed upon plans and resultant actions. It is important to turn the details of the final negotiation into actions. Talk about the who, what, where, and when of any decisions.

There are many styles and techniques of negotiation. We happen to subscribe to the school of win/win negotiation where both sides emerge feeling that they have what they need, are ethical in their dealings, and are respectful of each other. It is hard to predict what others will do in their style of negotiation, but it is our experience that everyone fares better when no clever schemes, tricks, or politics designed to outwit the other party in the negotiation are involved.

Negotiation clearly requires careful forethought and personal planning. A mentor once told us never to go into any kind of meeting without knowing ahead of time what we would like the outcome to be. A woman who has taken the time to determine what her goals are (as well as those of the other party) has a distinct advantage in the actual negotiation. Knowing the facts and having a sense of her negotiating self gives her increased self-confidence. She can then concentrate on the process of thoughtful and careful listening and responding, instead of feeling panicky.

The following exercise will help you understand the issues and clarify your negotiation plans. It can be used to prepare for many types of negotiation, including salary, benefits, conflict, and personal relationship issues. You may find it helpful to review your thoughts and responses to exercises in chapters 3 and 4 before jotting down your responses to these questions.

Negotiating Fact-Finder Exercise

1. Clearly define the issue, needs, and your personal goals before beginning a negotiation.

What do you want?

What do you think the other person wants?

2. If this is a negotiation about an issue with a conflict, how do you think others who are involved or know of the situation might see the problem? (It may be helpful to gather other legitimate insights.)

3. What characteristics and beliefs do you have that might contribute in a positive way to the success of the negotiation?

4. What characteristics and beliefs do you have that might hamper the success of the negotiation?

5. What characteristics or beliefs does the other person have that might be positive for the negotiation? How could you encourage these qualities in the other party?

6. What characteristics and beliefs does the other person have that might hamper the success of the negotiation?

7. Define what areas of difference or disagreement exist or might arise between you.

8. Define what areas of agreement exist or might arise between you.

9. Define what your boundaries or limits are in the items or issues you want to negotiate.

10. Define what you think are the boundaries or limits for the items or issues for the other person involved in the negotiation.

Using this planning list will give you an advantage in the process. If the other side hasn't planned, then you are way ahead. If they are prepared, they will respect you for your forethought, as you will them for theirs. The best scenario is for all sides to be prepared. The process proceeds more smoothly when people can clearly articulate their goals. Negotiation is not as easy when there is confusion about the desired end result.

In an ideal negotiation, a positive climate of mutual respect and trust has been established before the actual negotiations begin. Work toward building a relationship with the other party that allows both of you to feel comfortable, trusting, and free enough to honestly reveal all the issues and positions. *The point of negotiation is to work together toward resolution through dialogue.* It is essential that you maintain your personal integrity, sincerity, and honest commitment to the process, as well as using your listening and observing skills. Imagine how you would like to be treated and then apply those same principles to the other party. It can be very helpful to use creative visualization (see chapter 1) if you are having a difficult time imagining how you will fit into the negotiation. Set the scene in your mind and actually "listen to" the conversation that will take place between the two of you.

> *Elizabeth found out that Ethan Benson, whom she was to meet with later, was a great Red Sox fan. She was quite a baseball buff herself. She checked out the statistics on the sports' page and sat down, relaxed, and visualized how she would enter the room and greet him. "Hello, Ethan. How are you? What a great day. This is the kind of day to have tickets for Fenway Park."*
>
> *"Hey Elizabeth," said Ethan, "I didn't know you were a Red Sox fan."*
>
> *"I've been following them since I was a kid. My Dad used to take us to many of the home games at Fenway. I see that the Sox are gaining on Toronto. Do you think they have a chance of pulling it out?"*
>
> *The conversation in her mind continued on with an exchange of*

each of their favorite players and how they were doing. Ethan reminisced with her about visits to the ballpark as a boy, and how he loves to take his own son to games when he has time. When Elizabeth actually met Ethan to begin their negotiation process, the conversation that she had envisioned followed right along those lines, because she had taken the time to do some preplanning by visualizing the getting-to-know-you scenario.

Sometimes you will have a chance to meet the person with whom you will be negotiating. If that is not the case and if you have reliable sources, you can try to find out some information about the unknown party. Reliable is the key word here. It is best to have more than one source. (Remember how Sally got stung in her negotiations with the Playful Creations Company when she relied on the information from one unchecked source.)

If a friendly relationship is established, then the stage is set to reach agreement on the issues, interests, and needs of both parties. *It is very important to research or at least anticipate the other side's position.* As you recall, the issue at stake in Kay's negotiation with Mr. Parker of Moose Environmental was agreement on Kay's salary. Parker's particular interests and needs were to get a product developed in a timely manner and to hire a qualified person at a salary level the company could afford. Kay's goal was to be offered a job by a company whose needs and objectives were compatible with her personal and professional goals at a salary level that would justify her moving and changing jobs.

When it appears that the two sides in a negotiation are initially far apart, as in this case, it takes some good selling and creativity to promote your point of view. *Remember that a negotiation won't work well unless both sides come out feeling good about what they have agreed upon.* Kay proposed a win/win solution when she agreed to take a smaller, but still adequate salary if she couldn't deliver on her promise to have the product ready in eight months. Parker's company would really stand to gain financially if they could beat out the competition. If Kay did come through, she would have earned the higher salary many times over, and if she didn't, her starting salary was reasonable.

Never leave a negotiation without agreeing upon the details of implementation. When negotiating the terms of employment, make sure you have a written job description. Verify the details by restating your understanding of the agreements that you have made. If you have agreed on a new salary, when will it begin and when will you be eligible for your next salary review? What tasks and duties will you perform when you start your job?

Janet had just landed her first job, reentering the work force, after *fifteen years of raising children. She was so excited about landing her first job after so many years that negotiating a salary was not even in her consciousness. She had read that the job was offered at $17,800, and this was what she assumed was fair and what she would get. When it came time to talk with her boss about the specifics of employment, he offered her $17,500, $300 less than expected. Janet told him she thought the figure was supposed to be $300 more. And he said, "No, $17,500 was to be the salary." She didn't argue for all the reasons that women don't usually dispute money issues ("it's not polite to discuss money"; "it might seem aggressive, and therefore unfeminine"; "if the salary is set, it must be fair"; "it is an unfamiliar process").*

After she had been on the job a few weeks and had discovered that the tasks were different from those originally described to her, Janet began to feel she had not been told the truth about the job. This really hit home when she came across the original advertisement for the job, and indeed the salary for the position had been $17,800, as she had thought. She immediately began to feel taken advantage of and began to resent her boss. She never trusted him again, and the excitement for the job quickly waned. She performed at a level of adequate expectations, never putting forth the usual commitment and energy evident in all other areas of her life. Within the year, she left the job, feeling beaten, doubting her competency, and seeking the support of a counselor.

There are more than a few simple lessons here for us to learn from both the boss and the employee. Let's examine the role of the boss first. He knew that this employee was reentering the work force and had been employed at a much earlier time when women had accepted what was handed to them. He figured he could save the $300 and apply it toward a badly needed computer printer. He also figured that she wouldn't challenge the job description and that he could load extra duties on her after she started work. This would enable him to postpone hiring another person. He felt smug with himself for being able to outwit his new employee. He regarded his employees more as chess pieces to be played to his advantage than as people. You can guess that the turnover in this office was high and the productivity low. The boss assumed that if he could replace his personnel with machines, he wouldn't have the hassle of the ever-present personnel problems in his office. Somehow he never equated the difficulties with his employees to his own attitudes and lack of respectful behavior toward them.

Now, let's look at the employee. She was in a tough spot as a new person in the paid work force. Things had happened quickly, and she never had the time or inclination to consult friends who were working, resource books on the subject, or a career counselor. First, she should have researched this company and other similar companies to learn what salaries were offered at her level or grade. Second, it may have been possible to negotiate beyond the $17,500 level, given her experience accumulated through the years, if she could have demonstrated how that experience enabled her to be of greater value to the company. If she had researched the office more by talking to contacts who knew people there or even other workers, she might have discovered that the boss needed more done than the job description required. She might have enhanced her salary request by offering to take on more tasks for more salary (if she felt she could handle it). All of this wouldn't have changed the boss, but it could have changed how she felt about herself and her job.

This is an example of a salary and job situation where the boss felt he came out the winner. But in the long run, both he and his employee came out with a true no-win situation. He lost the services of an excellent employee because of his ethics, and she lost an opportunity to have work that was meaningful and compensated her justly. More importantly, she lost her self-esteem because she knew she was being taken advantage of. Clearly, the most important point is that if she had known what she was getting into and had laid all the cards on the table, she could have taken it or left it and would not have ended up resenting her boss.

The Art of Negotiating

We interviewed a lawyer who is well known for his negotiation skills. He shared some excellent pointers with us about the negotiation process. He aptly described the process as a kind of exercise in which you take different steps to get where you want to go.

He emphasized the necessity of being prepared as key to the whole process. The first step to being prepared is defining your goals. It is important to define your negotiable spectrum from the least you will settle for to the most you would hope for. Be aware of how you feel about different points between the two extremes. As he said, "It seems to be human nature that in negotiation the other party expects to do better than to accept your first offer. What you have to offer – the strengths and weaknesses – will largely determine where you will have to settle on the spectrum of possibilities." How independent you can be or how desperate you are also determines where you will end up. Your first offer, then, is a beginning, not a bottom-line last resort stance. Strive for a figure that is closest to the best rather than too willingly settling for the least you will accept. Your attitude and belief in yourself will have a lot to do with your ability to settle on the upper end of your spectrum. (Use some creative visualization to prepare yourself before a hard negotiation.)

You can always move downward with your position, but you can never go up or obtain more than your initial offering. For this reason, it is important to have the confidence and fortitude to stick with your upper range; lower it only if absolutely necessary. If you come down too quickly, then the other party will conclude that you do not have much confidence or that your position is desperate. The other party will often make lower offers than you are willing to accept. "People are often trying to gain the best advantage they can, rather than the fairest agreement; therefore, they will take advantage of what they perceive to be weakness, whether that weakness be in the negotiating process, the confidence of the other party's position, or simply the perception of a desperate or untenable stance."

The lawyer further stressed that negotiation works best if you can structure the agreement in a win/win solution, benefitting both parties. *It helps your negotiating stance to point out the benefits of agreement to the other party while subtly suggesting their risks in not reaching an agreement.* The other party must be given a reason to settle, and the best reason is concern that if he or she doesn't reach an agreement with you, he or she would be worse off. Negotiating with integrity works to your advantage in many ways. If you speak truthfully, the other side is more likely to accept what you are saying, so always avoid exaggeration and unsubstantiated claims. As the lawyer said, "It is often an accepted fact that both parties go home from a good negotiation thinking that it was not the best that they could do, but it was a good agreement under the circumstances. If the parties get this close, it is a win/win situation."

If the negotiation is multi-faceted, meaning that a number of items are to be negotiated (such as salary, title, benefits, perks), you can exchange settlement objectives. Plan to give in on some areas that may be important to the other party, but are not as important to you. When you are engaged in this kind of process, prepare ahead of time by evaluating which objectives are important to you and which are important to them.

This introduces you to the timing factor in negotiation. There are more favorable and less favorable times to make a concession that will be to your advantage. For example, you could do something early on or wait until the point of near hopelessness to make concessions. Timing is determined by both the person with whom you are negotiating and the situation itself. It is important to evaluate just how much the other party wants to reach an agreement, as well as the other person's bottom line. In essence, you are leaving room to move closer to the other person's objective. The other person, then, would have a positive feeling about his or her success in moving your initial offer closer to an acceptable level. Now how's that for a little reverse feel-good psychology?

Occasionally, the going can get tough. You need to gently remind the other party of the advantages of negotiation without resorting to any hint of coercion. If the other party is being rude, impatient, or coercive, don't fall into the trap of being more concerned with the personality of the person than with what you are trying to achieve. If an unpleasant situation begins to develop, disengage yourself from harassing behavior. Force yourself to focus on the issues. Just as in an interview falling into the trap is fatal to the process and the outcome.

As you can see, negotiating requires a lot of give-and-take and a fair amount of psychological maneuvering. Women are extremely sensitive to the subtleties of communication and can use this to great advantage in the negotiating process as long as they do not revert to nurturing or subservient roles. You will be able to handle any type of negotiation as long as you are well prepared, rehearsed, and have a positive frame of mind. It is important to examine your mind-set, your perceptions, and approach the process with calm and integrity.

Chapter 9

Reentry: Women at the Crossroads

Joan Smith

Navigating by chart and chance and passion I will know the shape of the mountains of freedom, I will know. — Marge Piercy

Very likely there will come a day when you realize it is time to change what you are doing. Whether you are entering the crossroad from full-time parenting, studying, a career as a housewife, or a job that you have outgrown, you will share some experiences common to all women. The wisdom of those women who have gone before is a legacy you can draw on to help recognize the crossroad and success-fully choose your pathway.

The day came for me one October afternoon while I lay sobbing desperately on my daughter's bed. I had just turned thirty. Our new house was exquisitely decorated; the freezer was full of homemade Christmas cookies; and my two preschool children were playing in the backyard. My other life as a community organizer and lobbyist for the local League of Women Voters had stimulated my talents for thinking and doing on a larger scale, and I was hungry for more of that kind of challenge. I knew my family would not like it; I knew, too, that I would be intensifying the conflict I felt between what seemed at the time to be disparate worlds. But I made a decision that day to trust my ability to create a life that included meaningful work in addition to my home and parenting responsibilities. The alternative seemed like living as a shallow breather. The path since then has been both difficult and rewarding, but I have never doubted my choice.

On the surface, the decisions made at any crossroad may seem the same as other job or career decisions but any woman who thinks twice knows in her bones it is more than that. She can sense the magnitude of the opportunity to put what she knows about herself and the way the world works to use, and to see what happens. A woman at the crossroad can become the author of the next chapter in her life.

The terms "reentry women," "women returning to the workplace," or "going into the real world" are phrases that should be used cautiously. They imply that the woman who has been a student, household manager, parent, or the volunteer fund-raiser for the local library has been doing something other than work, something less important and less real. This is simply not so. *When a woman begins to look for different tasks to which she will commit her time and talents (which may or may not include paying work), she is changing her workplace, not entering it.*

"The workplace" is also a misleading term, an overweight abstraction that does not exist. An office building full of suited men and women is a workplace. A factory where people work physically hard and sweat is a workplace. A mother's household-garden-carpool-community is a workplace. A workplace is anyplace where things of value get done. This chapter focuses on women seeking satisfying paid work, but the process of reflecting encouraged here could just as easily lead a woman to choose the opposite direction.

When a woman successfully changes what she is doing with her life, several fundamental things happen. She experiences the satisfaction and untidiness of navigating a normal transition. She comes to know more about her own abilities and purpose, as well as her own resident demons that work against her. Her world expands as she explores unfamiliar corners to find what she is looking for, and she becomes wiser about its realities and distortions. Eventually she joins what often feels like another culture, a workplace or project that has language and customs that both use and challenge her own.

These fundamental processes – navigating transitions, knowing one's essentials, and linking to a new work culture – are our focus. Since most adults will change their work at least three times in a lifetime, and women currently move in and out of workplaces more often than men, we can expect to be at a crossroad at least several times.

A wide number of catalysts for change exist. They work together and build momentum to get our attention. Some are obvious, such as the completion of something important – building a house, receiving a college degree, or paying off a loan. Others are subtle, like the sense of having closed a certain chapter in life and being called to something new. Some have to do with people – the beginning, shifting, or ending of important connections with partners, children, parents, or friends. Others have to do with money — a loss of expected financial support, a special new need for income, or even an increase in monies through an inheritance or a business windfall. Some changes in life direction after recovery from addiction, illness, or burnout are both jarring and potentially healing.

A twenty-nine-year-old woman who has been waitressing and skiing for a decade begins to have the feeling of time running out, and talks about finding a career with a future. A fifty-year-old woman who is a veteran community volunteer, recently divorced, says she needs to find a way to support herself while doing something that matters. But they both will have to answer the same basic questions. What is actually changing? Why is this happening? Do I have a choice? How much do I rely on others, how much on myself? What direction do I choose? What practical steps do I take? What will I leave behind? What will I take with me? Can I do it? What will it be like?

No matter what direction she chooses, a woman must first understand the inner workings of change in order to have a chance to make a satisfying, long-term decision. Transitions are messy, but fertile. What looks chaotic actually has an order of its own. During ten years of work with over 1,000 adults in transition, I have repeatedly seen people discover the inevitable phases of the change cycle as well as their intrinsic ability to make successful changes.

Each person has her own characteristic way of moving through the change cycle, repeatedly visiting or getting stuck in certain parts, touching down lightly or completely avoiding others. There is no recommended amount of time in any phase nor a prescribed sequence. Look rather for the effectiveness of the time spent. Leave what works alone, and experiment with what doesn't. Do you spend some time in each phase? Do you spend enough time, but not too much, in order to reap its benefits? Do you take time out to rest when needed? Change — even thinking about change — consumes valuable energy. Keep in mind that this is a productive expenditure.

Changing the way your life is structured takes time, anywhere from the length of a full-term pregnancy to two years. Finding where you are in your change cycle can be useful in crafting appropriate strategies and in being patient with yourself for not being somewhere else.

The Signals of Change

The first clue that something major is coming to an end is a vague discomfort which can take the form of boredom, free-floating anxiety, compulsive busyness, or flashes of excitement. What used to be invigorating is flat. Usual coping strategies don't work. And there often doesn't seem to be a logical reason.

> *Lisa is a talented craftswoman whose quilts are sold throughout New England. She is exasperated with herself. She talks about how long it took her to take her own work seriously, about eventually showing her work and winning awards, and finally founding a successful crafts school. But now she is bored and restless. "I have done it. It is finished and I don't know what is next." Lisa alternately ignores and embraces her dilemma, an ambivalence many of us share. She wants to find a salaried job in order to leave her marriage and support her two sons in relative security. But she also needs a new direction because she has learned and challenged herself to the full extent in her craft.*

The only purpose of this phase is to get our attention and tell us the time is ripe to start thinking. Some key questions to consider: What actually needs to change? Is it the kind of tasks I am doing? Or my connection with people? Or the purpose to which my efforts are going? If a woman ignores the signals for too long, she is likely to see signs of depression, irritability, or physical illness. There is always a cost for not paying attention. It is as if we have a muscle that allows us to do marvelous things, but unused begins to atrophy and eventually to poison our system.

It helps to talk to others about what we think is changing and to hear reassurances about the process and the goals. Women and men who have weathered major life changes are particularly helpful at this time. A person who has been on the fringe of our lives, or whom we meet fresh at this time, often turns out to be a wise guide and companion, fading into the background as we come out the other side. Family and friends are sometimes too close to see clearly and too affected by the change to have an unbiased reaction.

If the phase of our lives that is ending is harsh or unwanted, such as a death, an accident, or being fired, the grieving work will have to take precedence for a while. Getting on with the career change may take longer, because making authentic change after a loss requires a shift from despair or resignation to acceptance. This change of perspective is the difference between "You can make me do it, but you can't make me like it" to "I would have chosen otherwise, but I'm willing to see what this change has to offer."

Peggy Capitano is a woman who has learned to recognize the signs of impending change early and respond to them with anticipation. In her twenties, she was a full-time mother and house manager. Later, as a human services counselor and administrator, she helped to foster innovative programs, such as a pilot project that matches college students in need of housing with elders who have a house, but can't live in it without help. When most of her programs were firmly established, she recognized the need for a new focus. She allowed herself to be drafted to run for the legislature even though it meant overcoming her fear of public speaking.

After five years of a very satisfying and challenging legislative life, she is starting to notice the signs of completion again: vague impatience with people who would have been a welcome challenge in the past, boredom with tasks that used to be interesting, a desire to delegate as much as possible. As these clues appear, she talks with her husband and trusted friends who have made major changes themselves. She asks questions to find her answers: Is it time to leave the legislature, to stay and develop a different emphasis within it, or simply to start something new to complement it? She makes note of anything that is a magnet for her attention—the tenement housing that moves her to tears, the stunning consultant she watches orchestrate a national level negotiation, a desire to paint again. She takes more time for reflection and thinks about taking time out to let things simmer. Her crossroads may be a gentle one, because she has learned to recognize the signals early and to rely on friends who have made changes to support and spark her. Most importantly, she assumes the process will be invigorating.

Break Apart

For some women the process is rockier. They make a subtle shift from a general sense of discomfort to an angry, staccato breaking apart, as they begin to identify what they *don't* want. Absolute statements are hurled at whatever seems to be the culprit. "No more long hours . . . I'll never work with someone like that again . . . I'm not getting up one more day to look at an empty house!"

Condemning, exaggerating, and pronouncing serve to hammer out answers to the key question: What is it about this situation that needs changing? Knowing what isn't right leads to seeing what its opposite might be. The vehemence dislodges us from the comfort of the familiar, which otherwise might seduce us into avoiding new territory. A particularly private person may appear very absent-minded during this time, taking long thoughtful walks and carrying on this conversation in her own mind. A people-oriented person may think out loud and may be surprised at her supposedly unwarranted angry outbursts as she tries to get at the heart of discontent.

This is not a time for problem solving and decisions. It is a time to take things apart to see what is going on, while keeping all the pieces on the table, like emptying out a pocketbook and sorting. An outside person who can find the kernels of truth in the barrage of verbiage, without getting caught up in the anger or feeling personally attacked, can be extremely helpful. It helps to spread the frustration around among friends, so no one gets overloaded.

> *After trying out three different colleges, Kit Woolman has a lot of information about what doesn't work for her. Learning by reading isn't her way. And after one year in three temporary jobs, she knows even more about what she doesn't want. None of these settings sufficiently used her ability to find and implement unusual solutions to real-life problems. The colleges and workplace settings were not experience-oriented enough for Kit. With a handle on what isn't right, Kit can now reverse the negative and find a place for what might work better. Kit's imagination can now work on what it would be like to be a problem solver par excellence and how she can find a workplace that needs her abilities and talents.*

Exploration

The work of breaking apart and naming what is not right gradually provides the momentum and focus for exploring. This is a time to move in and out of short-term projects, workshops, and experiences. The purpose of taking a course is to learn what a new area is like and to see if it fits well enough to warrant more intense exploration. Be prepared to leave projects once you have learned what you came to learn, even before they are over.

A woman in the exploration phase often has wide mood swings. One moment she is certain . . . This is it! The next moment she is discouraged . . . I'll never find it! Definitive statements seem like attempts to stabilize this roller coaster, but they are actually perceptions being tried on for size. At this stage, "I have decided to go into marketing," usually means, "Given what I know so far, this is my favorite idea." Ideas are best shared with people who understand they are trial balloons and not decisions. The most helpful people at this time are those who can add to our fund of new possibilities and give us a lot of room to try things out, without asking the dreaded question, "Well, what are you going to do?"

Anchor yourself by scheduling a little time to enjoy those parts of your life that are not in flux, such as your perennial garden or a regular walk with an old friend. Or construct a temporary scaffolding that gives extra support, such as a regular swim at the "Y" or a support group for women in transition. This is a good point in the change cycle to read about the process. Books such as *The Evolving Self* (Robert Kegan), *The Hero Within* (Carol Pearson), and *Transitions* (William Bridges) have been useful to many women. And talking with someone else who has weathered a transition is always energizing.

Knowing how long to stay in this exploratory phase is a delicate issue for many women. For some, the idea of becoming a part of a new workplace seems so alien and frightening that they make a career of "living on possibilities." Other women cannot tolerate the ambiguity of exploration and move on too quickly, making a choice that usually has to be remade within months.

Salome Patton is on a sabbatical from her position as director of the physical therapy department of a major hospital. She is feeling very restless in a field that she had found quite satisfying for fifteen years. She decides to use her sabbatical as exploration time to experiment with different daily schedules and to try out some interests that seem like radical departures. While still working, she had started building sets for the local theater group in order to try out an interest in carpentry. In the process, she learned how much she liked seeing immediate results for her efforts, working with a tightly knit group, and being in on an intense project that had a beginning and an end.

Salome starts her sabbatical with a telephone campaign to find out what it is like to be a self-employed woman in a trade. She learns a lot from a psychologist who now has her own wallpaper-hanging business. A temporary placement agency leads to several jobs at minimum wage, including packing Christmas hams for a mail order business. That particular job helps with expenses and also shows her that she doesn't mind repetitive physical work as much as she had assumed. She also starts a course in horticulture offered at a vocational center as a way of both trying out and building experience toward an interest in owning her own green-house. Salome makes exploration her job for a few months and learns more than she could have by thinking about it for years.

Sally Cartney also takes time out from her lifetime job as a social worker to explore, but for different reasons. She has never explored a major choice as an adult. She always took what was available. She has no clues about what she wants, feels, or values. As a child, most important decisions were made for her. As a college student, she began a parallel career of alcoholism that lasted until her recovery at age fifty. Her inability to test out her ideas as a child and her numbness to her limited activities as an adult left her without a bank of basic information. Anyone coming out of a narrowly prescribed life, a long period of physical or mental disability, or a history of addiction needs a long and thorough period of exploration before long-term commitments can be made.

Narrowing

Once curiosity begins to wane and little new information is turning up, choices usually narrow down to one or two particularly attractive ones. It is time to stop exploring and begin testing. One person might prefer a short-term commitment that allows her to reserve final judgment, while accumulating necessary experience. This tryout might be an apprenticeship in a graphic design studio, a contract to write the report for a time-limited research project, or a one-year acting directorship of a nonprofit agency. Another person might be ready to make the commitment and dive in; she then begins the process of finding or creating a specific position in the field she has identified. It may be right under her nose, or she may be embarking on another process that will take time. As the search narrows, there may be yet another step to negotiate.

The Wall

There is something about getting close to a commitment that brings out the demons and danger signals. Even as we feel excited and relieved to see the light at the end of the tunnel, we often hit "the wall." It can happen early, late, or repeatedly throughout the cycle, but it is most predictable at this point.

"The wall" is a collection of our worst fears, made up of useless barricades, as well as legitimate warnings. It is worth taking the time to separate the kernels of truth from the false prophecies. If we believe successful people are lonely people, we may fear that moving on means loss of our friends. If we believe there is a scarcity of satisfying jobs, we may fear that we won't find one. If we don't trust our own judgment, we may fear we will make a terrible mistake. Our fears can masquerade as confusion, a sudden disinterest, procrastination, or physical and emotional crises. An insightful friend, an hour of writing, or a hard run followed by some reflection can sometimes slice through the fear and help to name it, deal with it, and move on. The following checklist can be helpful:

★ Are there genuine competing priorities – a health problem, financial debt to be paid off, attention to a shaky relationship – that should be dealt with first?

★ Are there familiar but unfounded fears that surface any time you take a risk – "I am not smart enough or strong enough," "People like me don't do things like that," "People will laugh at me" – suggesting they are old messages that can be disregarded?

For example, a woman in a career planning seminar explained that she had been a lawyer in a group practice, taken five years out to begin a family, and now was thinking about opening her own office. But she was obsessed with the idea that she wasn't smart enough. When others in the group reminded her that she had finished law school, passed the bar the first time around, helped develop a town plan, and successfully represented several clients earlier in her career, she was able to see how exaggerated her fears were. This kind of reality checking is essential during and after a change, particularly for women going into male-defined fields such as law, finance, science, medicine, and academia.

★ Do you need more information or preparation for the choice you are making, or are you beginning to repeat yourself and know it's time to move on?

★ Are you aware of actual limitations for women in your chosen field that will require extra energy? Do you need to talk to more women about the costs, rewards, and strategies of being a change agent, as well as doing the job?

★ Are you experiencing the classic fears of success and failure that deserve to be heard, shrunk to size, and addressed? Common concerns among men and women of all ages, from any work or socioeconomic background include:

Will friends fall away because I am not as available or feel I have moved beyond them? Will I lose them when I need them the most?

Will I get so absorbed in this new direction that I neglect loved ones?

Can I handle the increased challenge? What if I blow it? If I do a good job, will people just expect more and more? Will it be too serious and no fun?

Will it turn out to be a terrible decision, not at all what I expected?

The most useful tools I know to deal with all of these fears are the following three questions:

1. What is the worst thing that can happen?
2. What can you do ahead of time to minimize this danger?
3. If the worst happens, what are your options?

For women who are in a relationship or are parents of dependent children or are children of dependent parents, the fear of neglecting these relationships (or being seen as negligent) is often the most inhibiting. Our fear can range from concern to immobilizing terror. We may doubt our ability to combine it all. We worry that those we love will be damaged in some fundamental way. Even if we suspect this change will actually be beneficial to each person in our family, we anticipate they will feel neglected anyway, and that they – or others judging us – will punish us directly or indirectly. There is no simple answer to this overwhelming concern, but there are many of us working out creative, jerry-rigged solutions that seem to work. We can all take solace and be inspired by those who have gone before us and are managing and loving every minute of it.

A prerequisite for creating such workable solutions is the establishment of a regular, quiet personal time before your new work ever starts. Most women who gracefully orchestrate their lives, with or without a partner, have learned to take a few minutes every day to themselves to clear their minds and be refreshed. Sitting down with the adults and children involved to discuss how the changes you are initiating will affect each of them is a good place to begin preventive maintenance. It is also a chance for everyone to brainstorm ways to minimize difficulties, to gripe, ask questions, be reassured, and even offer to help. Most families need to do this regularly to fine-tune the new arrangements and give everyone a chance to be heard.

Talking with single women, single parents, couples, and families to collect solutions is also good research. Parents with children in their early twenties are particularly useful, as they have gained insight into how their family's system worked in retrospect. Their young adult children can also provide their own views on what worked and didn't work for them, often dispelling some of our worst fears about how women working affects the children. Reading research can be depressing and misleading. Books can be helpful, but be wary of those that outline solutions that sound good to the author but haven't been tested at home. Do your research with real people.

This conflict is not actually between home and work, but between the human desire to set one's own course and the expectation that women should defer to others. Once we understand this, it is no longer a matter of choosing between home and work, but of creating a collage that includes both home and work. A successful collage of this kind does not, however, lend itself to the long work week and skewed priorities of a "company man" or "company woman." The woman setting her own course has to remember that departing from traditional roles at home and at work is a necessary part of changing her image and defining success in both roles.

I have struggled with this question for twenty years. Finally, my own children are old enough to report in. It turns out my son is grateful he knows how to cook for himself and do his own laundry, after years of telling me that, if I were any kind of mother, I would do it for him. In addition, his photography, creative writing, and living in two other cultures tell me he has learned to be loyal to a personally intuited course that may appear impractical to some but inspires me.

My daughter, on the other hand, took her engineering degree and became one of three women in a training program for operating ocean-going research vessels. Her phone calls home are a mixture of stories about surviving the smoke-filled fire-fighting chamber and dropping anchor for the first time, requests for a family cheesecake recipe, and frustrated observations about how hard it is to be a woman in a man's world, while not being seen as a witch or a pushover. Throughout her training, I notice she tackles navigation, emergency repair, and the struggle to avoid the stereotyped female labels with equal vigor. She sometimes mentions other women friends to whom she has given support for taking risks in their own lives.

As we sat down to a recent Thanksgiving dinner the three of us had planned and cooked, I found myself thinking, "I think we are home free! Not only are they all right, but they are thriving." I hope other women with young children will experiment at their crossroads, for the sake of their kids, not in spite of them – as well as on behalf of their own dreams.

Once the mixture of valid womanly and human concerns embedded in your wall is addressed and the inflated fears are punctured, a time will come when no more exploring, sorting, or preparing needs to be done. Your desire to test your preparations begins to prevail. The stage fright that is left after a thorough preparation will dissolve only after you make the leap. Half of the work of a major transition is the information gathering and decision making. The other half is working with your hammer and chisel to understand and dismantle the wall we each build.

Commitment

Clearing away the fear and the fog usually frees us to make a commitment to a plan and move into action. The plan may be to prepare for a job, to find a job, or to begin a position that has already materialized. Three important aspects of this moment of commitment bear some thought.

First, making a decision and a plan in itself is a major accomplishment. Most people have a desire to celebrate this in some way, to mark the fact that they have weathered the amorphous half of the change cycle and have something to show for it. Making a phone call to a valued friend, gathering people for a get-together, or hiking to the top of a favorite mountain are all symbolic ways of relishing one's persistence and anchoring the fact in our memories for our next time around. Other women will be disturbed, taught, and inspired by a woman changing her life, whether words are exchanged or not. Celebrating and publicizing this turning point will be a beacon and anchor to others who are just beginning the process and need proof that it can be done.

Second, the inner act of commitment, combined with an outer acknowledgment, create a focus and magnetism that begin to attract the resources needed to reach the goal. Tell people and take the first step. Commitment organizes our attention, and often things begin to happen very quickly. People start to pass on opportunities they have heard of, and we become more sensitive to books, events, or people that might be useful. We instinctively know this, and sometimes cringe as we tell the first person, as if steeling ourselves for a barrage of events that will be unleashed. If a woman hasn't told at least one person about her goal, she is probably not yet committed to it.

Finally, a person often feels the need for a time-out at this point, as well as at other times during the process. A thick novel, a bike trip, or a lot of extra sleep can all serve the purpose. This is not procrastination or laziness, but a legitimate need to rest and integrate all the changes and conclusions of the previous months.

The remainder of the cycle has to do with what happens with our commitments. Once a particular involvement has run its course, it is up for negotiation, and we are ripe to go around again. It will never be as difficult as the first time. We are born to make these kinds of circles, and change flows naturally once we allow ourselves to get the hang of it. The most challenging phase of the change cycle for many women is the process of linking what they want with what is in the world around them.

Linking

Linking is simply the process of translating and documenting what you can already do with learning or demonstrating what you would like to do, all with the purpose of finding work. The chapters on networking, planning, and presenting yourself in person and on paper give a wealth of information. The following discussion deals with some of the links that don't fall easily into those categories, but can make a critical difference in your finding a job, career, and life-style that suits you. These are the links that women at the crossroads are most likely to overlook and underestimate. These are the links that often give validity to your goals.

Finding the links that already exist between past experience and a future goal is like a treasure hunt. It is often a process of making visible what has gone unnoticed, naming it, and translating it into words that allow a prospective employer to see what you can do. Acquiring the needed links that are not a part of past experience can be turned into a short-term goal, through training, volunteering, joining, part-timing, developing a seed idea, or apprenticing. Start first with what you have.

Translating

Many of the activities a woman does naturally with friends, family, and community aren't even noticed enough to be called volunteering. The comment, "Oh, well, I've just always done that... I mean, doesn't everyone?" veils many transferable abilities such as organizing a yearly dinner dance for a group of friends; being sought after by coworkers to help them buy clothing and create outfits for special occasions; serving as resident counselor for all your teenager's friends; doing the family bookkeeping and making decisions about investments; or completely designing, landscaping, planting, and caring for extensive gardens. Each of these abilities can be broken down into specific skills and knowledge that could be transferred to several jobs. In the landscaping example, a few obvious skills include designing, locating resources, planning, organizing, doing hard physical labor, and knowing about growing conditions, soil science, cultivation, growing seasons, and diseases. This could translate into related work at a garden center, horticultural research project, landscaping service, floral shop, or even interior design.

A person changing careers can find these same treasures by renaming some of her current responsibilities to make their transferability to a different workplace more obvious. For instance, as a school guidance counselor, I was responsible for individual counseling and classroom teaching. But I also designed and taught an occasional in-service program for teachers or a workshop for parents, and facilitated many group discussions with students. Describing my skills as a trainer, facilitator of group organization and development, and program designer helped a prospective employer see me as a human development trainer for his employees.

Joining

Women can connect with a field by participating in activities that bring them shoulder to shoulder with others involved full-time. Joining a related trade, business, or professional organization can provide a bridge. If a person has been in a career at some time in her life, she may still belong to organizations that link her to that world. When a woman leaves a career, if she has any interest at all in returning to it, keeping up membership and participation in such a group is worth the investment.

If you are planning on finding employment in a new field, go ahead and join whatever organizations are open to you. As an aspiring writer, I can fully partici-pate in the statewide League of Writers, a group of beginning and widely pub-lished writers that provides biannual meetings, a newsletter of who has published what, an annual workshop with nationally known authors and agents, and a reading service.

Whether you are maintaining a membership or joining for the first time, become active. Attend different levels of conventions and workshops, volunteer to serve on committees, and read newsletters and journals. Lasting links are formed when people work together on a committee or a project. This is a surprisingly efficient way to learn the language and customs of the field, get a sense of the new developments and concerns, learn the different forms work may take in that field, and, obviously, to meet and network with people.

Seed Ideas

Another way to bridge where you are and where you want to be is to just begin. Some ideas are like seeds; they lend themselves to beginning with something simple and allowing it to grow. This could be teaching an evening workshop at the local adult education center on cooking meals for one; designing greeting cards and selling them to friends; or writing a short story. You may have a specific goal when you begin, such as starting a culinary school or having your own graphic design studio, or you may just want to go in that direction and see what happens.

Anna had an idea that grew out of boredom. After she moved to a small town in New England, she missed the stimulating discussion centering around books and issues that she had enjoyed in a university town. She had an image of a group of people getting together to read a series of books focused on a topic, hearing the perspective of an expert, and then discussing the group's reactions. At the urging of a friend, she wrote a small grant to the state Humanities Council for funds to create one four-session series at the local library. It was funded. Anna's idea met the needs of many people beyond herself. Within five years, she was writing and managing similar grants for state library systems all over the country. She never dreamed or intended that her seed would become a beanstalk, but she was willing to follow where its growth seemed to lead.

Women can also expand an idea within their present job by taking a new area of interest seriously and finding ways to relate this interest to functions going on in and around their workplace. A woman may be interested in doing more financial planning, which is technically outside her responsibilities. Looking for an opportunity to get involved, she might find a supervisor who would appreciate some late night help putting together the department's financial report. Or asking for more responsibility in this area might lead to a request when a special project arises that would otherwise require hiring temporary help.

In the midst of thoroughly enjoying owning and running a small town newspaper, Cary Witten noticed she was beginning to lean toward a totally new career. She was spending more time at selectmen's meetings, following up with questions for the town manager far beyond what was needed for the article in the paper. Keeping her opinions out of the articles was becoming more difficult. She wanted to be in there helping to make the decisions. So she used her reporting privileges to learn as much as she could, went back to school for a degree in public administration, and ended up as the town manager in a neighboring town. Sometimes a career change can be as natural as rolling down a hill.

Training

As with Cary, it may be that additional education, training, or experience are needed to be well prepared for a successful job search. The academic route was indicated for Cary because a master's degree was a necessary credential and allowed her to fill gaps in her knowledge, such as fiscal planning and federal regulations. But it was her prior community experience and her internship with a town manager that proved she could do the job.

If a woman is excited about the intellectual exploration of an academic two- or four-year degree program or is pursuing a goal that requires a degree as a credential, college can be a rewarding choice. For most adult students, however, a more practical approach is to build experience in the field before starting an academic program in order to be sure the actual day-to-day work experience meets your expectations. Some colleges and universities offer internships in specific departments, such as education, clinical psychology, or business.

Service learning and cooperative learning programs are more intensive work experiences and serve as excellent links after graduation. Service learning programs are relatively new vehicles for placing students in full-time internships with nonprofit organizations, such as the Department of Mental Health or the United Way. Students are trained by the employer and supervised by the college. This gives students an opportunity to discuss their experiences as they go. Cooperative learning (often referred to as co-op) usually means alternating two full-time semesters in classes with one full-time semester in an internship, such as physical therapy, engineering, or marketing. Northeastern University in Boston has a highly respected co-op program and also maintains an office providing information on co-ops in other institutions.

If financial aid is required, take the time to comb through *The Foundation Directory* in the reference section of the library for the names of foundations, such as the American Association of University Women Fellowship and the Ms. Foundation, that award grants to women wanting to further their education.

Recently the U.S. Department of Education has been funding innovative programs for low income women who want to complete a college degree. These programs are jointly supported by one or more colleges, the federal government, and state departments of human services and education. The best ones offer career counseling, day care, and personal support groups along with small stipends for books and transportation. The most likely source of information should be the local office of the state departments of social services or employment or the nearest community action office. One particularly exciting option is the Ada Comstock Scholars Program at Smith College in Northampton, Massachusetts 01063. This program gives women who have completed up to two years of a strong college career without obtaining a degree, a chance to finish their liberal arts degree. The 380 women currently enrolled include both part- and full-time students, with single, married, and single parent women equally represented.

Financial aid packages, including Pell grants, loans, and work study are also available to adult women. It is often easiest to apply to the financial aid office of the schools receiving your applications; counselors are available to explain eligibility and to assist with filling out the forms. If one office is not helpful, try another.

There are so many other ways to obtain training and experience that all of them cannot be listed here. A few of the most available and sometimes most overlooked include the following:

■ **Specialized schools and institutes.** Typical of these are Emerson College in Boston for broadcasting and journalism, and New England Culinary Institute, Montpelier, Vermont for cooking and restaurant management.

■ **Local vocational schools.** Many now admit adults to all of their programs, and some have special evening programs just for adults. Training starts with basics and is usually thorough, often leading to job offerings through local employers who have connections with the instructors. Typical offerings include culinary arts, drafting, horticulture, printing, and health occupations.

■ **Women's vocational programs.** There are a growing number of federal and state funded training programs for women entering specific fields, such as the trades, small business, and nursing. Many of these are open but not restricted to low-income women. One such program in Vermont is Step-up, a six-month intensive for women to try out and be trained in three trades – printing, welding, and carpentry – while participating in ongoing workshops on working in male-defined jobs and personal development.

Metropolitan and suburban areas through county or public school facilities often provide programs specifically for women looking for their first jobs or returning to paid work. A community college, women's counseling service or health service, office of economic opportunity, or state department of education should know what and where such programs are in your area.

Women in rural areas might find similar services through the state agricultural college extension service, or state departments of employment or social welfare. Women who are currently receiving social welfare, a large but often hidden group, should check into state-administered programs sponsored by the federal Job Training and Partnership Act. They often operate under the name WIN (Work Incentive), which is being renamed JOBS. These programs focus on the exploration and decision-making process and provide some support in finding actual job experience and training.

Catalyst, an organization based in New York City, was formed as a national clearinghouse for information about programs, career counseling services, and printed material regarding women's efforts to integrate work and family. They will provide information by mail or phone (Catalyst, 250 Park Avenue South, New York, NY 10003, 212-777-8900).

■ **Apprenticeships and internships.** An apprenticeship implies that you will be paid while you learn, ideally working alongside someone who is a good teacher and skilled. An internship provides learning while you are a supervised volunteer and usually requires some sort of written report at the end. Some states have organized apprenticeship programs (check with your local state employment office); some unions and trade organizations provide structured apprenticeships, and some companies have comprehensive in-house on-the-job training. General Electric, for instance, has two- and three-year training programs in areas such as manufacturing management, mechanical/electrical engineering, financial management, and technical sales. Employees are either hired into these programs out of college or are allowed to apply after employment begins.

Satisfying apprenticeships can often be set up informally on your own. A first step is to identify someone who is highly respected in the area in which you want to become competent and to ask to shadow her for a day. If she appears to be a good teacher, she may be willing to train you as you do entry level work.

Sharon, an elementary school art teacher, thought she wanted to become a graphic designer after taking a series of courses at the local community center. On that experience, she talked a well-known graphic design firm into hiring her as a six-month apprentice during their busy season. As it turned out, she learned from working in the studio that it wasn't right for her. Had she wanted to continue, she would have had excellent experience and a good recommendation to link her to a new career.

Sometimes finding out what isn't right is as valuable as finding out what is.

Volunteering

Volunteering is a social bargain: a chance to have responsibilities available only after many years in a formal job; an opportunity to learn as much as you have time to do; a place to demonstrate what you know you can do with an endless variety of tasks to choose from. Through volunteering, you can build a network that can vouchsafe for you when you need recommendations while you discover exactly what it is you like and don't like.

All past experience as a volunteer should be combed, broken into skills and special knowledge, and translated into terms that will make sense to anyone interviewing you in your desired workplace. The process is the same as discovering your hidden specialties discussed in chapter 3. It is often fun to sit down and do this with a friend, perhaps someone who worked on the same project.

> *Sue Levinson is forty-five, married, and has spent most of the past fifteen years raising her two children, now young adults. She is proud of having finished her college degree recently, but beyond knowing she wants to do some kind of organizational planning, she feels somewhat aimless. While she was figuring out what she was really going to do, she decided to serve on a volunteer council exploring city compliance with the needs of the disabled population. She had no prior experience in this field, but the issue seemed important to her the day she read the notice for the meeting. Since then, she has become assistant to the chairman, helped draft ordinances and regulations, written a handbook, and participated in negotiations with local officials. Her skill list might include:*

> *researching new content areas*
> *organizing information*
> *drafting detailed regulations and ordinances*
> *writing handbooks*
> *producing printed documents*
> *devising strategies*
> *being prompt, hard-working, and reliable*
> *special knowledge: needs of disabled*
> *experiences of physical disability*
> *regulations regarding disabled*

> *For Sue, the development and documentation of these skills is the link to the paying part-time job she is seeking.*

Part-Timing

Part-timing, or doing temporary work, may seem like a rather obvious link. But I want to emphasize the often-neglected ways this link may be used to good advantage.

A woman who is taking a long time out from paid work for any reason might benefit from occasionally taking a part-time or temporary job. This allows her to explore other fields or roles that may be interesting and makes the transition back to a formal workplace more graceful and less rushed. She has been accumulating information and experience all along. Volunteering certainly falls in this category.

A woman who is taking time out from a field she knows she will want to rejoin may want to think about doing consulting, contract, part-time, or free-lance work in her specialty. Doing a few challenging projects is more important than doing a lot. Later, this will show prospective employers she has remained active and up-to-date in the field at a high level; for her benefit, she knows she is still competent. This is especially important in fields that are information heavy, such as medicine, research, academics, or law, or in fields where technology changes quickly, such as computer operations or communications. In general, it is usually easier to join or rejoin a field that uses a process, such as counseling, writing, marketing, or managing, than a field that uses a lot of information or technology.

The woman who wants to take time out to get a new perspective, but can't afford the complete loss of income, can often survive on a series of jobs from a temporary service. The use of temporary services is increasing, and they usually have a variety of interesting positions. This is another great way to explore unfamiliar workplaces and roles. And you always have the option of saying, "Not today, thank you."

Beware of becoming stuck in velvet ghettoes. Some temporary or part-time jobs are easy to come by, but can become a trap for women. A woman typically enters them with a few immediate goals and ends up staying only because she becomes comfortable, and there are no obvious attractive alternatives. This tends to happen in large institutions such as hospitals, colleges, and religious organizations whose "good works" image often veils rigid hierarchies that exploit staff; professional offices where separation between the professional (lawyer, doctor, psychologist) and support staff is absolute and allows minimal job development (a secretary does not move up to lawyer); manufacturing plants where the office staff are mostly women and most production, supervisory, and management personnel are men; or single large employers in a small town who hire the bored wives of top management into lower level jobs. It is fine to work in these settings in order to accomplish a specific plan, such as learning bookkeeping or gaining formal work experience. But be careful about choosing to stay if you have no further goals that can be realized there. This kind of stagnant cul de sac can sap your energy and confidence, and before you know it, you are looking back on ten years of marking time.

Janet Coolidge is a woman in her fifties who is successfully making her way through a personal crossroads, drawing alternately on intuition, careful reflection, advice from others, and a willingness to notice and seize opportunities as they appear. She lives in Stockton, a small southwestern town whose largest employer is a prestigious liberal arts college. Because her husband is on the faculty, she has been a part of that culture for twenty-five years. After their recent divorce, she almost accepted an offer to work in one of the college offices as support staff. She decided against it.

Since then, she has set about finding or creating most of the links discussed earlier in the chapter in order to create a work life that matters to her. Each morning she goes to the college library and uses it as her "office." She makes a list of skills gained from her past experience as a parent, cartographer, board member for several state-level planning commissions, officer and newsletter editor for the local and state Audubon Society, and most recently, office manager and bookkeeper for a paving company.

She has a long list of organizational and data collection skills, but her passion is birds. Her hope is to find a career doing field work of some kind and to use her writing skills. The list of possibilities includes regional planning, archaeology/anthropology, environmental planning, or research project manager. Still, it is difficult to see where the birds could fit in.

For weeks, Janet puts off taking an interview with a woman she spoke with by phone who does research management; she is concerned she will stutter with a stranger. She does apply for several planning positions in her town and an assistant's job at a local museum, but not with much enthusiasm. None of them comes through. In between she investigates the possibility of working/volunteering as a research assistant to a local professor studying creek vegetation, suggesting they barter her services for his teaching her how to use a new computerized cartography program. He is encouraging, but the timing is not right. Some days she feels hopeful, other days she is discouraged.

Finally, she decides to spend part of the summer as a volunteer on a short-term archeological dig to see if that lures her. She makes arrangements for someone to stay with her ailing mother, has a wonderful summer learning about Shakers, and decides archeology is not for her. She worries about what she will do, if she does find an opportunity far from Stockton; her mother is not the understanding sort.

Upon her return, Janet's strategy is to find an interesting and benign part-time job to bring in money, but one that leaves enough time to travel three hours round trip to a natural science center to learn bird banding. She is beginning to admit she has her eye on finding a way to work with birds in the field.

The benign job turns out to be office manager for a new national magazine being published nearby. As Janet puts it:

★ *I can indulge my love of number crunching without getting back into administrative work.*

★ *It fills my need to belong, to identify, to have something to do.*

★ *With part-time, flexible hours, I have plenty of time to pursue things more central to my goals.*

★ *It pays pretty well and the people are compatible.*

★ *It exercises my organizational skills as I help to set up the system.*

★ *It gives me a front row introduction to the publishing industry and an entre, if I ever want to go in that direction.*

Eventually the bird banding ends and Janet asks the teacher (who happens to be in charge of research) if there is anything he needs to have done that she could do as a volunteer. He needs his cluttered office restored to sanity! So Janet continues to drive down once a week to sort and organize the piles and files stacked on the floor. He warns her repeatedly that there is no hope of hiring a second person in his department. Janet just keeps showing up on Thursdays.

Eventually, her quiet persistence pays off. A recent letter exclaims: "Look what I'm going to do this spring and summer! (She has become coinvestigator for the Migratory Bird Study.) I am helping Glen analyze the last summer's data on the Forest Bird Monitoring Program, and I'm hoping to write the report. He has

*said he'd give me coauthor status. I find now that I have tremen-
dous energy and the old self-confidence level is way up there. I'm
really flying!'*

Janet's saga is not over. I am inspired each time I read her letters. There are other
women whose paths have been more dramatic, but Janet leaves me feeling more
powerful about reaching my own goals. She is in it with her whole person, putting
herself on the line, drawing on both passion and logic. By chart and by chance,
she is providing a quiet heroine for all of us.

Bibliography

Allen, Jeffrey G. *How to Turn an Interview into a Job.* New York: Fireside Books, 1983.

Baer, Jean. *How to Be an Assertive Woman.* New York: Signet Books, 1976.

Bateson, M. K. *Composing a Life.* Atlantic Monthly Press, 1989.

Beattie, Melodie. *CoDependent No More.* New York: Harper & Row, 1987.

Beatty, Richard H. *The Complete Job Search Book.* New York: John Wiley & Sons, 1988.

Beatty, Richard H. *Five Minute Interview.* New York: John Wiley & Sons, 1986.

Belenky, Mary Field, Blythe McVicker Clinchy, Nancy Rule Goldberger, and Jill Mattuck Tarule. *Women's Ways of Knowing.* New York: Basic Books, 1986.

Bolles, Richard Nelson. *Three Boxes of Life.* Berkeley: Ten Speed Press, 1981.

Bolles, Richard Nelson. *What Color Is Your Parachute.* Berkeley: Ten Speed Press, 1990.

Braiker, Harriet B. *The Type E Woman.* New York: Signet Books, 1986.

Bramson, Robert M. *Coping with Difficult People.* New York: Random House, 1981.

Bridges, William. *Transitions: Making Sense of Life's Changes.* Redding, MA: Addison-Wesley, 1980.

Catalyst Staff. *What to Do with the Rest of Your Life.* New York: Simon & Schuster, 1980.

Cheng, Barbara Davis. *Trail-blazers: Vermont Women and Leadership Development.* Burlington, VT: Trinity College of Vermont, 1988.

Cohen, Stephen. *The Termination Trap: Best Strategies for a Job Going Sour.* Charlotte, VT: Williamson Publishing, 1984.

Cousins, Norman. *Anatomy of an Illness.* New York: Norton, 1979.

Dail, Hilda Lee. *The Lotus and the Pool.* Boston: Shambala Publications, 1989.

Davis, Martha, Elizabeth Robbins Eshelman, and Matthew McKay. *The Relaxation and Stress Reduction Workbook.* Oakland, CA: New Harbinger Publications, 1988.

Dawson, Kenneth M. and Sheryl N. Dawson. *Job Search.* New York: John Wiley & Sons, 1988.

Dewey, Barbara. *As You Believe.* Inverness, CA: Bartholomew Books, 1985.

Elsea, Janet G. *First Impression, Best Impression.* New York: Simon & Schuster, 1984.

Falvey, Jack. *After College: The Business of Getting Jobs.* Charlotte, VT: Williamson Publishing, 1986.

Falvey, Jack. *What's Next? Career Strategies after 35.* Charlotte, VT: Williamson Publishing, 1987.

Figler, Howard. *Complete Job Search Handbook.* New York: Holt, Rinehart & Winston, 1988.

Foundation Directory. 13th edition. New York: Foundation Center, 1990.

Freeman, Arthur, and Rose DeWolf. *Woulda, Coulda, Shoulda.* New York: William Morrow, 1989.

Fournies, Ferdinand. *Coaching for Improved Work Performance.* Blue Ridge Summit, PA: Liberty House, 1987.

Gawain, Shakti. *Creative Visualization.* Mill Valley, CA: Whatever Publishing, 1978.

Germann, Richard, Diane Blumenson, and Peter Arnold. *Working and Liking It.* New York: Fawcett Gold Medal, 1984.

Gill, Eliana. *Outgrowing the Pain.* New York: Dell Publishing, 1988.

Gilligan, Carol. *In a Different Voice.* Cambridge, MA: Harvard University Press, 1982.

Hennig, Margaret, and Anne Jardim. *Managerial Woman.* New York: Simon & Schuster, 1977.

Hochheiser, Robert M. *Throw Away Your Resume.* New York: Barrons Educational Series, 1982.

Hodgson, Philip. *A Practical Guide to Successful Interviewing.* London: McGraw-Hill, 1987.

Johnson, David N., and Frank P. Johnson. *Joining Together.* Englewood Cliffs, NJ: Prentice Hall, 1982.

Josefowitz, Natasha. *Paths to Power.* Reading, MA: Addison-Wesley, 1980.

Josselson, Ruthellen. *Finding Herself.* San Francisco: Jossey-Bass, 1987.

Kegan, Robert. *The Evolving Self: Problem and Process in Human Development.* Cambridge, MA: Harvard University Press, 1982.

Kopp, Sheldon. *Who Am I Really?* Los Angeles: Jeremy P. Tarcher, 1987.

Latthrop, Richard. *Who's Hiring Who?* Berkeley: Ten Speed Press, 1977.

Lerner, Harriet Goldhor. *Dance of Anger.* New York: Harper & Row, 1985.

Lerner, Harriet Goldhor. *Women in Therapy.* New York: Harper & Row, 1988.

McGarvey, Robert. "Getting Your Goals." *USAir Magazine,* July 1989.

Melia, Jinx, and Pauline Lyttle. *Why Jenny Can't Lead.* Saguache, CO: Operational Politics, 1986.

Michelozzi, Betty Neville. *Coming Alive from Nine to Five.* Palo Alto, CA: Mayfield, 1984.

Miller, Jean Baker. *Toward a New Psychology of Women.* Boston: Beacon Press, 1976.

Nierenberg, Juliet, and Irene S. Ross. *Women and the Art of Negotiating.* New York: Simon & Schuster, 1985.

Occupational Outlook Handbook. Annual edition. Washington, DC: U.S. Department of Labor, 1990.

"Office Professional." Round Rock, TX: Professional Training Associates.

Parker, Yana. *Damn Good Resume Guide.* Berkeley: Ten Speed Press, 1986.

Parker, Yana. *Resume Catalogue.* Berkeley: Ten Speed Press, 1988.

Pearson, Carol. *The Hero Within.* New York: Harper & Row, 1986.

Pieczenik, Steve. *My Life Is Great. Why Do I Feel So Awful?* New York: Warner Books, 1990.

Plas, Jeanne M., and Kathleen V. Hoover-Dempsey. *Working Up a Storm.* New York: W.W. Norton, 1988.

Reck, Ross R., and Brian G. Long. *The Win-Win Negotiator.* New York: Simon & Schuster, 1987.

Sanford, Linda. *Women and Self-Esteem.* New York: Penguin Books, 1984.

Scott, Niki. "Working Woman." Universal Press Syndicate.

Sinatar, Marsha. *Do What You Love, The Money Will Follow.* New York: Dell Publishing, 1987.

Stechert, Kathryn. *On Your Own Terms.* New York: Vintage Books, 1987.

Steinam, Gloria. *Outrageous Acts and Everyday Rebellions.* New York: Holt, Rinehart & Winston, 1983.

Tannen, Deborah. *You Just Don't Understand.* New York: William Morrow, 1990.

Wegamann, Robert, Robert Chapman, and Miriam Johnson. *Looking for Work in the New Economy.* Salt Lake City: U.S. Olympus, 1985.

Weinberg, Janice. *How to Win the Job You Really Want.* New York: Henry Holt, 1989.

Win, David. *International Careers.* Charlotte, VT: Williamson Publishing, 1987.

Woititz, Janet Garinger. *Adult Children of Alcoholics.* Deerfield Beach, FL: Health Communications, 1983.

Woititz, Janet Garinger. *Home Away from Home.* Deerfield Beach, FL: Health Communications, 1983.

Woititz, Janet Garinger, and Alan Garner. *Life-skills for Adult Children.* Deerfield Beach, FL: Health Communications, 1990.

Yate, Martin John. *Hiring the Best.* Boston: Bob Adams, 1988.

Yate, Martin John. *Knock 'Em Dead.* Boston: Bob Adams, 1988.

Ziv, Avner. *Personality and Sense of Humor.* New York: Springer Publishing, 1984.

About the Authors

Gerri Bloomberg, M. Ed., CCMHC, CEAP, is a nationally certified clinical mental health counselor working with individuals, couples, and families. In addition, she is a nationally certified employee assistance professional and serves as a consultant, counselor, facilitator, and trainer. She is the founder of Workplace Solutions, a company that provides employee assistance programs (EAPs), organizational consulting, training, problem-solving, conflict resolution, outplacement services, and personal and career counseling to private sector and non-profit organizations. She has conducted workshops, seminars, and training sessions, and has written articles on work-related issues for magazines, newspapers, in-house publications, and professional journals. Gerri and her husband reside in Vermont. They have three grown children – a daughter and two sons.

Margaret D. Holden, M.Ed. has combined her work with individuals and groups in career development with many years of experience in marketing, fund-raising, public relations, organizational development, and volunteer management. She has been the director of a community based internship program for high school students, a career counselor in a university center, and a consultant designing and presenting career workshops. She has held executive positions in both private and nonprofit sectors.

She is presently affiliated with Workplace Solutions where her primary responsibility is to direct the outplacement and career counseling function. She has also reserved a portion of her work time this year for individual thought and planning.

Margy lives on an island on Lake Champlain in Vermont and has two grown daughters and four stepsons.